Anne Waldschmidt, Hanjo Berressem, Moritz Ingwersen (eds.)
Culture – Theory – Disability

DISABILITY STUDIES • BODY • POWER • DIFFERENCE • VOLUME 10

Editorial

The scientific book series *Disability Studies: Body – Power – Difference* examines disability as an historical, social and cultural construction; it deals with the interrelation between power and symbolic meanings. The series intends to open up new perspectives to disability, thus correcting and extending traditional approaches in medicine, special education and rehabilitation sciences. It views disability as a phenomenon of embodied difference. Fundamental cultural concepts of »putting things into order«, for instance normality and deviance, health and illness, physical integrity and subjective identity are thereby discussed from a critical point of view. The book series *Disability Studies* aims to contribute to the study of central themes of the Modern age: reason, human rights, equality, autonomy and solidarity in relation to social and cultural developments.

The scientific book series *Disability Studies: Body – Power – Difference* is published by Professor Anne Waldschmidt (iDiS - International research unit in Disability Studies, Faculty of Human Sciences, University of Cologne), together with Professor Thomas Macho (Institute for Culture and Art Sciences, Humboldt University Berlin), Professor Werner Schneider (Faculty of Philosophy and Social Sciences, University of Augsburg), Professor Anja Tervooren (Department of Education, University of Duisburg-Essen) and Heike Zirden (Berlin).

Anne Waldschmidt, Hanjo Berressem,
Moritz Ingwersen (eds.)

Culture – Theory – Disability

Encounters between Disability Studies and Cultural Studies

[transcript] DISABILITY STUDIES

Funded with generous support by the UzK Forum Initiative, University of Cologne

 An electronic version of this book is freely available, thanks to the support of libraries working with Knowledge Unlatched. KU is a collaborative initiative designed to make high quality books Open Access for the public good. The Open Access ISBN for this book is 978-3-8394-2533-6

Bibliographic Information published by the Deutsche Nationalbibliothek
The Deutsche Nationalbibliothek lists this publication in the Deutsche Nationalbibliografie; detailed bibliographic data are available in the Internet at http://dnb.d-nb.de

© 2017 transcript Verlag, Bielefeld

Cover layout: Kordula Röckenhaus, Bielefeld
Cover illustration: Anonymous Artist, Year Unknown, Private Collection of Hanjo Berressem
Printed in Germany
Print-ISBN 978-3-8376-2533-2
PDF-ISBN 978-3-8394-2533-6

Content

ENCOUNTERING ...

Dedicated to Tobin Siebers
(1953-2015)

Acknowledgments

The rewarding process of guiding this project to publication would have been impossible without the invaluable support and assistance of many sets of hands, ears, and eyes. We are grateful to Mary Jane Radford Arrow for her commitment, patience, and keen eye for detail in conducting the English language proofs. Thanks go to Barbara Gehlen for her organizational support during various stages of this project and to Eleana Vaja for her translation of Karin Harrasser's essay into English. We are grateful to David Bolt, the editor of the *Journal of Literary & Cultural Disability Studies* at Liverpool University Press, for his support of this collection and the generous permission to reprint adapted versions of the articles by Kateřina Kolářová and Ria Cheyne that were previously published in *JLCDS*. Furthermore, we would like to thank Vicki Lee at Palgrave Macmillan for the kind permission to reprint Tobin Siebers' article, and Michelle Whittaker at Routledge, Taylor & Francis Group for the kind permission to reprint Dan Goodley's article in this collection. Finally, we are indebted to our publisher and their great trust in this project and to the University of Cologne for supporting both the conference *Contact Zones* and the publication by generous funding from the UzK Forum initiative.

Foreword: Culture – Theory – Disability

Hanjo Berressem, Moritz Ingwersen, Anne Waldschmidt

The seed for this collection was laid at the international conference *Contact Zones: Encounters between Disability Studies and Cultural Studies* which was hosted and co-organized by the International Research Unit in Disability Studies (iDiS) and the Institute of American Literature and Culture at the University of Cologne in 2012. It is noteworthy that this project has its own history. While the interrogation of disability in traditional (special needs) educational environments had long been on the research and teaching agendas at Cologne's Faculty of the Human Sciences housing the Departments of Psychology and Education (*Humanwissenschaftliche Fakultät*), the focus was significantly expanded with the faculty's establishment of the first university position for disability studies in a German-speaking country in 2008, specializing in the sociology of disability and disability policy. Since then, this position has proven a stimulus for spreading the approach of critical disability studies across the university and beyond. In parallel, the Literature and Philosophy Departments of the neighboring Faculty of the Humanities (*Philosophische Fakultät*) had discovered disability as a critical category of cultural analysis. As a result, a productive dialogue between graduate students from both faculties emerged, addressing disability from the perspectives of literary and film studies, sociology and political science, inclusive and special education.

Eventually, this conversation led to this collection, which aims to encourage the problematization of disability in connection with critical theories of literary and cultural representation, aesthetics, philosophies and sociologies of the body, the study of society and politics, science and technology. It links up with the interdisciplinary approaches to disability that can be found at the center of such foundational publications as Lennard J. Davis' *Enforcing Normalcy* (1995), Rosemarie Garland-Thomson's *Extraordinary Bodies* (1996), David T. Mitchell and Sharon L. Snyder's *Narrative Prosthesis* (2001), Robert McRuer's *Crip Theory* (2006), Margrit Shildrick's *Dangerous Discourses of Disability, Subjectivity and Sexuality* (2009), Tobin Siebers' *Disability Theory* (2008) and *Disability Aesthetics* (2010), and David Bolt's *Journal of Literary & Cultural Disability Studies* (since 2006).

The aim of this collection is to provide a platform not only for the thought of many of the leading scholars in the comparably young discourse of cultural disability studies, but also for some of the innovative voices at its disciplinary fringes. In this sense, it is set up to facilitate a dialogue between scholars working from within British, Czech, German and US-American discourses. Many of our contributors have chosen to focus their interrogation of disability through readings of the visual and literary arts. Our goal was to encourage contributions anchored in practice as well as theory-driven contributions. As a result, a number of essays show a self-reflexive engagement with disability studies not only as a heterogeneous transdisciplinary academic apparatus, but also as an expression of the social, political, cultural, and corporeal experiences of persons living with impairments and disabilities.

Drawing inspiration from Erving Goffman's interaction theory and taking up his idea of a party, this collection is organized along the triad of an *introduction*, the establishment of *contact*, and a series of prolonged *encounters*. It opens with two introductory essays by Anne Waldschmidt and Hanjo Berressem. **Anne Waldschmidt** explores the potentials of a cultural model of disability by discussing existing versions and the strengths and weaknesses of the 'social model.' Following a broad notion of culture, she argues for an analytical perspective that investigates the relations between discourses of categorization and institutionalization, the material world, 'ways of doing things,' modes of subjectivation, and their consequences for persons with and without disabilities. Tracing a link between disability studies and poststructuralism, **Hanjo Berressem** finds in the work of Gilles Deleuze and Félix Guattari a productive framework to replace the nature|culture binary with a multiplicitous field of "machinic production" within which all life articulates itself as "differently constrained." With recourse to examples that range from constrained writing to the aesthetics of stumbling, stuttering, and the prosthetic soundscapes in William Gibson's cyberpunk fiction, he illustrates how positions of alleged disability emerge as sites of creativity and production.

Establishing a contact with the field, three figureheads of cultural disability studies, Lennard J. Davis, Rosemarie Garland-Thomson, and Robert McRuer, provide entry points into *Culture – Theory – Disability* with contributions that exemplify what it means to read disability through culture. With reverberations of Sharon L. Snyder and David T. Mitchell's literary analysis of disability as a 'narrative prosthesis,' **Lennard J. Davis** builds on the observation that "media loves disability" and takes a critical look at the casting of non-disabled actors for roles with disabilities in a wide selection of mainstream film and television productions ranging from *The Big Bang Theory* to *Pandora*. Drawing attention to fair employment discrepancies in the movie business, he makes a call similar to that of **Rosemarie Garland-Thomson**, who advocates for what she calls "inclusive world-building." In sharp contradistinction to eugenic agendas, such an initiative would emphasize the generative rather than the restrictive potential of disability in contributing to the "community of embodied human-kind." Through a close reading of Pedro Almodóvar's film *La Mala Educación*, **Robert McRuer** develops a "critically disordered position" that aligns disability interests with positions within queer theory that are similarly in favor of a non-universalizing critique of neoliberal politics of tolerance and identity.

The subsequent contributions are to be read as *encounters* which, in the sense of Goffman, imply 'focused gatherings' of diverse groups and involve conversations, debates, and controversies. Six 'keynotes' are each complemented by a two-tier set of responses from established and emerging scholars who offer ways to make the disability paradigm productive within their own fields of expertise.

Dan Goodley provides a detailed account of the transformative factors within the field of disability studies that have contributed to the emergence of *critical* disability studies in the 21st century. Contextualizing the work of Garland-Thomson, Shildrick, Davis, Siebers, and McRuer, among others, he spells out some of the challenges and potentials of theorizing disability beyond what is known as the 'social model,' without losing touch with its embodied reality in activism and practice. Following the trajectory of Goodley's overview, **Konstantin Butz** highlights the concept of intersectionality to locate sites of revolutionary potential in the gap between a movement's physical materiality and its codification as a discursive gesture. With recourse to the Frankfurt School and the works of Michel Foucault, Judith Butler and Jacques Derrida, **Rouven Schlegel** interrogates the notion of 'critique' in critical disability studies and offers a deconstructionist approach to impairment.

Tobin Siebers argues against the perception of a metonymical relationship between disability and pain, shifting away from the portrayal of bodily pain as an individual identity marker towards the experience of "epistemological pain" as a common thread which unites people with disability in a political struggle for recognition. Following Siebers' claim that personal experiences of pain and disability identities are interrelated, **Andreas Sturm** explores the implications for the identity politics of disability rights movements, while considering that due to the United Nation's Convention on the Rights of Persons with Disabilities collective identities are in the foreseeable future likely to be framed through human rights discourses. With reference to the performance artist Bob Flanagan, **Arta Karāne** uses Siebers' article as a springboard to offer an example of how the experience of pain may serve as a source of self-empowerment and as a critique of normative performances of masculinity.

Margrit Shildrick mobilizes the thought of Deleuze, Guattari and Derrida to conceptualize life with prosthetic aids in terms of "a potentially celebratory re-imagining of the multiple possibilities of corporeal extensiveness." As a proponent of critical disability studies, she points to the ways in which the discussion of disability even within the discourse of disability theory sometimes unquestioningly subscribes to a modernist notion of selfhood. In his response, **Jan Söffner** strengthens the phenomenological tradition in Shildrick's account of embodiment and suggests alternative theoretical frameworks beyond the writings of Deleuze and Guattari pointing to the work of Evan Thompson and Francisco Varela. **Moritz Ingwersen** connects Shildrick's proposal of transcorporeal subjectivity to a paradigm shift in the natural sciences that highlights the role of open systems, in order to distill an appeal to ethics that can also be found in the disability rights activism of Amanda Baggs.

Taking as a starting point a comparative reading of the athletes of the 2012 Paralympics and the protagonists of the X-Men movie franchise, **Karin Harrasser** offers a critical perspective on the semantics of disability in the context of technological enhancement. In resonance with Shildrick's account of prosthetic corporeality and with reference to Bruno Latour and Deleuze, she draws attention to the problematic distinction between human and technological performance. **Eleana Vaja** uses the work of French philosopher of technology Gilbert Simondon to further illuminate the relationship between body and prosthesis and to understand the reciprocal determination between the technical object and its physical milieu. With particular attention to Harrasser's notion of 'the parahuman,' **Olga Tarapata** explores similar lines by drawing on the poetics of American cyberpunk author William Gibson in order to offer an alternative model for non-normative engagements between bodies and environments.

Ria Cheyne's article is an example of the incorporation of disability into the toolbox of literary criticism. She attends to the popular genre of the romance, noting that "romances featuring disabled heroes or heroines are uniquely positioned to challenge public perceptions of disabled people as asexual." Via a close-reading of novels by Mary Balogh, Cheyne illustrates a literary attitude that breaks with the dominant depiction of disability as a metaphor of insufficiency. Contrasting Cheyne's analysis with a reading of Franz Kafka, **Martin Roussel** responds by problematizing the relationship between the interpretation and the representation of fictional scenes of disability. Similarly, **Benjamin Haas** highlights the active role of the reader in the construction of literary meaning and points to the necessity of critically reflecting current concepts of normalcy beyond the level of fictional narrative.

Kateřina Kolářová dissects the political rhetoric of the post-socialist transformation in the Czech Republic to reveal a correspondence between a semantics of illness, disability, cure, and neoliberal austerity policies. Borrowing from the vocabulary of affect theorist Lauren Berlant and McRuer's writings on crip theory, Kolářová proposes a "cripistemological" recoding of what neoliberalism seem to leave by the wayside. **Heidi Helmhold** responds to Kolářová's analysis by suggesting different interpretations of Lauren Berlant and Jan Šibík's photographic art. Reflecting on the value of disability in the political context of post-socialist Czechoslovakia, she furthermore builds a bridge to the devalorization of education in the wake of recent university reforms in Germany. With reference to the sociology of Pierre Bourdieu, **Arne Müller** supplements Kolářová's analysis by positing the merits of an intersectional approximation of the categories of disability and social class.

Introducing ...

Disability Goes Cultural

The Cultural Model of Disability as an Analytical Tool

Anne Waldschmidt

Even today, with the United Nations Convention on the Rights of Persons with Disabilities (UN CRPD) adopted in December 2006 and disability-related discourses, structures, and practices gradually changing throughout the world according to the new human rights approach, there are many people who still take disability as a simple natural fact. Not only myself, but probably other critical disability studies scholars also feel that Lennard J. Davis expresses a common experience:

"When it comes to disability, 'normal' people are quite willing to volunteer solutions, present anecdotes, recall from a vast array of films instances they take for fact. No one would dare to make such a leap into Heideggerian philosophy for example or the art of the Renaissance. But disability seems so obvious – a missing limb, blindness, deafness. What could be simpler to understand? One simply has to imagine the loss of the limb, the absent sense, and one is half-way there." (xvi)

However, it is not only 'normal people' who tend to underestimate the complexity of disability. Academia itself often chooses to apply somewhat undifferentiated approaches to this phenomenon. When it comes to disability, rehabilitation sciences, medicine, psychology, education, and social policy research dominate the field. To avoid misunderstandings: Social protection and rehabilitative assistance are important; persons with disabilities do rely on societies committed to the principles of solidarity and equality instead of leaving them to a destiny of negligence and ignorance. Still, this is only one side of the coin. Traditional approaches ignore that impairment is a common experience in human life and that we all are differently able-bodied. At the same time, it is important to acknowledge that while most people are likely to be impaired at some point during their lifetime being disabled is, as Tom Shakespeare puts it, "a specific social identity of a minority" (295). Why then are certain differences subsumed under the label 'disabled' and others considered as 'normal' manifestations of diversity? Why do modern societies see the need to categorize people as 'normals' and 'deviants'? Why and how is disability negatively valued? In which ways is 'otherness' – and disability is a form of alterity – (re-)produced in history, society and culture?

To answer these questions, we ought to take notice of discourses other than just those of traditional rehabilitation sciences. We need encounters between disability studies and those disciplines that at first sight seem to have nothing to do with disability, such as philosophy and anthropology, history and sociology, ethnology and archaeology, literary studies and linguistics, media studies and religious studies, etc. At the same time, we have to bear in mind that doubts are also raised about such an interdisciplinary approach: What can disability studies gain by incorporating culture as an analytical tool more fully into its work? Is it truly important that disability studies meet cultural studies?

With sociology as my academic background, this discussion is familiar to me. In its founding phase at the beginning of the 20th century, sociology was originally considered one of the humanities. However, in the 1950s and 1960s as a side effect of the then dominant empirical approach that was interested primarily in quantifiable data, the issue of culture was pushed into the background in mainstream sociology. It needed the cultural change of the 1970s and the birth of cultural studies to make possible a renewed attention to culture as an analytical category essential for a comprehensive understanding of society. In short, I am arguing for an interdisciplinary approach which I believe useful and relevant for shedding new light on our contemporary societies, cultures and histories. This approach assumes that impairments and disabilities are structuring culture(s) and at the same time are structured and lived through culture. And it is not only myself who is of this opinion. For example Rosemarie Garland-Thomson was already calling for "New Disability Studies" in 2001 (see Joshua and Schillmeier 4). However, many works are still being published that apply traditional ways of thinking and more established approaches, such as the social model of disability, still remain at the centre of most scholars' attention.

APPRECIATING AND CRITIQUING THE SOCIAL MODEL OF DISABILITY

Since its introduction in the late 1970s, the social model of disability has changed international disability discourses. This model, as academics and activists with a disability studies background well know, emphasizes that disability is a social construction. Basically, it implies three assumptions. First, disability is a form of social inequality and disabled persons are a minority group[1] that is discriminated against and excluded from mainstream society. Second, impairment and disability need to be distinguished and do not have a causal relation; it is not impairments *per se* which disable, but societal practices of 'disablement' which result in disability. Third, it is a society's responsibility to remove the obstacles that persons with disabilities are facing.

When this model of disability was introduced by disability rights organisations and developed further by activists and academics in parallel processes in both the United Kingdom and the United States, it offered a fundamental critique of capitalist society and a new way of thinking. However, in the course of the last 40 years this approach has somewhat become the victim of its own success. It has proven an 'all-rounder,' a useful tool for both academic discourse, disability rights activism and, last but not least, for laypersons and their identity politics. Moreover, the incorporation of its basic ideas into transnational policies, such as the UN CRPD and the two disability classifications of the World Health Organisation of 1980 and 2001, has resulted in pragmatist policies and the opinion that disability as a social problem can be 'solved' through accessibility and participation, mainstreaming and human rights policies. Especially in recent years, many interpretations have tended to ignore the revolutionary impetus of the social model and have watered it down to reformist aspirations of social inclusion and participation. Against this background, the social model seems 'a little dusty' today and it may be time to rethink or amend the concept.

In the following, I refrain from discussing merits and weaknesses of the social model at length. Instead, I will focus on the aspect of culture, which is itself a multifaceted phenomenon in need of specification. Before providing a definition, it is worth mentioning that the social model has frequently been criticised, as Katie Ellis contends, for "neglecting cultural imagery, certain personal experiences and the impacts of impairment" (3). Michael Oliver, one of the British originators of the social model, has reacted to this critique by pointing out that the model emerged directly out of the personal experiences of disabled activists and does indeed allow for the study of impairment effects. Regarding the argument that cultural representation has been neglected, however, he confirms the view of his critics as he does not consider "cultural values" to be crucial, at least as long as so many persons with disabilities are

---

1 | As the British version of the social model of disability is implicitly based on the minority group theory, I cannot see a big difference compared with the US-American minority model and will for this reason not follow Goodley (Disability 11-18) in this point. There are other disability models, often established in competition to the social model, but they are also disputable. Be it the minority model or the relational model, the social policy model or the civil rights model and the human rights model, they all are more or less variants of a social science (sic!) perspective on disability.

still suffering from poverty and material deprivation (49). This assessment, although understandable in terms of practical politics, is astonishing from a sociological point of view: It clearly underestimates the role and the relevance of cultural practices in and for society and their influence on our understanding of disability. My feeling is that this lack of regard may be traced back to some shortcomings of the cultural studies approach. But before I elaborate this point, let me trace the contours of a cultural model of disability.

DRAFTING A CULTURAL MODEL OF DISABILITY

Until today, efforts to develop a cultural model of disability have been rare. However, in parallel with the development of the social model and its critical discussion and partly independent of them, the past decades have witnessed an increase in cultural studies oriented works with regard to disability and we can already identify cultural disability studies as an innovative and prolific research field carried out in the humanities. Yet, it is striking that in contrast to the social model of disability, which is characterised by strong coherence and therefore often accused of dogmatism, the field of cultural disability studies still looks more like a patchwork quilt. It has not yet found its unique contours, despite an ongoing discussion on the implications of culture for disability constructions.

As early as 1994, Tom Shakespeare called for a greater attention to cultural representations of disabled people. Inspired by feminist debates he discussed different theoretical approaches and suggested "that disabled people are 'objectified' by cultural representations" (287), under which he subsumed theatre, literature, paintings, films, and the media. In the following years, prominent scholars in the Anglo-Saxon world such as Lennard J. Davis, Rosemarie Garland-Thomson, Robert McRuer, David T. Mitchell and Sharon L. Snyder, Margrit Shildrick, Tobin Siebers, Shelley Tremain, and others (for an overview, see Goodley, *Disability* 14-15) published a wide variety of cultural and literary analyses showing the value and productivity of treating "disability as a cultural trope" (Garland-Thomson 2). In 2006, Snyder and Mitchell explicitly introduced a "cultural model of disability" but they defined it narrowly as an approach that was primarily associated with US-American disability studies. In terms of content, they remained rather vague:

"We believe the cultural model provides a fuller concept than the social model, in which 'disability' signifies only discriminatory encounters. The formulation of a cultural model allows us to theorize a political act of renaming that designates disability as a site of resistance and a source of cultural agency previously suppressed [...]." (10)

In introducing the phrase "cultural locations of disability," referring to "sites of violence, restriction, confinement, and absence of liberty for people with disabilities" (x), Snyder and Mitchell offered a tool for interdisciplinary work on disability within and beyond cultural studies. Additionally, some scholars have argued for the usefulness of a cultural model of disability to study intersections between migration, ethnicity, 'race,' and disability. In 2005, Patrick J. Devlieger, who teaches cultural anthropology in Leuven (Belgium), pleaded for a dialectical cultural model focussing on communication and cultural diversity, following Michel Foucault, Jacques Derrida and Karl Marx. Recent works in postcolonial studies ask the question "how disability is figured in the global, postcolonial history of the modern" and aim "to highlight specific located examples of disability in cultural contexts" (Barker and Murray 65). Meanwhile, the cultural model of disability has also been acknowledged in religious studies as a 'key term.' In this context, Nyasha Junior and Jeremy Schipper define it as an approach which analyses "how a culture's representations and discussions of disability (and nondisability or able-bodiedness) help to articulate a range of values, ideals, or expectations that are important to that culture's organization and identity" (35).

We can state that there is an ongoing reflection on the strengths of a cultural approach to disability. The Liverpool-based *Journal of Literary & Cultural Disability Studies*, which celebrated its tenth anniversary in 2016, is a witness to this lively debate. At the same time however, the respective 'model' still seems to have rather blurred features. Further, the debate tends to reproduce the dominance of English-speaking disability studies (see for example Goodley *Disability*) and overlooks contributions from other countries, such as the longstanding works of French philosopher Henri-Jacques Stiker. With regard to Germany, both the interdisciplinary book series "Disability Studies" published since 2007 by *transcript* and the Edinburgh German Yearbook's fourth volume on disability in German literature, film, and theatre from 2010 attest to a great wealth of works drawing on a cultural studies approach. The editors of the yearbook, Eleoma Joshua and Michael Schillmeier, define the cultural model as "the analysis of the representations of disabled people in the cultural spaces of art, media, and literature" (5) and even speak of a "cultural turn" in disability studies (4).

It is beyond the scope of this essay to discuss these different proposals extensively. Instead I will, in what follows, explain my own approach. Based on contributions published in 2005 and 2012, the latter together with Werner Schneider, I develop a cultural model of disability for the purpose of providing a joint framework for the already numerous contributions which analyse disability with the help of methodologies and approaches originating from cultural studies. My intention is not to suggest that a cultural model should replace the social model of disability. Rather, critical disability studies should acknowledge that disability is *both* socially and culturally constructed (on this point, see also Ellis 2).

THE CULTURAL MODEL OF DISABILITY AS AN ANALYTICAL TOOL

What is the core of a cultural model of disability? My starting point is that such a model needs to reflect first of all its own understanding of culture. As both a social practice and an analytical category, culture not only implies cultural activities in the narrow sense, be it so-called high culture or popular culture. Instead, for innovative research it is much more productive to apply a broad conception of culture that denotes the totality of 'things' created and employed by a particular people or a society, be they material or immaterial: objects and instruments, institutions and organisations, ideas and knowledge, symbols and values, meanings and interpretations, narratives and histories, traditions, rituals and customs, social behaviour, attitudes and identities (see Moebius 7-9; Schneider and Waldschmidt 146).

In my opinion, if we were to use such a general understanding of culture, a cultural model of disability would not be dismissed as focalising only symbols and meanings, but could broaden our analytical perspective to investigate the relations between symbolic (knowledge) systems, categorization and institutionalisation processes, material artefacts, practices and 'ways of doing things,' and their consequences for persons with *and* without disabilities, their social positions, relations and ways of subjectivation. Such a cultural disability model thus differs from other approaches in important aspects: It considers disability neither as only an individual fate, as in the individualistic-reductionist model of disability, nor as merely an effect of discrimination and exclusion, as in the social model. Rather, this model questions the other side of the coin, the commonly unchallenged 'normality,' and investigates how practices of (de-) normalization result in the social category we have come to call 'disability.' As a consequence of this shift in focus, four programmatic ideas arise.

First, a cultural model of disability should regard neither disability nor impairment as clear-cut categories of pathological classification that auto-matically, in the form of a causal link, result in social discrimination. Rather, this model considers impairment, disability *and* normality as effects generated by academic knowledge, mass media, and everyday discourses. These terms are 'empty signifiers' or blurred concepts referring to a mixture of different physical, psychological and cognitive features that have nothing in common other than negative or, as in the case of ability and normality, positive attributions from society. In any culture at any given moment these classifications are dependent on power structures and the historical situation; they are contingent upon and determined by hegemonic discourses. In short, the cultural model considers disability not as a given entity or fact, but describes it as a discourse or as a process, experience, situation, or event.

Second, from this premise arises the notion that disability does not denote an individual's feature, but an always embodied category of differentiation. Disability is taken as 'true' because it is not a natural fact but a naturalized difference. It is ascribed to the evidence of physical or embodied expression (even in the case of not directly observable alterities), and it is interpreted within a dichotomous framework of bodily differences: healthy, complete, and normal versus diseased, deficient, and deviating. It exists only when and insofar as certain (bodily and embodied) differences can be distinguished and thought of as 'relevant for health' within a given cultural and historical order of knowledge.

Third, both disability and ability relate to prevailing symbolic orders and institutional practices of producing normality and deviance, the self and the other, familiarity and alterity. By assuming a constructivist and discursive character of disability, the historical contingency and cultural relativity of inclusion and exclusion, stigmatization and recognition can come into consideration, as well as socio-cultural patterns of experience and identity, meaning-making and practice, power and resistance. Furthermore, from this perspective disability is connected to specific social imperatives addressing all relevant parties, on the one hand the experts for support and the rehabilitation business, and on the other hand the laypersons, whether able-bodied or disabled, with their desire or their defiance to adapt and comply to socio-cultural normative expectations. Thus, a cultural model of disability shows that the individual and collective subjectivities of 'disabled' and 'nondisabled' persons are interdependent.

Fourth, when one employs such a 'de-centring' approach, surprising new insights become possible, insights into our late modern societies, their trajectories and processes of change. Instead of continuing to only 'stare' at persons with disabilities, asking what kind of problems they are confronted with and how society should support them, the focus can widen to a look at society and culture in general, aiming to understand the dominant ways of problematizing issues of health, normality, and functioning; how knowledge of the body is produced, transformed and mediated; which and how normalities and deviations are constructed; how exclusionary and including practices in everyday life are designed by different institutions; how identities and new forms of subjectivity are created and shaped.

In sum, the cultural model of disability implies a fundamental change of epistemological perspective since it does not deal with the margin but rather with the 'centre' of society and culture. As a consequence, it changes disability studies into 'dis/ability studies' (for this approach see also Goodley *Dis/ability*). The introduction of the slash indicates that one should no longer problematize just the category of disability, but rather the interplay between 'normality' and 'disability.' In short, the transversal and intersectional should become the actual object of research. Dis/ability understood as a contingent, always 'embodied' type of difference relating to the realms of health, functioning, achievement and beauty (and their negative poles), offers essential knowledge about the legacies, trajectories, turning points, and transformations of contemporary society and culture.

CONCLUSION

This essay has discussed the relevance of culture as an analytical category for the study of disability. It has attempted to show that a cultural model of disability has emerged over the last two decades, cross-cutting different academic disciplines and transnational with regard to languages and contexts. Of course, bringing disability and culture together does not progress smoothly; it involves "contact zones," i.e., "social spaces where cultures meet, clash and grapple with each other, often in contexts of highly asymmetrical relations of power [...]" (Pratt 34). This volume offers these conflictual yet productive spaces through which new ways of seeing and thinking can emerge. Let me finish my contribution citing Davis again: "[W]hile most 'normals' [and academics] think they understand the issue of disability" and can "speak with knowledge on the subject," we need to commence from the assumption that "in fact [we] do not" (Davis xvi). The belief that one is lacking knowledge seems a good point of departure for new journeys into the worlds of dis/ability.

REFERENCES

Barker, Clare and Stuart Murray. "Disabling Postcolonialism: Global Disability Cultures and Democratic Criticism." *The Disability Studies Reader*. Ed. Lennard J. Davis. New York, Milton Park: Routledge, 2013 (4th ed.). 61-73. Print.

Davis, Lennard J. "Introduction." *The Disability Studies Reader*. Ed. Lennard J. Davis. New York, Milton Park: Routledge, 2006 (2nd ed.). xv-xviii. Print.

Devlieger, Patrick J. "Generating a Cultural Model of Disability." Paper presented at the *19th Congress of the European Federation of Associations of Teachers of the Deaf (FEAPDA)*, October 14-16, 2005. Web. 02 June 2011. <http://feapda.org/Geneva%20Files/culturalmodelofdisability.pdf>.

Ellis, Katie. *Disability and Popular Culture: Focusing Passion, Creating Community and Expressing Defiance*. Farnham: Ashgate, 2015. Print.

Garland-Thomson, Rosemarie. "Integrating Disability, Transforming Feminist Theory." *Feminist Disability Studies*. NWSA Journal 14.3 (2002). 1-32. Web. 25 Feb. 2013. <http://www.jstor.org/stable/4316922>.

Goodley, Dan. *Dis/ability Studies. Theorising Disablism and Ableism*. London, New York: Routledge, 2014. Print.

Goodley, Dan. *Disability Studies: An Interdisciplinary Introduction*. Los Angeles, New York: Sage, 2011. Print.

Joshua, Eleoma and Michael Schillmeier. "Introduction." *Disability in German Literature, Film, and Theater. Edinburgh German Yearbook. Volume 4*. Rochester, New York: Camden House, 2010. 1-13. Print.

Junior, Nyasha and Jeremy Schipper. "Disability Studies and the Bible." *New Meanings for Ancient Texts: Recent Approaches to Biblical Criticisms and Their Applications*. Eds. Steven L. McKenzie and John Kaltner. Westminster: John Knox Press, 2013. 21-37. Print.

Moebius, Stephan. "Kulturforschungen der Gegenwart – die Studies." *Kultur. Von den Cultural Studies bis zu den Visual Studies: Eine Einführung*. Ed. Stephan Moebius. Bielefeld: transcript, 2012. 7-12. Print.

Oliver, Michael. *Understanding Disability. From Theory to Practice*. Basingstoke, London: Palgrave, 2009 (2nd ed.). Print.

Pratt, Mary Louise. "Arts of the Contact Zone." *Profession 91*. New York: MLA, 1991. 33–40. Print.

Schneider, Werner and Anne Waldschmidt. "Disability Studies: (Nicht-) Behinderung anders denken." *Kultur. Von den Cultural Studies bis zu den Visual Studies: Eine Einführung*. Ed. Stephan Moebius. Bielefeld: transcript, 2012. 128-150. Print.

Shakespeare, Tom. "Cultural Representation of Disabled People: Dustbins for Disavowal?" *Disability & Society* 9.3 (1994). 283-299. Print.

Snyder, Sharon L. and David T. Mitchell. *Cultural Locations of Disability*. Chicago: University of Chicago Press, 2006. Print.

Waldschmidt, Anne. "Disability Studies: Individuelles, soziales und/oder kulturelles Modell von Behinderung?" *Psychologie & Gesellschaftskritik* 29.1 (2005). 9-31. Print.

The Sounds of Disability

A Cultural Studies Perspective

Hanjo Berressem

While Anne Waldschmidt has approached disability studies from within, my side of the introduction comes to disability studies by way of literary and cultural studies, a field whose history for about the last 60 years has been defined by a number of diverse theories bundled under the term 'poststructuralism.' This occurred more in American discourses than in the UK, which witnessed the development of a number of Marxist and post-Marxist approaches that were only later aligned with poststructuralist concepts. The historical vector of Poststructuralism went roughly from Michel Foucault, Jacques Lacan and Jacques Derrida to Gilles Deleuze and Félix Guattari. In its gradual unfolding it became the theoretical spine not only of literary studies, but also of minority studies, such as critical ethnic studies and queer studies. When I began reading works from within the field of disability studies a number of years ago I realized that, at least in theoretical registers, much of it followed the gradual unfolding of that spine. At that moment, disability studies had just turned towards Deleuze and Guattari.

Before Deleuze and Guattari, much of poststructuralism was defined by a deep unease about the concept of 'nature,' which was often assumed to imply characteristics such as 'inevitability' or 'essentialism.' To a large degree, the poststructuralist fear of nature resulted from the assumption that if nature was indeed considered as essentialist, critical cultural agency could always be kept in check by references to purportedly 'natural' and 'unnatural' practices. And indeed, for a long time the notion *of* – and often a belief *in* – an essentialist nature was the weapon of choice wielded by almost any politics of discrimination. Even while the poststructuralist fear of nature was understandable, therefore, it ultimately revealed more about the political and cultural misuse of the term than about the reality of how nature, whatever that might be, 'in actual fact' operates.

This reality has come into focus not only by way of Deleuze and Guattari, who replaced in *Anti-Oedipus* the distinction between nature and culture with a general field of 'machinic production:' "[T]here is no such thing as either man or nature now, only a process that produces the one within the other and couples the machines together [...] the self and the non-self, outside and inside, no longer have any meaning whatsoever" (2). A similar view is held by scholars such as Gilbert Simondon, Michel Serres and Donna Haraway, who proposed the term "naturecultures" (Haraway 15) for this field. Such conceptual superpositions resonated well with disability studies, where it also makes little sense to categorically, or even empirically, separate the fields of nature and of culture. According to the 'new machinic natureculture,' the world consists of an infinitely complex arrangement of machines, ranging from physical, chemical, biological to cultural machines. In Deleuze and Guattari, the machinic field is made up of a combination of both 'autopoietic, living machines' and 'allopoietic, industrial machines' that together work according to a general machinism that defines the world from its most microscopic to its most macrocosmic levels. As Deleuze notes in *Dialogues*, "each individual, body and soul, possesses an infinity of parts which belong to him in a more or less complex relationship. Each individual is also himself composed of individuals of a lower order and enters into the composition of individuals of a higher order" (59).

While the world is indeed everywhere a singular 'field of production' that consists of a diversity of site- and time-specific, inherently dynamic and constantly changing machinic assemblages, it is, at the same time, filled with an unlimited potentiality for change that destabilizes every machinic arrangement and that allows for always new and surprising alignments to emerge. Also, the machinic world is inherently 'constrained' in that it *affords* certain operations and modes of life, but also *prohibits* others. In fact, the world might be described as the arena of the constrained and interrelated play of human and non-human life.

If that sounds too celebratory, we must be aware that we cannot 'trust in the world,' because the world is nothing that exists outside of us and it is 'itself' not an agent, because the world is just the name for what is brought about, at every moment, by the totality of its creations. All it does, therefore, is to express itself *by way of* and *in* its creatures, which means that it is, like them, invariably constrained and 'disabled.'

It is not only that all of individual life is 'constrained life,' it in fact *depends* on specific constraints, be these temporal, spatial or operational. From such a position, the field of disability can be defined, in very general terms, as a multiplicitous field of site- and time-specific constraints that play themselves out on an infinite number of levels simultaneously.

Conceptually, the notion of 'differently constrained lives' defines not only 'lives with disabilities,' but *all* forms of life in relation to an impossible 'non-constrained,' 'non-disabled' state. As all lives are subtractions from such an ideal state, each life needs to be considered as a 'singular life' with singular constraints, which means that in the gradations of constraint it is no longer a question of 'the normal' set against 'the abnormal,' but one of specifically constrained positions within a given multiplicity. In this context, in *A Thousand Plateaus* Deleuze and Guattari set off "the Anomalous" (242) – a term that refers initially to specific animals in a pack, with the pun operating between the French *anomal* and animal – against the French term *anormal*. The word *anomal* ('anomalous'), they note, "is very different from that of *anormal* ('abnormal')" (243). While the latter "refers to that which is outside rules or goes against the rules" (244), "*an-omalie* [...] designates the unequal, the coarse, the rough, the cutting edge of deterritorialization" (ibid.). If the topological logic of the *an-omalie* is transferred to the field of disability studies, a specific disability is no longer considered as being excluded from a field of normalcy, but rather as in "a position or set of positions in relation to a multiplicity" (ibid.). It is, in fact, that multiplicity's "borderline" (245) or "peripheral" (ibid.).

To stress the inherently disruptive force of an-omalies as destabilizing given fields, Deleuze and Guattari use the term 'deterritorialization.' They deterritorialize the 'expected,' habitual movements – the territories within a given space – that define a given multiplicity. Let me set up an example to which I will return in more detail. Picture how a person engaging in what is labelled as 'spastic' dancing will destabilize the general multiplicity of a dancefloor (a scene that will be qualified below), not by being excluded from that floor but by bringing it into a different rhythm. By making, perhaps, the habitual rhythm 'stumble.' Sometimes, one imperceptibly small stumbling may cause a marching group to begin to dance.

In the following, let me offer a number of modes in which the notion of a constrained and disabled world insists on artistic productions and how these 'construct' constrained and disabled worlds. The first example is obvious, in that I have taken the notion of 'constraint' from literature, where it designates an experimental writing strategy: Consider the alphabet as a system of communicative affordances and constraints – affordances, in that it allows for a specifically human mode of constructing and moving meaning; constraints, in that there are, in any given language, only a number of letters, as well as rules of grammar, syntax, word-order, etc. In analogy to an individual, specific style of life, an individual style of talking and writing positions an individual in a general, machinic multiplicity of discourses. Within this field, the reasons for 'linguistic impairments' might lie on cellular, genetic and chemical levels (autism: presumably genetic, synaptic, environmental; dyslexia: presumably genetic and environmental), on cultural levels (an insufficiently developed educational system), or a mix of any number of in-between levels (a dysfunctional family, a drug habit, anatomical alterities affecting the vocal chords, etc.).

Such linguistic disabilities are usually seen as constraints. They might, however, also be seen from the point-of-view of 'creative deterritorializations.' In fact, as with life in general, the constraints themselves might be seen as sources of creativity. It is in the context of such a logic that, in order to bring about artistic deterritorializations, the French literary movement of *L' Ouvroir de Littérature Potentielle*, abbreviated as *OuLiPo*, developed the notion of 'constrained writing,' which is based on a poetics of the willful 'disabling' or 'constraining' of one's linguistic agency. *La Disparition* by Georges Perec is written without the letter 'e.' Christine-Brooke Rose's 1998 novel *Next* is written without the verb 'to have' and her novel *Between* is written entirely without the verb 'to be.' Ironically, her memoir *Remake* is written without the pronoun 'I.'

The perhaps most elaborate *tour de force* of constrained writing is Walter Abish's novel *Alphabetical Africa* (1974), which tells its story in 52 chapters. The first chapter contains only words that start with the letter 'a,' the second uses words that start with 'a' or 'b' and so on until it reaches, in the 26th chapter, the freedom to use all letters. But then Abish subtracts letters again, with the final chapter using once more only words that start with the letter 'a.' The novel starts "Ages ago, Alex, Allen and Alva arrived at Antibes, and Alva allowing all, allowing anyone, against Alex's admonition, against Allen's angry assertion: another African amusement ..." (1) and it ends with "another Africa another alphabet" (152).

Initially, these experiments sound weird. One should remember, however, that a sonnet also allows only a certain number of lines, that a tragedy asks for a crisis at a certain point and that a short story should be, well, short. In fact, what constrained writing teaches is that any form is nothing but a complicated set of constraints, which means that 'de-formation' is nothing but a shift in the architectures of constraint that have come to be considered as 'good form.' Ultimately, constrained writing throws the notion of good form into perspective by a willful act of deformation. However, this deformation does not 'impoverish' the multiplicity of discourses. Rather, it adds to it in many unexpected ways. It unsettles and invigorates language. It makes language new and it makes it *sound* differently. Who has ever listened to four pages of text in which every word starts with the letter 'a' before *Alphabetical Africa* came along?

My second example also has to do with how 'disabilities' unsettle a multiplicity. It comes from the science fiction subgenre of cyberpunk. In his 1982 short story "Burning Chrome," William Gibson's narrator, when he talks about his artificial arm, does not talk about the clichés of disability with their images of loss and pain. In Gibson's world, which is a world pervaded by a multiplicity of man-machine assemblages and interfaces – from artificial memories and synaptic plug-ins to mobile life-support systems and corporeal prostheses – where both psychic and physical prostheses are no longer related to a logic of making up a lack, but rather understood as a 'given' within an overall man-machine multiplicity.

Against this background, Gibson develops a new aesthetics of prostheses, both in the sense of a machinic beauty and in the sense of a new set of perceptions. Like much of constrained writing, Gibson's text concerns the 'sound of disability,' this time however from the position of the new technological sounds produced by prostheses. The narrator's prosthesis, in fact, heralds the meeting of a 'differently constrained' body, a new electric soundscape, and a new vocabulary of human motion: "The servos in the hand began whining like overworked mosquitos" (199), he notes. Together with this new aesthetics, there are also hints toward a new prosthetic erotics, such as when the narrator describes a girl's fingernails as laquered in a color that is "only a shade darker than the carbon-fiber laminate that sheathes" (205) his arm. What Gibson creates, from within the field of 'differently constrained lives,' however, is not only the perception of new sounds and new, machinic colors. Perhaps most interestingly, he also develops a prosthetic, machinic unconscious. In the face of an unwelcome surprise, the narrator notes laconically: "I stood there. My arm forgot to click" (210). In Gibson's work, 'differently constrained lives' are invariably vistas into such new experiences and affects, literature being a mode of staging these constraints in their singularity and in their 'monstrous' – in the sense of the Latin *monstrare* – technical splendor.

My final example comes from music and it shows how each singular differently constrained individual brings about a singularly 'disabled' environment. In 1969, the Electronic Music Studio of Brandeis University became the setting for the premiere performance of American composer Alvin Lucier's work "I Am Sitting in a Room." The piece consists of Lucier sitting on stage tape-recording a text he speaks into a microphone. The taped text is then played back into the room, where it is once more picked up by the microphone, recorded, and played back into the room. This procedure is repeated until Lucier's voice has completely vanished into an anonymous sound that corresponds to or, as Lucier notes, more precisely "articulates" – in terms of 'making audible,' or 'actualizing' – the resonant frequency of the room. The text spoken by Lucier provides a very concise description of the acoustic process that is at work in the composition:

"I am sitting in a room different from the one you are in now. I am recording the sound of my speaking voice and I am going to play it back into the room again and again until the resonant frequencies of the room reinforce themselves so that any semblance of my speech, with perhaps the exception of rhythm, is destroyed. What you will hear, then, are the natural resonant frequencies of the room *articulated by speech*. I regard this activity not so much as a demonstration of a physical fact, but more as a way to smooth out any irregularities my speech might have." (Lucier 31; emphasis added)

Although the internal field of resonances might be broken down into its acoustic components – its landscape of frequencies – by way of what is called a Fourier analysis, Lucier's piece develops not only 'within' these tones, but also, and more importantly so, between these tones and their acoustic environment. It concerns both the single tones and the acoustic architecture – the sonorous ambience – within which these sounds are produced.

In the context of this introduction, two aspects interest me in particular. First, the notion that, as Lucier notes, the operation should "smooth out any irregularities my speech might have." Of course this is not a plea for order, regularity or normalcy. Rather, it is the attempt to let his speech interact actively with the environment. Even more, it is a way to let the environment – the world, that is – speak through one's own speech. To channel the disabled world, in that the eigenfrequencies of the room are "articulated by speech" in his performance. The second aspect that interests me is Lucier's remark "with perhaps the exception of rhythm." To understand this exception, one needs to know (or listen to the performance) that Lucier stutters – the linguistic equivalent of stumbling – making his voice different from the statistical voice, which it deterritorializes. It is an *an-omalie* in that it destabilizes the general, given multiplicity of voices. In particular, of course – and Lucier, as a musician, is very aware of this – it does so in terms of rhythm, because stuttering is, musically, a rhythmic *an-omalie*. Within the poetics of the piece, therefore, the particular 'differently constrained' parameter remains as the only element that retains a singularity. All other speech vanishes in the process of articulating the room. At the end of the piece, then, it is quite literally Lucier's impairment that reverberates through the concert hall. It has been *dis-attached* from Lucier to become pure rhythm. The room whose sound is articulated by Lucier's 'differently constrained' voice articulates, in return, Lucier's 'differently constrained' voice. It is 'articulated by space.'

In his essay "He Stuttered," Deleuze writes about an analogous stuttering not in terms of speech, but of language: "It is no longer the character who stutters in speech, it is the writer who becomes *a stutterer in language*. He makes the language as such stutter: an affective and intensive language, no longer an affectation of the one who speaks" (107). Although Deleuze remains within the medium of language, he also opens this language up to its environmental aspect. To make language stutter brings out in language "an atmospheric quality, a milieu that acts as the conductor of words – that brings together within itself the quiver, the murmur, the stutter, the tremolo, or the vibrato, and makes the indicated affect reverberate through the words" (108). Lucier, however, goes even further. With Lucier, it is not so much about "a *minor use* of the major language" (109; emphasis added), nor is it about what Deleuze calls "a music of words" (113). In fact, it is not about making language stutter at all, but rather about making 'the world' stutter. With this move, Lucier brings stuttering to its extreme. If for Deleuze stuttering implies bringing language and sense to their limit, Lucier literally 'disables' the world through his speech. He singularizes the world through its articulation, by way of a 'differently constrained' speech, operating at the limit of anonymity and singularity – the singularity of a speech impediment.

It is not difficult to transpose these 'differently constrained poetics' onto other artistic fields, such as dance, where the kinetic room that is articulated by the dance is also a 'disabled' room. Here as well, the disability is expressed as the residue of singularity within an anonymity or multiplicity – the two are, of course, ultimately the same – of movement.

A more thematic instance of such an expression is Ian Dury's song "Spasticus Autisticus" that was played during the Opening of the 2012 Paralympics. Linking a political agenda to a bodily performance, Dury, who contracted polio when he was young, expresses both in the movements of his body and in his music the 'spastics' of rock 'n' roll. He articulates an *anomal*, disabled dancefloor. Symptomatically, one might easily misunderstand – mis-hear, that is – the title as "Spasticus Artisticus."

My examples have all stressed the sense of hearing, not so much from within the problematics of deaf- or muteness as from within an expansion of the spectrum of sound. As Deleuze notes, "Dante is admired for having 'listened to the stammerers,' and studied 'speech impediments,' not only to derive speech effects from them, but in order to undertake a vast phonetic, lexical and even syntactic creation" (Deleuze, "Stuttered" 109).

Already my digression into the field of dance has implied that such expansions of sensuality might also be 'applied' to the other senses and thus to other, new surfaces of sensation. Without forgetting the pains that often surround impairments the 'expression of disability' widens the spectrum of sensation for both artist and audience. It also widens the self-expression of an inherently disabled world. If we come to love this disabled world, we have come a long way toward an adequate treatment of people with disabilities. There is a line that goes from Lucier to Herman Melville's stuttering hero Billy Budd to the notion of a 'minor,' inherently stuttering, disabled literature, and finally, to a disabled world.

REFERENCES

Abish, Walter. *Alphabetical Africa*. New York: New Directions, 1974. Print.

Deleuze, Gilles. "He Stuttered." *Essays Critical and Clinical*. Trans. Daniel W. Smith & Michael A. Greco. Verso, New York, 1998. Print.

Deleuze, Gilles and Félix Guattari. *A Thousand Plateaus: Capitalism and Schizophrenia 2*. Trans. Brian Massumi. Minneapolis: University of Minnesota Press, 2005. Print.

Deleuze, Gilles and Claire Parnet. *Dialogues*. Trans. Hugh Tomlinson and Barbara Habberjam. New York: Columbia University Press, 1987. Print.

Dury, Ian. "Spasticus Autisticus." *Lord Upminster.* Polydor, 1981. CD.

Gibson, William. "Burning Chrome." *Burning Chrome.* Gollancz, London, 1986, 195-220. Print.

Haraway, Donna. *When Species Meet.* Minneapolis: University of Minnesota Press, 2008. Print.

Lucier, Alvin. "I Am Sitting in a Room" *Chambers: Scores by Alvin Lucier, Interviews With the Composer by Douglas Simon.* Middletown: Wesleyan University Press. 1980, 30-31. Print.

Contacting …

The Ghettoization of Disability

Paradoxes of Visibility and Invisibility in Cinema

Lennard J. Davis

Perhaps every theory has to contradict itself. If I have been saying that dismodernism allows for a flexible and malleable sense of identity in relationship to disability, then when I think about the notion of actors playing disabled characters, it would seem I would be open to any kind of actor playing any kind of part. Is not identity what you make of it, rather than an absolute and essential category? You would think so, but in this essay I am going to be arguing that only disabled actors should play disabled roles.

It is not like we do not see a lot of people with disabilities in film. In some sense, disability is one of the sub-specialties of the visual media. From Lon Chaney, Jr. playing the Hunchback of Notre Dame to Daniel Day Lewis' portrayal of Christie Brown in *My Left Foot* to Sam Worthington playing Jake Sully in *Avatar,* from the wheel-chair using dancer on *Glee* to the son with cerebral palsy on *Breaking Bad,* media loves disability. People with disabilities are portrayed in the media as present, in the sense of ubiquitous, always marked as different, and yet rarely if ever played by actors with disabilities. Why is that?

Cinema and television use popular and knowable narratives and then tweak them a bit here and there. Disabilities are part of that narrative. Physical disabilities appear in the popular imagination in a variety of ways, notably as challenges or tragedies, and affective and cognitive disorders have a somewhat different role. Intellectual disabilities, most particularly in the case of people with Down syndrome and non-verbal autism tend to function in the media as states of existence designed to evoke the compassion of the viewer. Most commonly audiences are called upon to produce a limited range of responses from sympathy or pity to some kind of beneficent granting of limited personhood to such characters. The more lovable and understandable the characters become, the more likely the film or television will succeed. And the ultimate point about the function of such narratives is that they end up making the audience feel good about itself and its own *normality.*

Affective and anxiety disorders seem to provoke a different audience involvement than that with intellectual and cognitive disabilities. If the affective disorder falls into the realm of an anxiety, depression, delusion, or schizophrenia, the film or television special (never a series) will revolve around that character *going mad*. The madness, in turn, will then symbolize the response we might all have to a dehumanizing, stressful, disabling and demeaning society. The character becomes a tragic stand-in for any viewer facing the human condition. Some movies like *A Beautiful Mind, The Soloist,* and *The Fisher King* follow the descent of the character into madness while trying to offer some kind of cure, control, or redemption at the end.

Obsessive-compulsive disorder (OCD) seems to straddle the divide between tragedy and redemption as well as between tragedy and comedy. The standard representation of OCD in film and other narrative forms is to see the obsessive behavior as a combination of amusing and yet debilitating. One scenario turns the person with OCD into a kind of lovable nut or what I like to call a disability *mascot*. The mascotization of disabilities produces warm, cuddly, lovable representations. The television show *Monk* mainly does this, while also showing how disability can itself be ability. Monk is a detective whose Holmes-like skills are aided by his obsessive behavior. Monk can notice things that others cannot, and like Sherlock Holmes has a kind of autistic intensity that aids his detective work but hinders his life. Monk *suffers* from his disability and cannot function without a personal assistant who hands him sanitizing wipes and coaxes him through his fears. Yet, in this case, cure is not an option. In one episode, for example, he decides to use medication, and although he is personally happier as his symptoms diminish, he becomes a terrible detective. So he eventually renounces the medication, goes back to his tortured but amusing self, and returns to super-sleuthing. Shows like *The Big Bang Theory*, a sitcom that focuses on the social lives of scientists and engineers, group conditions like Asperger's Syndrome with OCD in loveable and amusing characters like Sheldon. Sheldon is the lead character in the show and one of the most popular comedic figures in American television because his behaviors lend themselves to comic situations.

Reality TV shows have even gotten into the affective disorder act. *Obsessed* was a series that followed people with OCD and other compulsions. These include people who are agoraphobic, those who pick their faces or pick their hair out, count compulsively, hoard, and so on. The series did not turn people with OCD into mascots, but rather portrays them as symptoms in need of cure. This is also true for a show like *Hoarders*. This program profiles those who compulsively hoard objects and form attachments to an array of junk stashed in their homes. Usually, family members or friends attempt to forcibly change this behavior. Any individual episode is painful to watch, but the people themselves become objects of interest, compassion, fear and pity. The aim of the show is to let us know that cures are readily available for scary diseases.

In my book *Obsession: A History* I raised the point about how we categorize being obsessed. In one sense, we live in a culture that values obsession. We think that the best and brightest should be obsessed with their work, their lives, their sex lives and so on. At the same time, we sub-categorize a section of such behavior as *too much*. Those who are too obsessed fall into a clinical category. The social, political, and ideological surround creates a state of desire for obsession and fear of obsession. The key way to tell if you are too obsessed is to note whether you feel pain or suffering in regard to your obsessions and compulsions. If you do, then you are clinically obsessed.

This concept that the ability to choose is the difference between good and bad obsession is a crucial point. If you choose to be obsessed in work, athletics, or sex, that is a good thing. If you cannot help but count the number of times you brush your teeth or the number of steps you need to cross a threshold, and you cannot stop, then you are pathological. Your ability to choose is the key between pathology and passion. Linked to this is how you feel about it. If you do such things, are happy about them, then you will not choose to stop. If you do such things, want to stop, or are told by family members, friends, or lovers that you should stop, and you cannot, then you are pathological or, putting it another way, disabled.

It should not take too much effort to see that the element of choice of a lifestyle through consumerism and the element of *how you feel about it* are key signposts along the way of neo-liberal, consumer society which is based on the idea of the consumer who has the power to choose to buy products that confirm a lifestyle and who is happy to do so. So with OCD personal suffering comes from wanting to stop but being unable to. And suffering comes from being in an environment that pinpoints the kinds of things you are doing as unproductive and worthy of stopping. An article in the *New York Times* for example showcases a man who obsessively builds large gardens with mosaics made from small pebbles. Jeffrey Bale is described as picking through 400 pounds of pebbles "and found only two dozen stones that would work for this project, an ornate pathway and sunken garden mosaic" (Murphy) in the garden of Tony Shaloub, ironically or perhaps not – the actor who plays Monk. The article makes the obvious connection between such painstaking activity and OCD, and Mr. Bale responds, "It's not a disorder if you channel it into something productive" (ibid.).

OCD as it is understood by the general public is a discrete disease. It has developed over time into something incontrovertible and recent work seeks to locate its origin in brain chemistry, structure, or genetics. It feels palpable and real, and the suffering it produces is real as well. In that sense, OCD is primed to be sucked into the media mill. It has dramatic possibilities as ordinary people seem to be fingered for torment by mysterious and diabolic forces. However, my own work suggests that the causes are not mysterious. In fact, I argue, that there is a deep cultural involvement in the genesis and production of this illness. And the media, for one, is both implicated for publicizing it as the disease of the month, for narrativizing it in familiar ways, and for dramatizing the dilemma of the person with the disorder. I am not blaming the media here but just pointing out how a disease can be proliferated through the dispersal of images and stories about it. In the case of OCD, for example, the disorder has gone from an extremely rare disease in the 1950s to one of the four most common disorders in our time. In a mere 50 years or so, OCD has gone from something *had* by one out of 1000 to one in 10. People now routinely say, 'I'm so OCD.'

The point I want to make is that OCD is a clinical entity, which can mean many things, but one thing it means is that it is part of a social, cultural, medical – that is to say biocultural – milieu. As such it is produced by conscious and unconscious cooperation between medical establishments, individuals, social networks, families, and their intersections with governmental, media, and corporate entities. This is a complex process that is both essentialist on some level and performative on another. OCD then becomes both a disorder and by extension an identity or a set of identities. How do people who *have* OCD know that they have it? How do they enact their symptoms? How do family members and friends help them to *identify* it?

In this sense the media is more active than simply holding up the proverbial mirror to life. The media is deeply involved in the proliferation of images that help people in the general population diagnose themselves. And the direct-to-consumer advertising for psychoactive drugs such as antidepressants, antipsychotic, and sleeping pills is an intimate part of the matrix that is television viewing. In a sense, the media is not simply about the portrayal of disabilities but the de-facto advocate of contemporary treatments for affective disorders as well.

Linked to this hegemonic activity is the development of identities to correspond with this citizenship in which one becomes a card-carrying member with *depression* or OCD along with other disorders you have seen on television and in film. That is, one's identity iterated and reiterated on television and in film as a trope and a dramatic plot element – particularly in the form of a knowable, understandable, and delimited character – becomes a familiar feature of everyday life. In turn, television and film narratives often center on how people chose to live with these disease entities, now seen as freestanding and independent of any social or economic forces. For example, there are cinematic possibilities in portraying someone with OCD or depression, but no possibilities of showing in film how OCD developed over time in complex ways and also no possibility of dramatizing the life of someone who is depressed not by a putative bio-chemical imbalance but because he or she is poor, part of the

99 percent of Americans facing economic inequality, and so on. In the media, poverty, as with disability, is something to be overcome. Both are rarely if ever portrayed as systematic problems; rather they are routinely seen as individual ones. And we never have a TV series about poverty, only about the side-effects of poverty – drugs, prostitution, crime – just as we never have a TV series about disability, only about how a disabled character, often minor, makes other *normal* people feel good about themselves.

At this point, I want to explore a contradiction in what I have been saying in this essay compared to what I have said in my earlier work on identity. That is, I have spent a fair amount of time in my work and writing deconstructing the idea of a monolithic disability identity. I have claimed that what characterizes disability is that it is a shifting, changing, morphing notion of identity that distinguishes itself from other identity categories that seem to have developed, over time, a certain rigidity in definition.

So the example I have often used is that you can become disabled over night by a car accident or a fall from a horse, while if you are a woman or a person of color, you cannot wake up the next day and find yourself a man or a white person. I have said all of this with a lot of qualifications about the shiftiness of all identity categories, but with the assertion that disability identity can lead us to rethinking all identity categories, and I have coined the term *dismodernism* to point out the way that disability as a category can help us find a postmodern perspective on the aging, antique and antiquated categories of race, gender, and so on.

Yet recently I have been blogging about the necessity for Hollywood and other large media conglomerates to rethink their attitudes toward having non-disabled actors play disabled characters ("Let Actors"). But is it a contradiction for me to claim that there is no essential identity to disability and then insist on disabled actors playing the role of disabled characters? If I am using critics like Judith Butler to claim that there is something non-essentialist and performative about disability and normality, then why ought non-disabled actors avoid performing the roles of disabled people? And if I maintain the necessity of disabled actors playing disabled roles, am I being rather crudely essentialist?

You could argue that since disability, according to the social model, is in the environment not in the person, then creating an accommodating environment in which all can perform any theatrical or cinematic role regardless of their physical status would be an appropriate action. So if I say that only disabled actors can play disabled parts, am I in effect saying that only some people should be accommodated?

Before I come to grips with this problem, I think it will be necessary to present the lay of the land as concerns disability and acting. For a non-disabled actor to take on the role of a disabled person, there are huge incentives. If you want to try for an Academy Award, you would do well to portray a person with a disability. Notable movies of this kind fill the silver screen from Patty Duke's

Helen Keller to Dustin Hoffman's Rainman, from Daniel Day Lewis' portrayal of Christie Brown to Tom Cruise as Ron Kovic in *Born on the Fourth of July*. Yet, in all these cases, the people who starred in these films were non-disabled actors playing disabled roles. So the take-home message here is that films that focus on disability in a central way continue to be made and remain star-vehicles for high profile non-disabled actors.

You would think then given the appeal of these roles that characters with disabilities should be rife in the media. Only they are not. Although disability can provide acting opportunities, on television, at least, according to *The Hollywood Reporter*'s survey for the 2011 season, which noted out of a total of 600 repeating characters on US prime time television shows, only six were characters written to have a disability. And of those, only one was actually played by a disabled actor (*Hollywood Reporter*). Most of the supporting roles in movies will be played by non-disabled people. And the default status for the stereotypical roles – the best friend of the main character, the mother, father, siblings and so on – will all be conceived of normal and not disabled.

The reason has something to do with the economy of visual storytelling in an ableist culture. This in turn comes out of the legacy of eugenics and the current hegemony of ableism itself. If you want to make a film that is about disability in such a culture, then every part of the story has to do with disability. The film has to be, in some sense, obsessed with disability. But if the roving eye of the camera takes its focus off of disability, then disability has to disappear or it will create a buzz of interference in the story telling. Instead of disability, to illustrate this point, think of pregnancy. It is quite normal to see a pregnant woman on the street, but if you make one of the characters in a television show pregnant, then you have to provide a whole rationale and back-story for the pregnancy. That is why generic mothers in cinematic narratives about children are never pregnant, unless the pregnancy figures into the plot, whereas in real life mothers might be pregnant or not depending on a host of completely random factors. The same might be said of acne, sore throats, and other bodily ills. Likewise with disability – if the mother of a child in a movie has a disability, and the film is not about the disability, then the audience will be distracted from the narrative arc by the disability. They will wonder why the *normalcy* of the film is being tampered with. In an ableist culture disability cannot just *be* – it has to *mean* something. It has to signify.

In this sense, disability is allegorical – it has to stand for something else – weakness, insecurity, bitterness, frailty, evil, innocence, etc. – and be the occasion for the conveyance of some moral truth – that people are good, can overcome, that we shouldn't discriminate or despair. But, to paraphrase Sigmund Freud, sometimes an amputated leg is just an amputated leg. That obvious statement can never be true in the world of media narrative, and so an amputated leg is never just that. It must be a character trait, a metaphor, and fit into a plot point, or be a *reveal* to some other character who has not seen it, or to the main character who discovers new things about himself or herself in the process of triumphing over the disability. Yet, possessing a functional leg is never allegorical, needs no interpretation, and is basically a degree-zero signifier without a referent.

So when an actor takes on a role as a person with a disability, he or she is entering a world of signs and meanings that encapsulate the larger society's attitude toward disability. This system of signs and meanings participates and encourages the non-disabled person's fantasy about disability. Just as Edward Said pointed out in *Orientalism* that the East was made into the projected fantasy of the West, so has film and television, and the ableist media projected its image of disability. You learn much more, according to Said, about the West by studying orientalist works than you learn about the East. And with ableist narratives you learn much more about the mindset of a *normal* than you do about the real experience of being a person with a disability. So it might well be that only a non-disabled actor could in fact portray that distorted and biased disability that lives and breathes in ableist culture and that translates so easily to the standard Hollywood film or television series. Just as only someone like Rudolf Valentino could portray the orientalist sheik in the silent movies – being the eroticized but very Western heart throb who could convey the mytheme of the sexuality of the orient. In the same way, the non-disabled actor can eroticize and embody the stereotypes and clichés inherent in the regnant ideology around disability.

A non-disabled actor has literally to transform him or herself in order to portray a disabled person. Audiences and critics enjoy that transformative ability, and it is surely tied up with our basic ideas of theatricality. We are used to the idea that an actor transforms him- or herself by means of make-up, mental preparation, and even now computer-graphical assist. In fact there is something mercurial and protean about being an actor. We admire the hours of cosmetic and prosthetic work that goes into transforming the likes of Brad Pitt into the likes of the aged Benjamin Button.

But we are now less willing to approve, and this is where the complexity comes in, when we transform actors from a dominant identity group to one that is not. So for example, the practice of using blackface was widely appreciated and prized by white audiences of theater and film until attitudes toward people of color became much more changed beginning in the 1930s. Despite performances by Al Jolson in the 1929 classic *the Jazz Singer*, Fred Astaire in *Top Hat*, and, as late as 1938 to 1941, Judy Garland repeatedly in *Everyone Sing* (1938), *Babes in Arms* (1939), and *Babes on Broadway* (1941), the latter two directed by Busby Berkeley, the practice faded out entirely from dramatic works by the 1950s and 1960s. Blackface may have taken a very late bow, but having white actors portray Native Americans, Asians, Indians, Arabs, and others continued well into the latter half of the 20th century until consciousness raising and awareness of racism ended that practice only as recently as 25 years ago.

It is now almost universally acknowledged that when it comes to most racial groups, actors from within the tradition of those groups are preferred to actors from outside. No one doubts, for example, that Ben Kingsley can do a pretty good job of playing Gandhi, but in 1982 such a practice was tolerated whereas now it might not be. It is currently acceptable for Morgan Freeman to play Nelson Mandela in Clint Eastwood's *Invictus*, although South African actors had decried the limited roles for them in this film. Freeman as an African American is seen as having enough kinship with black Africans to make the transition by Hollywood, at least by US if not by South African standards. The Creative Workers Union in South Africa protested saying "we want more South African actors because we do have some great talent to take on these strong roles in these stories" (*PRI*). South Africa actor Florence Mesebe analyzed the situation as this: "South African actors are never going to be good enough, because we don't have the Hollywood tag. We are tired of the Hollywood box office excuse" (ibid.).

These arguments concerning ethnicity and national origin seem to ring less forcefully to the public because those in the English speaking world routinely see US, UK, Australian, and New Zealand actors playing each other's nationality, as well as playing Russians, Eastern Europeans, Greeks, Italians, Jews, and the like (*11 Points*). Within the larger category of those who are currently considered *whites* there is less trouble with interchangeability.

So how do we parse these predilections and taboos? Again, I would return to the issue of choice. Nationalities and even ethnicities, particularly where there are no overly stereotyped physical features are not seen as rooted in the concept of normality but rather in the concept of diversity. One can choose to move from South Africa to the UK, and if one is white, there is little discrimination to be faced, particularly in the assimilated generations. Actors, therefore, are well within their rights to play these kind of parallel roles, and their skill in adopting accents, as actors like Meryl Streep or Jude Law do routinely, is part of their mimetic profession. Thus nationality does not seem inappropriate for actors to take on in their roles, although race does. Disability has been seen as fair game for actors, but in a sense it is ontologically more like race in the sense that it is not a state of being one can choose.

This element of choice is paramount in something like Clint Eastwood's, now infamous in disability circles, *Million Dollar Baby*. When it was released it was roundly criticized for its pessimistic vision of life for a disabled woman. But few criticized Eastwood for not casting a disabled actress in the main role. The reason for that is obvious – Maggie had to go from a physically intact athlete to a quadriplegic in the course of the film. The skill of the actor and the director would involve a transformation that had no element of choice in it (except of course the choice to die). So a central concept in a film like this is that the disabled person is a person without a choice, and therefore the actor who plays the person has to be normal to counter, in some sense, this message of hopelessness (lack of choice) by letting the audience know in a de facto way that the actor, while playing someone who has no choice, himself or herself does have a choice.

That is, although the character is without a choice regarding his or her disability, the audience will always know that the actor has many choices. In fact, to return to the issue of the transformation of the non-disabled actor into a person with a disability, which is often the subject of film publicity, the salient point for the audience is that the actor is not disabled – but that the magic of computer generated imagery, make-up and prosthetics magically and cinematically transforms the actor into the disabled character. The audience can rest comfortably assured that the central character may appear to be disabled but is not really a disabled person, only a non-disabled actor playing the role. The cinematic experience is a form of make-believe whose fantastic nature is revealed when the time comes for Hillary Swank to stride across the stage and accept her Oscar. We know she will not be ambulating using a wheel chair with a sip-straw control. She will not choose to die in obscurity over a disability, but rather will live in Hollywood glory to accept her award.

The star system makes it hard for disabled actors to fit in. Stars tend to be interchangeable parts in a system of production. Their *normality* is a sign of their ability to transform. Transformation and choice, two basic tenets of the neoliberal system based on lifestyle and niche marketing, are touchstones in a system that promotes individuality and self-actualization. Interestingly, class is never portrayed in film as operating in ultimately disabling ways. One's class in this view is only the place where you start as you transform through choice and hard work. And if you are upper class in film, then your narrative will be about how you suffer from being too rich and have to find yourself through adopting the values and viewpoint of a middle-class or poor person. Each of us, so the story goes, can become anything we want if only we have the will, the drive, and the dedication. The *normal* actor then embodies this mythology of class and bodily open-endedness, while the disabled actor is seen as a grim reminder that transformation is not possible, except in limited ways.

If disability represents, in the popular imagination, a tragic fate in which choice is removed while at the same time a kind of frightening and disfiguring prospect for audiences who can only too easily imagine themselves transformed into a disabled person by the simple swerve of a car on the highway, a virulent disease, or a malfunction of the body, then the role of the media historically has been to provide comfort to them. The comfort comes from the triumphant scenario in which the main disabled character overcomes the limitations of the impairment to become the leader of, say, the anti-war movement, or a famous blind-deaf writer, or any other accomplished professional. The comfort also comes from seeing that person accepted with all their limitations by friends, family, lovers, and the general public – which includes the audience who learns to see that person as *human*. Indeed, the greatest comfort comes from knowing that the character is being play-acted by a normal person. The fear of fragmentation and destruction of ego is compensated for by the notion that *it's only a movie.*

Some of these points are illustrated in the film *Avatar*. Jake Sully, played by Sam Worthington a non-disabled actor, is a paraplegic who lost the use of his legs in war as a marine. At one point in the film, we see his atrophied legs as he wheels his chair frontally toward the camera. This shot is in some sense the *money shot* which verifies to the audience that the physical body of the actor is indeed that of a paraplegic – while of course in reality it is not. Part of the visual frisson of seeing those atrophied legs is knowing that this is one among many other special effects that have no contractual bearing on the reality of the actor's actual body. In fact, the film is about nothing if it is not about transformation since Jake becomes a larger than life blue avatar through the miracle of both DNA, biotechnology, and of course computer generated imagery and 3D. In fact, the realism of the 3D effect guarantees the realism of the live action part of the film that also *guarantees* the character's disability. That disability disappears in the movie whenever Jake enters his avatar, and, given the film logic, the unreal world of the avatar eventually becomes more real than the live action part of the film. In the film's paradisiacal world of the primeval forest of Pandora, Jake is one with nature, able to perform acts of physical prowess and agilely use his super-human mobility. So the bargain with the audience is that you get to have a disabled character, who remains disabled at the end of the film, even turning down the villain's offer to give him back his legs through expensive medical cures, but that indeed that character can still transform to become a non-disabled character. And of course, in reality, Sam Worthington had the ability to walk into the Academy Awards on his own two feet. Everyone will be assured that the movie is after all only a movie. And disability is after all only a trope, a signifying event, an allegorical state of being.

To return to my main argument and contradiction, I think it fair and right that disabled actors should play disabled roles. In fact there is a movement to this effect in the UK and Australia called "Don't Play Us, Pay Us." The general public, however, based on responses to the blogs I have written, are torn about this proposition, and many feel that delimiting what an actor can and cannot do is an abrogation of freedom of speech and a denial of what it is that actors do. And then I myself have argued for the fluidity of the identity category of disability, so why would I then argue that we should limit roles to actors who are *actually* disabled in the particular way that the character is?

My response would be that in the best of possible worlds, all actors should play all parts. As my colleague Rosemarie Garland-Thomson questioned recently: Why should not disabled actors be cast in non-disabled roles? But the current state of affairs perpetuates ableism by reinforcing both the audiences' expectations that disability is a state to be magically transformed and that non-disabled actors are the high priests who reenact this sacrament every time they don a disability for a role and then remove it when they go home at night. This state of affairs also ghettoizes stardom so that only non-disabled characters can become stars, which in turn emphasizes that disability is an abnormal state that needs to be patrolled and marginalized by casting directors and unreceptive audiences.

Indeed, if we only consider issues of fairness, it would make sense that a discriminated against group of actors – those with disabilities – are in need of work. I am not suggesting a quota system or affirmative action, but some of the principles of those systems might well be applied to the casting of actors. Right now, it makes little sense for a young person with disabilities to imagine a career in acting. I recently asked Matt Fraser, one of the more successful disabled actors, whether things were improving for disabled actors, and he told me that he did not think they were. In what other profession would it be acceptable to discriminate against an identity and get away with it? In what other profession would we counsel young people to forget their hopes and dreams because of rampant prejudice against the kind of person they are? The state of affairs is not acceptable, and only when we routinely see disabled actors playing disabled and non-disabled roles will the stereotypes perpetuated in the media be eliminated. While it may seem like a rarified complain to lodge against Hollywood, it is actually crucial to the goals of disability awareness and disability studies.

REFERENCES

11 Points. "11 Best Jewish Movie Characters Played by Non-Jewish Actors." Web. 7 November 2014. <http://www.11points.com/movies/11_best_jewish_mo vie_characters_played_by_non-jewish_actors>.

Davis, Lennard. "Let Actors With Disabilities Play Characters With Disabilities." The Huffington Post. 2011. Web. 7 November 2014. <http://www.huffing tonpost.com/lennard-davis/let-actors-with-disabilit_b_380266.html>.

The Hollywood Reporter. "GLAAD: Only 6 disabled primetime characters." Web. 7 November 2014. <http://www.hollywoodreporter.com/news/glaad-only-6-disabled-primetime-15312>.

Murphy, Kate. "Turning Every Stone for the Perfect Fit." The New York Times. 2009. Web. 7 November 2014. <http://www.nytimes.com/2009/12/24/ garden/24mosaic.html?pagewanted=all&_r=0>.

PRI. Web. 7 November 2014. http://www.pri.org/arts-entertainment/movies/ clint-eastwood-invictus1771.html>.

Building a World with Disability in It

Rosemarie Garland-Thomson

In this essay, I consider the question of why we might want disabled people in the world.[1] I begin with the 1568 Peter Bruegel painting, *The Cripples*. This painting suggests a fundamental contradiction about disability as a human condition. *The Cripples* shows a humble group of four men, with what we today call mobility impairments, using a variety of prosthetic devices that range from crutches to a proto-wheelchair. The men are out and about in the public world amongst fellow subjects and public buildings, perhaps scouting out the area for the best begging situation. The faces of two of the gnome-like figures express a confused attentiveness, with mouths agape and searching, if perplexed, eyes. The other two seem concentrated on the task at hand – getting about in inaccessible terrain. Although this is most probably a scene of begging, all four are deeply engaged in the challenges of navigating their world with a disability. This representation expresses uncertainty rather than assurance, humility rather than entitlement, persistence rather than privilege, and ordinariness rather than distinction. In short, the parable I wish to draw from these paintings is that disability presents at once a problem and an opportunity for solutions. There inheres, in other words, in all things disability a contradiction.

This contradiction is summed up in the following two assertions from disability studies scholars: Disability is "the master trope of human disqualification" (Snyder and Mitchell 125), and "What we call disability is perhaps the essential characteristic of being human" (Garland-Thomson, "Integrating" 21). Sharon Snyder and David Mitchell's claim suggests that disability restricts, excludes, renders one exceptional: disqualifies. But, at the same time, my own assertion suggests that disability gathers us into the everyday community of embodied humankind. If disability is inherent in the human condition, how can it simultaneously disqualify us from full membership in the human community? How can disability be both an occasion for inclusion and exclusion?

---

1 | Portions of this essay appeared in "The Case for Conserving Disability," *Journal of Bioethical Inquiry* 9.3 (2012): 339-55.

WORLD BUILDING

This contradiction inherent in disability can be found in what I call world building, the shared project of making and using our world together. The premise of world building is that the shape of the material world we design, build, and use together both expresses and determines who inhabits it and how we use it to exercise the duties and privileges of citizenship within that world.[2] Modern culture in the U.S. and other developed and developing societies is now undertaking two contradictory world building initiatives that are expressed in social, legislative, material, cultural and attitudinal practices.

One initiative, which I call inclusive world building, seeks to integrate people with disabilities into the public world by creating an accessible, barrier-free material environment. Inclusive world building frames disability as valued social diversity and supports the civil and human rights-based understanding of disability encoded in legislation like the Americans with Disabilities Act of 1990 and 2009 and broader initiatives, such as the United Nations Convention on the Rights of Persons with Disabilities of 2006, which aims to integrate people with disabilities as full citizens.

In contrast to this inclusion initiative, is the initiative I call eugenic world building, which strives to eliminate disability and, along with it, people with disabilities from human communities through varying social and material practices that range from seemingly benign to egregiously unethical. Restrictive environments that segregate people with disabilities from one another and from the nondisabled are one form of eugenic world building. Scientific and medical technologies are another form – for example, genetic manipulation, selective abortion, and medical normalization justified by the idea that social improvement and freedom of choice require eliminating devalued human traits in the interest of reducing human suffering, increasing life quality, and building a more desirable citizenry. Eugenic world building, in short, is the ideology and set of practices that control who enters and participates in the shared public spaces of a democratic order.

---

2 | This essay follows on an earlier discussion I presented in "Welcoming the Unbidden: The Case for Conserving Human Biodiversity" (2006).

INCLUSION AND EXCLUSION

This material contradiction between inclusive and eugenic world building suggests that the world we are making at this time and in this place simultaneously wants and does not want disabled people in it. In other words, in these two contemporary world building initiatives, disability is an occasion for both inclusion and exclusion. The question this contradiction raises, of course, is how we reconcile a world that rewards diversity of all types and still emphasizes particular standards of acceptable bodies.

One recent, specific example of this world building contradiction appears in a July, 2011 *New York Times Magazine* article, reporting that the neuroscientist and physician Alberto Costa, whose daughter has Down syndrome, is researching drugs that he hopes will yield treatment (see Hurley). His aspiration is to increase the quality of life and develop the potential for inclusion of people with Down syndrome in a world that values intellectual capability. Costa explains that he is in a losing race for funding with scientists developing new prenatal genetic tests, which are less invasive and can be administered earlier to identify fetuses with Down syndrome for possible elimination. This funding disparity, he suggests, reflects our cultural preference for building a world without people who bear the human variations we think of as disabilities. Costa's story suggests that the kind of research he is undertaking supports an inclusive world building initiative, whereas the preferentially funded prenatal testing research supports a eugenic logic that would eliminate people like his daughter from our shared world.

EUGENIC LOGIC

How then do we understand this eugenic logic, modernity's sustained commitment to eliminating disability from the human condition, this literalizing of disability as disqualification that Sharon Snyder and David Mitchell identify as the master trope of our shared world? Why, eugenic logic asks, should the world we build together include disability at all? Our dominant understanding is that disability confers pain, disease, functional limitation, disadvantage, and social stigma; limits opportunities; and reduces quality of life. Eugenic logic tells us that our world would be a better place if disability could be eliminated. Enacted worldwide in policies and practices that range from segregation to extermination, the aim of eugenics is to eliminate disability and, by extension, disabled people from the world. Eugenic logic is a utopian effort to improve the social order, a practical health program, or a social justice initiative that is simply common sense to most people and is supported by the logic of modernity itself.

COUNTER-EUGENIC LOGIC

Against the eugenic commonplace that assumes we should eliminate disability, I consider the bioethical question of whether disability and disabled people are something we might want to conserve rather than merely tolerate. To do so, I take up an eclectic, rather than systematic, variety of counter-eugenic positions and perspectives, ranging from instrumental to pragmatic, ardent to skeptical. Taken together, these perspectives honor the complexity of how disability acts as "the master trope of human disqualification" and also constitute a conversation asserting that disability might better be conserved (Mitchell and Snyder 3). These speculations about what disability might be good for reframe it as a resource rather than restriction, offering a reading of disability as generative rather than limiting. In other words, this conversation asks what cultural and material work disability does in the world.

What I endeavor to explicate here are 'because of rather than in spite of' counter-eugenic positions. In other words, I explore what disability-as-disability and what disabled people-as-they-are contribute to our shared world. By this, I do not mean productivity in capitalist economies, nor contribution through individual agency or acts, but I want, instead, to think about the generative work of disability and people with disabilities through their presence. Put another way, I ask what we lose besides the individuals themselves if we eliminate disability and disabled people from the world.

Attending to what disability contributes requires focusing on its generative potential rather than its restrictive potential. The tension between disability as a universal and persistent human experience and disability's cultural work as a disqualifier intensifies its generative potential, I suggest. As disability studies has amply pointed out, once we begin to attend to it, disability is everywhere in the cultural products arising from our collective consciousness. As both a generative concept and a fundamental human experience, then, disability creates circuits of meaning making in the world. The meaning-making potential of disability can be organized into a taxonomy of three interrelated registers – the narrative, epistemic, and ethical. Under these rubrics, I find sustained and complicated counter-eugenic arguments for disability conservation.

DISABILITY AS NARRATIVE RESOURCE

From the unsettling contradiction of disability's universality and disqualifying potential come some of our most enduring and canonical cultural narratives. Disability is apparently close to the quick, a perpetual narrative resource. Perhaps something resolutely human and inherently interesting inheres in disability itself and the lives we make with disabilities. Sophocles's tragic figure, Oedipus, for example, is one of the founding protagonists of Western culture. Oedipus's tragic flaw is of course hubris, the Promethean aspiration to know the terrible truth of his own fate. Oedipus's life journey is also bookended by disability: his parents, the King and Queen, expose their newborn to die on a mountaintop with his ankles bound together, for which he is named Oedipus, meaning swollen foot. The mark of his damaged foot provides the irrefutable evidence of his identity and terrible fate. Laden with this inescapable self-knowledge, Oedipus seizes the truth of who he is, knowingly taking his fate into his own hands by gouging out his eyes and heading down the road alone. As such, disability defeats hubris. With this dramatic act, Sophocles expresses an alignment of the hero's body and identity by making Oedipus, like Tiresias before him, into one of the canonical figures of classical Greek tragedy, the blind seer.

In another example, Arthur W. Frank's *The Wounded Storyteller: Body, Illness, and Ethics* (1995) puts forward a strong argument for disability as a narrative resource in the form of self story. Frank values the narrative potential of disability for disabled people, and the contribution of disability narrative in Frank's account is to counteract disability's social disqualification. As Snyder and Mitchell suggest, few of us willingly welcome disability into life today. The birth of a disabled child or the onset of disability is seen as a catastrophe or a failing. This is so because being disabled shifts one into an unappealing and unexpected social position.

Narrative is a productive rather than compensatory resource in Frank's ardent defense of disability's contribution to self-understanding and identity formation. Using the more belletristic language of 'wound' and 'illness,' rather than the politicized and rights-invoking language of 'disability,' Frank asserts that being the author of one's own disability story "transforms fate into experience" through narrative's restorative potential (Frank xi).[3] Frank considers the narrative of his own wounding and the proposed utility of a wound-telling story to be a "survival kit" (xiii).

Disability in Frank's account is an opportunity to develop "voice" (109), by which he means the capacity for making a coherent, causal account from the arbitrary temporal incidents that compose acquiring, adjusting to, and experiencing the transformation of self that is becoming disabled. For Frank, voice expresses body in storytelling, redeeming through order making and reintegration into the human community. The work of narrative is selecting and linking random incidents to make a structured story with a beginning, middle, and end that puts retrospective order to the baffling chaos of experience that

---

3 | Independent scholar Terry Tracy makes a distinction between illness and disability narratives in an unpublished paper entitled, "Disability Narrative vs. Illness Narrative: Different Wounds, Different Stories," delivered at Columbia University in March 2012.

washes over us each moment. Fortified and calmed with story, we are equipped to navigate what happens next by folding it into our story of what has already happened and into the stories of those who have gone before and will follow us. Telling one's disability story is an antidote to disability disqualification, to the social banishment and apartness of the sick role and the stranger-making function of disability stigma. Making disability narrative integrates one into the human community by generating "the common bond of suffering that joins bodies in their shared vulnerability" (xi). Frank transforms the tragic narrative of disability as isolation into the comic narrative of disability as belonging. "Sooner or later," Frank assures us, "everyone is a wounded storyteller" (xiii). Thus, Frank's notion of wounded storytelling illustrates how disability can be an occasion for both exclusion and inclusion and that resolution of contradiction can come through the process of narrative making.

Disability as Epistemic Resource

For Frank, the generative work of narrative is to produce knowledge through rendering life experience into a coherent and usable form. Disability narrative can thus contribute to knowledge making as an epistemic resource. What psychologists call "embodied cognition" suggests that people draw on their bodily experiences not only to think and know but also to construct our social reality.[4] In other words, our bodily form, function, comportment, perceptual apprehension, and way of mind shape how we understand the world. The current critical generation's critique of objectivity, master narratives, and a universal standpoint has not only discredited 'the so-called view from nowhere' but has also advanced a material turn that furthers a phenomenological approach, bringing together epistemology and ontology in productive accounts of assemblages and material-discursive understandings. This critical exploration has yielded terms that range from oppositional consciousness, standpoint epistemology, outsider/insider perspective, privileged epistemic state, to subjugated know-ledge.

The bioethicist Jackie Leach Scully has argued persuasively that a distinctive and morally privileged knowledge can arise from the experience of living in a disabled body. In accordance with Scully and following Patricia Hill Collins, I maintain that the material experience of navigating a world built for the majority while living with a minority form of embodiment like disability can produce a politicized consciousness or epistemic epiphany regarding the relativity of exclusions that the status quo explains as natural or essentializes as inherent inferiority. Disabled bodies, as Scully explains it, produce "experiential gestalts" (91), or ways-of-knowing shaped by embodiment that are distinctive from the ways of knowing that the nondisabled body develops as it interacts

---

4 | See, for example, Gibbs (2005) and Shapiro (2010).

with the world built to accommodate it. This "thinking through the variant body," as Scully calls it, can be a resource (83).

For example, the deaf blind activist and writer, Helen Keller, gives an account of how embodied cognition generates subjugated knowledge in her 1908 collection of essays, *The World I Live In*. Keller's enforced unreliance on the dominant senses of hearing and sight provide her a generative opportunity to develop vivid tactile, taste, and olfactory knowledges that often remain dormant in sighted and hearing people. Keller narrates what one might call disability synesthesia when she smells horizons, recognizes people by the touch of a hand, and analogously knows scarlet from crimson through perceiving the olfactory distinction between the smells of oranges and grapefruits. Her well-developed subjugated knowledge leads her to the observation that the typically sensed are limited by being "smell-blind-and-deaf" (Keller 31). Touch, she concludes from her distinctive way of knowing, "is a great deal the eye's superior," as phenomenology has suggested (34).

Disability as Ethical Resource

This cascade of rationales for disability conservation I offer begins in disability's propensity to generate narrative, which in turn generates knowledge, and finally generates an explicitly ethical counter-eugenic logic. The final and most nuanced counter-eugenic argument I will offer comes from Emily Rapp's wrenching account of her experience and understanding of parenting a child with a fatal disease, which she published in *The New York Times* and *Slate Magazine Online*. In these two pieces, Rapp offers a humble argument for disability conservation that honors the pain, loss, and suffering that is fundamental to much disability.[5]

At nine months old, Rapp's son Ronan was diagnosed with Tay-Sachs, a rare genetic condition which causes a slow developmental regression into paralysis and sensory loss that is irrevocably fatal by the age of about three. The condition represents a perverse reversal of our imagined developmental trajectory, foreshortening an entire life course to a chillingly compact arc. With Tay-Sachs, the disintegration we expect to languidly stretch over seven decades instead rushes by in mere months. Tay-Sachs is, of course, the exemplary "worst-case" put widely forward in arguments for reproductive counseling, eugenic testing, and selective abortion. It is the anchor of any reasonable eugenic argument. As such, Rapp's son Ronan offers the most difficult and controversial case for disability conservation. Moreover, that Rapp had two screenings for the

---

5 | Rapp has since written in greater detail and at length about her experience of parenting a terminally ill child and about her son's short life in her memoir *The Still Point of the Turning World* (2013).

condition which did not indicate its presence complicates what is often taken to be a clear-cut case for genetic testing and selective termination. Rapp herself has said that had she known Ronan would have Tay-Sachs, she would have selectively aborted her pregnancy in order to prevent the suffering both her son and his parents have experienced.

The prevention of suffering is one of the major eugenic arguments for eliminating disability and disabled people at all life stages. The Nazis, Peter Singer, supporters of physician assisted suicide, and the reproductive rights movement have all used it in some way.[6] A wary Flannery O'Connor has even warned of the peril – rightly, I think – that sympathy for the suffering of others can lead to the gas chamber.[7] But Emily Rapp and her son's situation offer a consideration other than the well-worn conversation about suffering. While it would be wrong to reduce the complicated and contradictory understandings Emily Rapp offers about her son's condition, one point that her story makes clear is that suffering expands our imagination about what we can endure.

More than this, however, Rapp's account of what Ronan's disability imposes upon her clarifies a less-recognized aspect of disability's distinctive work in the world that is worth conserving. Disability in general, and Ronan's dramatic disability manifestation in particular, offers an experience-based counter narrative to the modern subject's understanding of the present moment as an opportunity to shape the future. Living with her son's disability compels Rapp to live "without a future," to cultivate a primary self-defining interpersonal relationship in the lived present that presumes no future (Rapp, *Still Point* 11). Rapp's forcible abandonment of the future stretches toward understandings and experiences that expand what she, and perhaps Ronan, might have had in an ordinary, nondisabled life together. The contribution of Ronan's disability is rooted in the present and in presence. Disability speaks only of the present; the prodigious cannot be prepared for and it anticipates nothing in our control.

---

6 | In Practical Ethics (2009), Peter Singer argues for selectively killing, in particular, infants and disabled people as a reasoned, utilitarian principle. He presents this case in order to argue against and refute the sanctity of human life principle as an absolute position uninflected by utilitarianism or liberalism. In order to put forward his position of secular speciesism, Singer argues for killing disabled people as conscienceless newborns or sufferers, which is related to his critique of vitalism as a bio-conservative position rooted in Judeo-Christian culture. His argument for killing disabled people, therefore, is less an argument for this position than it is one against the logical flaws in conservative, vaguely nonsecular positions holding to a moral boundary between human and nonhuman life forms.

7 | In "A Memoir of Mary Ann," O'Connor says: "In the absence of […] faith, now we govern by tenderness […]. It ends in forced labor camps and in the fumes of the gas chamber" (O'Connor 227).

Like Frank's wound-telling stories, Rapp's story of the "even blissful," "magical world" of the mundane and its "terrible freedom" from expectations could not be restorative, in Frank's sense, but may indeed be transformative (Rapp, "Notes" n. pag.).

One might say that Rapp's story could be just one more version of lessons from the disabled for the nondisabled. I want to suggest, instead, that the forcible abandonment of the future that Rapp explains constitutes something more complex and capacious: it is a modern counter-eugenic ethics. Eugenics is about controlling the future; it is the ideology and practice of controlling who reproduces, how they reproduce, and what they reproduce in the interest of controlling the composition of a particular citizenry. The very idea of shaping a community or a national citizenry through the technological and legislative practices that control reproduction is distinctly modern. This understanding of the relationship between present actions and future outcomes is expressed in many aspects of modern cultures and is one of the hallmarks of modernity, codified in modern nation states, modern culture, and modern subjectivity – even modern design. Zygmunt Bauman finds modern genocide, for example, rooted in rationality, efficiency, science, bureaucracy and its manifestation in the nation state – in short what Max Weber called "rationalization," the hallmark of modernity. The interrelated concepts of evolution, progress, and improvement comprise a temporal aspiration for both individuals and societies that is crucial to modernity. The insistence on control in the present over the outcomes of the future – what James R. Beniger calls the "control revolution" and what Thomas Haskell shows to be the relationship between benevolence and capitalism – is perhaps the fundamental aspect of modernity and modern subjectivity. This impulse to control the future is the overreaching that Michael Sandel has so effectively decried in his case against perfection.

Disability is, then, a conceptual category that represents something which goes beyond actual people with disabilities. It represents a problem with temporality as it is formulated in modernity. Disability and illness frustrate modernity's investment in controlling the future. Douglas Baynton argues that the efficiency and increased pace in task performance in all aspects of daily living which became the dominant value and way of life during 19th century modernization shaped the cultural understanding of disability as representing inefficiency and intractability. Baynton's historical account suggests that as the modern understanding of time as a commodity – of the present moment as an opportunity for investment in the future – developed, disability came to be seen not just as a misfortune, punishment, blessing, or omen from an either benevolent or angry God, but rather as intransigence embodied. Disability and people with disabilities are eugenic targets because we embody the unpredictable and intractable nature of temporality. We frustrate modernity's fantasy that humans determine the arc of their own histories.

Rapp's narrative confronts our collective investment in futurity, which I have suggested is distinctly modern and differs from traditional worldviews. Thus, disability becomes for modernity's Promethean aspiration to control the future at once its greatest opportunity and its greatest repudiation. Curing cancer, sundering the conjoined into singletons, and flushing out the elusive gene for Tay-Sachs are challenges in the interest of controlling the future by shaping how human beings are and who we have among us. I object less to the idea of controlling outcomes in the future in general than I do to the problem of what outcomes we attempt to influence. In other words, it is not so much making a future we want that is the problem but, rather, the problem lies in how we go about deciding what that future might be.

So, disability's contribution – its work – is to sever the present from the future; more precisely, it is to be a narrative resource that does not mortgage the present on the future. Not simply an antidote to modernity's overreaching, disability contributes a narrative of a genuinely open future, one not controlled by the objectives, expectations, and understandings of the present. Disability, then, rescripts modernity's and the modern subject's temporal practices and understandings. Ronan's imminent and vivid mortality – indeed, people with disabilities and disability in general – present the difficult challenge for modern subjects not only to live in the moment but also to engage in a relationship not based on the premise of the future. Disability demands that we all might imagine a subject without a future life trajectory that is perpetually managed in the present moment. The important complexity of Rapp's story of her son and family is to be able to hold the contradiction (the Keatsian negative capability) of the work disability does the world; for Rapp, it is suffering entangled with joy. Rapp's navigation of this contradiction is her story of Frank's woundedness, both hers and Ronan's. This, I offer, is what Michael Sandel calls the "giftedness" of disability (Sandel 27 and 91).

References

Bauman, Zygmunt. *Modernity and the Holocaust*. Ithaca, NY: Cornell University Press, 1989. Print.

Baynton, Douglas. "Disability and the Justification of Inequality in American History." *The New Disability History*. Eds. Paul Longmore and Lauri Umansky. New York: New York University Press, 2001. 33-57. Print.

Beniger, James R. *The Control Revolution: Technological and Economic Origins of the Information Society*. Cambridge: Harvard University Press, 1986. Print.

Frank, Arthur. *The Wounded Storyteller: Body, Illness, and Ethics*. Chicago: University of Chicago Press, 1995. Print.

Garland-Thomson, Rosemarie. "The Case for Conserving Disability." *Bioethics, Sexuality, and Gender Identity.* Special issue of *Journal of Bioethical Inquiry* 9.3 (2012): 339-55. Print.

—. "Welcoming the Unbidden: The Case for Conserving Human Biodiversity." *This is What Democracy Looks Like: A New Critical Realism for a Post-Seattle World.* Eds. Amy Schrager Lane and Cecelia Tichi. New Brunswick: Rutgers, The State University, 2006. 77-87. Print.

—. "Integrating Disability, Transforming Feminist Theory." *National Women's Studies Association Journal* 14.2 (2002): 1-32. Print.

Gibbs, Raymond W. *Embodiment and Cognitive Science.* New York: Cambridge University Press, 2005. Print.

Haskell, Thomas L. "Capitalism and the Origins of the Humanitarian Sensibility, Part 1." *The American Historical Review* 90.2 (1985): 339-36. Print.

—. "Capitalism and the Origins of the Humanitarian Sensibility, Part 2." *The American Historical Review* 90.3 (1985): 547-566. Print.

Hurley, Dan. 2011. "A Drug for Down Syndrome." *The New York Times Magazine* 29 July 2011. Web. 29 July 2013. <http://www.nytimes.com/2011/07/31/magazine/a-fathers-search-for-a-drug-for-down-syndrome.html?pagewanted=all>.

Keller, Helen. *The World I Live in and Optimism: A Collection of Essays.* 1905. Mineola: Dover Publications, 2009. Print.

Mitchell, David T. and Sharon L. Snyder. *Narrative Prosthesis: Disability and the Dependencies of Discourse.* Ann Arbor: The University of Michigan Press, 2000. Print.

O'Connor, Flannery and Sally Fitzgerald. "Introduction to *A Memoir of Mary Ann* and Sally Fitzgerald." *Mystery and Manners: Occasional Prose.* Eds. Robert and Sally Fitzgerald. New York: Farrar, Straus & Giroux, 1969. Print.

Rapp, Emily. *The Still Point of the Turning World.* New York: The Penguin Press, 2013.

—. "Notes from a Dragon Mom." *The New York Times* 15 October 2011. Web. 9 May 2012. <http://www.nytimes.com/2011/10/16/opinion/sunday/notes-from-a-dragon-mom.html>.

—. "Rick Santorum, Meet My Son." *Slate Magazine Online* 27 February 2012. Web. 29 July 2013. <http://www.slate.com/articles/double_x/doubl ex/2012/02/rick_santorum_and_prenatal_testing_i_would_have_saved_my_son_from_his_suffering_.html>.

Sandel, Michael. *The Case Against Perfection: Ethics in the Age of Genetic Engineering.* Cambridge, MA: Belknap Press of Harvard University Press, 2007. Print.

Scully, Jackie Leach. *Disability Bioethics: Moral Bodies, Moral Difference.* Lanham: Rowman & Littlefield, 2008. Print.

Shapiro, Lawrence. *Embodied Cognition*. New York: Routledge, 2010. Print.

Snyder, Sharon L. and David T. Mitchell. *Cultural Locations of Disability*. Chicago: The University of Chicago Press, 2006. Print.

Singer, Peter. *Practical Ethics*. 3rd ed. Cambridge: Cambridge University Press, 2009. Print.

Tracy, Terry. "Disability Narrative vs. Illness Narrative: Different Wounds, Different Stories." Columbia University. March 2012. Lecture.

Weber, Max. *The Protestant Ethic and the Spirit of Capitalism*. 1905. New York: Routledge, 2001. Print.

No Future for Crips

Disorderly Conduct in the New World Order; or, Disability
Studies on the Verge of a Nervous Breakdown

Robert McRuer

Although the title of this essay invokes disorder, it is ultimately quite skeptical –
or perhaps even agnostic – about the work of disorder or the place of 'disorders'
in disability studies. I would argue, in fact, for ambivalence about disorder and
disorderly conduct as both impossible *and* necessary. This paper ultimately
offers what we might call a critically disordered position: a position *critical of*
hegemonic deployments of 'disorder' but imagining, through the seduction
and transgression of 'disorderly conduct,' understandings of disorder that
might be *critically useful or even necessary.*

CRITICALLY DISORDERED

My main source for this analysis is Pedro Almodóvar's film *La Mala Educación*
(2004), released in English as *Bad Education*. The essay will use *Bad Education*
as a vehicle for reflecting on neoliberalism, tolerance, inclusion, and abjection.
Before approaching Almodóvar's film, however, I want to lay out three
theoretical points or theses that are behind my analysis of it.

First, whether rejecting or embracing discourses of 'disorder,' there is no
purity, no innocence. Consider how the rejection of 'disorder,' by any group,
whether lesbian/gay/bisexual/transgender (LGBT) activists, disability activists,
or anyone else, has functioned. 'We're not disordered' is always a dangerous
statement given the degree to which it depends upon conjuring up a 'real' or
'essential' disorder located and embodied somewhere else. Disability studies
scholars such as David Mitchell and Sharon Snyder or Douglas Baynton have
made similar points, drawing attention to the ways in which various groups
have claimed rights and identities based on the proud assertion 'we're not
disabled!' (instead, we're gay, we're lesbian, we're women, and so forth). These

scholars are really talking about discourses of disorder or pathology that are disavowed, however, not 'disability' in all its senses; in other words, the proud assertion 'we're not disabled!' has essentially meant 'don't understand us as disordered or pathologized.' When practices of disavowal are conceptualized or specified in this way, it is important to recognize that some disability activists have at times done the same thing – that is, they have distanced themselves from other groups that are then rhetorically associated with a 'real' disorder. Although perhaps less prevalent than in the past, there have likewise been disability activist assertions such as 'we're not perverse' or 'we're not sick!' (we are, instead, disabled, out and proud). The rejection of rhetorics of disorder, then, is never innocent of the very processes of stigmatization that speakers or thinkers are trying to renounce. The same can be said (no purity, no innocence) for the *embrace* of discourses of disorder. The current rejection by some of 'intersex' in favor of 'Disorders of Sexual Development' (DSD), for example, attempts to access a certain innocence, arguing that the embrace of 'disorder' is simply strategic: 'we know it's problematic language,' these activists are essentially saying, 'but we're going to use it for a different, unproblematic, goal – access to care for individuals with DSD.' This innocence, however, does not seem attuned to the dangers of redoubled stigmatization, whether of queers (and there have been claims that disorders of sexual development is preferred because most intersex people feel they are 'normal heterosexuals') or of non-Western (or even non-North American) peoples, some of whom feel a redoubled stigmatization because they had so little input into this new North American rhetoric of 'disorder'.[1] For these reasons, it is important to stress that there is no purity, no innocence, whether one rejects or embraces disorder.

Second, there may be other ways of embracing disorder, but they are *openly non-innocent* (or even – to gesture forward toward my reading of Almodóvar's film – a bit 'bad,' or evil, as in the seductive, desirable, disorderly conduct of my title) and, in some ways, anti-futural. My second point is about futurity because the rhetorics of beauty and order as we have inherited them from the nineteenth century, and as they have been packaged anew by neoliberal capitalism, are always necessarily about a normative future. Embracing disorder in non-innocent ways, then, entails engaging in some way with anti-futural thinking, even if – as I hope will be clear – I am disidentifying with the universalizing and psychoanalytic thought of Lee Edelman in favor of a materialist, crip anti-futurity.[2] Edelman, whom I will discuss more below, is the queer theorist most

---

1 | For an excellent overview of these controversies, see Alyson K. Spurgas's article "(Un)Queering Identity: The Biosocial Production of Intersex/DSD." See also my own "Afterword: The Future of Critical Intersex."

2 | For a related effort to analyze a crip anti-futurity, specifically through the work of disabled performer Greg Walloch, see my "Fuck the Disabled: The Prequel."

associated with a certain strand of 'anti-futural' thinking in the field. In his book *No Future: Queer Theory and the Death Drive*, he argues that the future is generally associated with heterosexuality, reproduction, and idealized notions of children and then positions queerness, via Lacanian psychoanalytic thought, as a negative force that continuously undermines this idealization. I will be recognizing the value of a theory critiquing an idealized future, but will not ground my own critique in the universalizing language of psychoanalysis.

Third, to make a point very similar to an earlier thesis in my book *Crip Theory: Cultural Signs of Queerness and Disability*: Given the political and cultural economy we currently inhabit, if we live long enough, we will *all* (eventually, repeatedly) reject or disavow disorder (see 198). The disability movement of course often says that if we live long enough, we will all become disabled, but my point is that the forces of normativity, of compulsory heterosexuality and compulsory able-bodiedness, encourage a sometimes-problematic rejection of disorder or disorders that is bigger than any individual and that is caught up in contemporary neoliberal biopolitics. My third point, then, is about the specific world, of neoliberal normativity, that we inhabit right now (and as Edelman consistently fails in *No Future* to attend to that specific world, it is here that the anti-futurity of this essay departs most directly from his). A fourth and final theoretical point, about *identity* and disorder, undergirds this essay, but will emerge organically over the course of it: I will be attending to the ways in which identity itself can be deployed in disciplining ways that attempt to disavow disorder.

La Mala Educación

I begin this section with a very specific figure who has no future. Although this essay is largely a theoretical reflection on the disability movement or disability studies in a moment of danger (our own), my primary text is not always clearly, on the surface, a disability film. *Bad Education*, moreover, is notoriously difficult to summarize, although I will do so, as concisely as possible. Remember as I do, however, that it is the figure in the film with no future that I want you to keep in mind as you read: a heroin-addicted, preoperative transsexual with pallid skin and dirty blonde, unkempt hair who dies of an overdose near the end of the film, as she is typing a letter to her childhood love. Of course, placing this figure in readers' minds paradoxically carries her (this figure with no future) into the future. Nonetheless, I hope to demonstrate just how difficult – well-nigh impossible – the conveyance of the drug-addicted tranny into the future is. Remember her if you can.

The plot of *Bad Education* interweaves three distinct periods: 1964, 1977, and 1980. In 1980, an actor claiming to be Ignacio Rodríguez (Gael García Bernal), but now going by the stage name of Ángel Andrade, arrives at the office of gay filmmaker Enrique Goded (Fele Martínez) to sell him on a script called "La Visita." It turns out that Ángel's script (which comes to life on screen as Enrique reads it) fictionalizes Enrique and Ignacio's experiences as boys together in Catholic school in 1964: their pre-adolescent love and sexual play; the discovery of their affair by their literature teacher, Father Manolo; Enrique's expulsion from the school; and Ignacio's sacrifice for his boyhood love by acquiescing to the predatory advances of Father Manolo in an attempt to keep the full details of their affair and sexual experimentation from emerging. The 1977 section of the story (continuing the script) has the adult Ignacio returning to the school in rural Valencia to blackmail Father Manolo. Now working as the transgender performer Zahara, and living as a woman, Ignacio demands money that will enable her to pay for sex-reassignment surgery. In return, she will remain silent about the abuse she survived as a boy.

The actor Ángel in the 1980 segments of the film and the performer Zahara in the 1977 segments are absolutely seductive, partly by virtue of Bernal's amazing performance and mostly by virtue of their function in the narrative. I argue, in fact, that audiences are – in a sort of trademark Almodóvar move – encouraged to fall in love with these offbeat gay and transgender figures. I call them gay and transgender pointedly to comprehend them contingently in relation to those identity categories, even though one (Ángel) is an actor and that the other (Zahara) is a performer – they are, in other words, in the business of taking on and off identities. With some qualifications, however, I argue that audiences are, in fact, encouraged to receive them as gay, or as transgender – identities increasingly tolerated in the New Spain, whether we are talking about the 'hedonistic' post-dictatorship, post-Franco days of the late 1970s and early 1980s or (even more) the neoliberal present, when the film was released (see D'Lugo 122). Even if, as with any film noir, you are always aware that something is amiss, you are seduced by their performance and you fall in love.

It turns out, however, that Ángel is not the real Ignacio. Through a bit of detective work in 1980, Enrique – who begins an affair with Ángel after reading the script – learns that the *real* Ignacio died in 1977, and that his younger brother Juan (again, Gael García Bernal) has assumed Ignacio's identity and his story to jump-start his acting career. A man named Mr. Berenguer (Lluís Homar), who formerly had been the priest Father Manolo but is now a successful and married business executive, arrives at Enrique's office and eventually tells him the truth: the real Ignacio had been a heroin-addicted transsexual who had attempted to blackmail Berenguer for a million pesetas. In the remaining 1977 scenes, which unfold for audiences through a series of flashbacks as Berenguer tells the (real) story, the actual Ignacio (Francisco Boira) plans to use the blackmail money on drug rehab and reassignment surgery. In the process of delivering what Ignacio demands, however, Berenguer becomes erotically obsessed with Ignacio's brother Juan and, as the two begin an affair, they plot to murder Ignacio and run off with the money Berenguer is acquiring from the bank. Juan and Berenguer provide the dosage of pure heroin that will lead to her death, and audiences watch as Ignacio overdoses at the typewriter, halfway through the first sentence of a letter: "Enrique, I think I have succeeded...."

In what follows, I read *Bad Education* as a crip film in and through what can be read as its critique of tolerance, identity, neoliberalism, and futurity. In preparation for that (concluding) argument, however, I turn first, in the next section, to a somewhat extended consideration of the antifutural or antisocial theses that I introduced above and that are, at this point, well-known in queer theory but that have not generally had a clear analogue in disability studies. Ultimately, even as I am critical of Edelman's version of anti-futurity in *No Future*, this essay – in the interest of *furthering* the critique of tolerance and neoliberalism legible in *Bad Education* and highlighting the problems neoliberalism has with disorderly conduct – provides some notes toward an antisocial thesis in disability studies or crip theory.[3] My subtitle for the essay, "Disability Studies on the Verge of a Nervous Breakdown," nods toward yet another Almodóvar film that writes breakdowns into its very title; my subtitle also metaphorizes disability in ways that the field generally disciplines or teaches us to be wary of. The metaphorization, however, is intended to suggest that a crip push toward the antisocial always has the potential to undo disability studies as we think we know it, questioning or unraveling both the identity of the field and some of the most recognizable identities *in* the field: proud, visible disability identities seeking inclusion in society as it is currently constituted; that is, society in its late capitalist, neoliberal form.

No Future for Crips

In *No Future*, Edelman calls on us to fuck the future (see 29). In a complex analysis of the figure of what he calls "the Child" in contemporary politics, culture, and society (with the capital C signifying that it is a figuration or ideal), Edelman argues against what he calls "reproductive futurism" (2). According to Edelman, reproductive futurism, across the political spectrum (indeed, defining politics as such), compels us, over and over, to invest in the future for the sake of our children. Founding what Edelman describes as the only permissible or imaginable future and the only imaginable social order, reproductive futurism requires us to "kneel at the shrine of the sacred Child: the Child who might witness lewd or inappropriate intimate behavior; the Child who might find information about dangerous 'lifestyles' on the Internet; the Child who might

---

3 | Other theorists in the field considering these issues include Anna Mollow and Fiona Kumari Campbell. Campbell's piece "Re-cognising Disability" is explicitly in conversation with an earlier (unpublished) version of this essay.

choose a provocative book from the shelves of the public library" (Edelman 19 et seq.). If the adult is always (regretfully) implicated in desire, the Child is the figure for the future who is always unmarked by desire and in need of protection from it. Queerness, in turn, is for Edelman always that which disrupts this phantasmatic figuration of childhood and innocence; queers, he claims, are phobically figured or produced by the social order as the primary threat to reproductive futurism and, consequently, to the sacred Child (14).

Blasphemously, Edelman calls on us *not* to resist or decry that phobic figuration, as – for example – normative movements for gay marriage, military service, or adoption invariably do, thereby jumping on the bandwagon of reproductive futurism and phobically shifting the burden of queerness to more abject others: don't worry, we're not like *that*, we're just like you, we're not your worst nightmare. Edelman, instead, wonders what it might mean to *acquiesce* to the charge that we are society's worst nightmare and to embrace our figuration as the negative force working against the social order: "without ceasing to refute the lies that pervade [...] familiar right-wing diatribes [about our capacity to destroy society], do we also have the courage to acknowledge, and even embrace, their correlative truths?" (22). In his most notorious (or nefarious) assertion, Edelman goes on to insist, "Fuck the social order and the Child in whose name we're collectively terrorized; fuck Annie; fuck the waif from *Les Mis*; fuck the poor, innocent kid on the Net; fuck Laws both with capital ls and with small; fuck the whole network of Symbolic relations and the future that serves as its prop" (29).

Although he does not say it directly in his litany of children being fucked, we might add, for our own purposes, following Anna Mollow, "fuck Tiny Tim" (Mollow 296), since earlier in his study, Edelman insists that pitiful and innocent literary characters such as Tiny Tim, from Charles Dickens's novel *A Christmas Carol*, are invariably endangered by evil, narcissistic (and, not incidentally, unmarried) men. Only when Ebenezer Scrooge renounces his queer, antisocial peculiarities and joins the community in an embrace of the figure of the Child is Tiny Tim ensured a future. Or, to again put it slightly differently for our purposes, through Scrooge's rehabilitation, the crip formerly known as Tiny Tim becomes the Child in whose name the only acceptable future can again be scripted. 'Fuck that,' Edelman implicitly says.

Edelman's argument in *No Future* is essentially exceptionalist (which, along with its psychoanalytic universalism, is my main critique of it). Edelman, in other words, sees queerness *in particular* as the (universalized) negative force that disrupts or destroys the social order and reproductive futurism. But as the location of the disabled Tiny Tim and other examples suggest (such as the first set of pictures in the book, which includes a still of Tom Hanks in an oxygen mask as his character is treated for HIV/AIDS in the 1993 film *Philadelphia*), *No Future* – and by extension, antifutural thinking in general – is saturated with disability, and the sacred Child, the one projected into the future, is *always* able-bodied: 'Everybody,' after all, or so the saying goes, 'wants a healthy baby.' At the same time, despite this commonplace desire, the imagined future is actually inescapably inaccessible; no real, flesh-and-blood child can ever embody the innocence, health, and ability associated with the sacred Child. This universal inaccessibility, however, does not stop (and in fact propels) the production of both queers *and* crips as scapegoats – monstrous figures endangering the Child and blocking access to the future we supposedly all desire.

Given the related antifutural function played by queers and crips in or against the social order, it is somewhat puzzling that the antisocial thesis is only barely legible in contemporary disability studies (although it is perhaps, in my mind, *because of* the limited usefulness of psychoanalysis for disability studies). It becomes all the more puzzling when we consider the particular array of illegitimate figures currently populating queer theory: over and over again, the queer theory we seem to want these days – again, in opposition to the normative thrust of the mainstream LGBT movement – is concerned with the invalidated and the unthinkable; with figures that are sick, infected, disordered, deranged, addicted, scarred, wounded, or traumatized (McRuer and Mollow 26-27).

Judith Halberstam, for instance (to bring forward a less problematic 'antisocial' queer theorist working in a more materialist and less exceptionalist vein than Edelman – and openly shaping alternatives to his particular anti-futurity), argues for what she calls "queer time" as that which is non-productive, wasteful, and even toxic. As I quote from Halberstam's *In a Queer Time and Place: Transgender Bodies, Subcultural Lives*, note two things: first, how able-bodied the *dominant* life cycle she sketches is and, second, how the figure or exemplar she imagines as *outside* this life cycle – a figure who indeed might be read as queer – might as easily (or, really, *more* easily?) be read as 'disabled' or crip. Halberstam writes:

"I try to use the concept of queer time to make clear how respectability, and notions of the normal on which it depends, may be upheld by a middle-class logic of reproductive temporality. And so, in Western cultures, we chart the emergence of the adult from the dangerous and unruly period of adolescence as a desired process of maturation; and we create longevity as the most desirable future, applaud the pursuit of long life (under any circumstances), and pathologize modes of living that show little or no concern for longevity. Within the life cycle of the Western human subject, long periods of stability are considered to be desirable, and people who live in rapid bursts (drug addicts, for example) are characterized as immature and even dangerous." (4-5)

Halberstam confirms here what I considered at the outset – how difficult it is to hang on to/convey into the future the figure of the drug-addicted tranny.

Following Halberstam, in fact, we might now read her as an *exemplary* figure against whom hegemonic, able-bodied notions of futurity are shaped. It is difficult to convey someone into the future if, by *definition*, the future is where and what she is not.

As I suggested, contemporary queer theory is full of exemplary figures, like Halberstam's drug addict, who are sick, infectious, obsessed, crazy, unstable, or deranged. It is fascinating to me both that we really do not question the queerness of such figures and that the more unusual academic argument is the crip theory argument I am making here, an argument that would read such figures, rather (or additionally), in relation to disability.

Ability Trouble; or, Disabled Liberalism

My critique in the previous section was, primarily, of elisions in queer theory, of an exceptionalism that makes it difficult to comprehend how disability is connected to our most central arguments. To excavate further why we have such trouble reading all the crips in contemporary queer theory in relation to disability, however, I turn now to some tentative, very qualified critiques of the disability movement. The absence of an antisocial thesis in disability studies, I argue, in part has to do with the dominance of liberalism in the field and movement. Although it is changing rapidly, it is still possible to say that, after other fields (feminism, critical race theory, queer theory) have sharply critiqued inclusion, tolerance, or multiculturalism, or have moved to more radical questions about the limits of tolerance or about figures who are always already excluded from, or sacrificed by, multiculturalism, the disability movement (in and out of the academy) at times remains a project largely indebted to liberalism.

One relatively famous example will have to suffice for my purposes, and poetically, the example will carry us back to 1977, the year of Ignacio's death. In April 1977, a month now often understood as a 'coming of age' moment for the disability movement in the United States (at least as the moment is narrated in disability studies), disabled activists demonstrated in Washington, D.C., at the home and at the offices of Secretary Joseph Califano of the Department of Health, Education, and Welfare (HEW). These activists were protesting the Carter Administration's failure to enforce section 504 of the Rehabilitation Act of 1973, which prohibited discrimination against disabled people by any institution receiving federal funding.

Demonstrations for section 504 took place at several other regional offices; in California more than 120 activists occupied San Francisco City Hall for almost a month. Since many of the protesters did not have attendants with them, or other necessary services or equipment, their lives were literally on the line. Joseph P. Shapiro calls the occupation "their own disability city, a mini Woodstock" and details how other groups (the Black Panthers, and a gay group called the Butterfly Brigade) expressed solidarity with the protestors and helped to facilitate the action (69).[4] For many of us (because I myself repeat what I am critiquing here, as I read, teach, or talk about the event), the City Hall take-over – with its emphasis on emerging disability identities and disability community – consolidated the disability movement for the future. Not only was section 504 successfully implemented (on April 28, 1977); so too was the Education for All Handicapped Children Act (later known as the Individuals with Disabilities Education Act). This legislation had passed earlier in the decade (1975) but was never enforced. And, perhaps, the poetics of an investment in futurity again bringing us back to children should not be lost.

I want to be very clear: I would never want to argue that these 1977 events were not important; I would never want to argue that they were not good, or even great. They were, however (and given the compulsory, celebratory position we are meant to have on these events, even saying this seems blasphemous and diminishing), in some structural ways, liberal appeals, first, to the state for inclusion and, second, to society (increasingly understood as multicultural) for tolerance of difference. And thus, inescapably, the contradictions of liberalism are apparent in the wake of these events: liberal tolerance, inclusion, and community all have clear limits. Indeed, President Jimmy Carter and Joseph Califano, Shapiro tells us, "were afraid of the public outcry if alcoholics, drug addicts, and homosexuals were to claim protection under the law" (66). Would the crips and queers from the previous section be understood as part of the disability community I am bringing forward, a community entering in the late 1970s, to ironically call back the language Halberstam used, 'a desired process of maturation'? Officially, and again this is not to diminish the incredible 'success' of the City Hall take-over, the answer was an unequivocal 'no,' since the Department of Health Education and Welfare had already concluded that

---

4 | For a critique of what she calls the "gay liberalism" of the Butterfly Brigade, a group whose motivation was to serve as a neighborhood watch keeping the streets safe for gay people, see Christina Hanhardt's Safe Space: Gay Neighborhood History and the Politics of Violence (81-116). To my knowledge, the Butterfly Brigade's participation in alliance with disabled activists in the City Hall occupation has always been read positively, and I would not argue otherwise, although I think it is important (especially in the context of what I am attempting in this section) to read them in the stories we tell as an ambivalent sign rather than as an easy guarantor of solidarity, coalition, and multiculturalism. Hanhardt's study is an important reminder that gay politics of the 1970s was complex and multi-faceted and that some campaigns for autonomous and safe (and identity-based) space, including the campaigns spearheaded by the Butterfly Brigade, materialized (often racialized) others as 'disorderly' (and even dangerous) and in need of stricter policing (policing that was carried out in the name of protecting newly-identifiable, 'safe,' gay spaces).

indeed (disorderly) alcoholics, drug addicts, and homosexuals would not be eligible to claim protection based on these documents (see Shapiro 66).

We cannot, currently, do without actions such as the HEW protests or documents such as section 504 or – to move a decade into the future, when other queercrips (most notably transsexuals), were explicitly excluded from a different state document even as some more, those with HIV/AIDS, were included – the Americans with Disabilities Act.[5] I am, however, as I move back towards some final reflections on *Bad Education*, extending Walter Benjamin's famous assertion that "there has never been a document of *culture* which is not at one and the same time a document of barbarism" (Benjamin cited in Spivak 168). Documents in disability history (those generated by, or as a result of, the movement) have not, to my knowledge, been analyzed for their 'barbarism.' A literal reading of Benjamin's dictum, however, does not really allow for a free pass: *there has never been* a non-barbaric document of culture.[6] Were I to trace the operations of Benjaminian 'barbarism' in relation to section 504 and the City Hall take-over, then, I would note two things: *whether necessary or not*, the ready sacrifice of alcoholics, drug addicts, and homosexuals is barbaric, and – even more – the always-celebratory, post-1977 narration of the events as *unequivocal* achievements carrying us into the future – a narration that erases the sacrifice upon which the achievement is founded (and thereby redoubles the sacrifice) – is barbaric. Do not get me wrong, I am certainly not advocating now reading 1977 as a bleak year in disability history. I am arguing that we should read that history rigorously, understand its connection to liberalism, understand how liberalism and neoliberalism continue to shape or found disability studies and the other fields in which we work, and always grapple with the sacrifices and erasures liberalism demands. Benjamin would argue that there are no unequivocal achievements in modernity. And I would add that it is simply bad education to suggest otherwise.

---

5 | The most important reading of these 1977 events is Susan Schweik's essay, which does in fact read beyond liberalism to what I would call excess, as she identifies the radical excess - the black power - undergirding the City Hall take-over. Schweik's analysis makes possible a key distinction between the specific goal (articulated through an appeal to the state) and excessive, unpredictable alliances and forms of solidarity that were made possible by the event.

6 | These points are adapted from Nicole Markotić's and my essay "Leading with Your Head" (167-168).

Volver; or, Almodóvar y los Minusválidos

My contention in the previous section was that the extent to which we have been defined by liberalism has largely precluded the development of an antisocial thesis in disability studies. In this final section, I return to *Bad Education* and the figure with no future in the Spain imagined by Almodóvar. Almodóvar himself articulates, as early as the late 1980s, some of the points about his films that are now foundational theses for those approaching his work: "[My films] represent more than others, I suppose, the New Spain, this kind of new mentality that appears in Spain after Franco dies, especially after 1977 till now. Stories about the New Spain have appeared in the mass media of every country. Everybody has heard that now everything is different in Spain [...]. I think in my films they see how Spain has changed" (cited in D'Lugo 131). Marvin D'Lugo underscores this assessment, not only in relation to the films of the immediate post-Franco period, but also in relation to more recent films, including *Bad Education*. The films *Bad Education* and *Live Flesh* (Spanish original: *Carne Trémula*), for instance, are examples for D'Lugo of Almodóvar wrestling with the ways in which "the demons of the past survive in new forms," and with "the problematic persistence of Old Spain in its varied disguises" (127 and 128). That the period between *Live Flesh* and *Bad Education* (1997-2004) is marked (like the period of this writing) by the dominance of the conservative Partido Popular suggests that Almodóvar continues to stand for some notion of an open and liberated "New Spain" as against what D'Lugo calls "the specters of Francoism" (127).[7]

While not disagreeing with D'Lugo (or Almodóvar himself, for that matter), I am uncomfortable, at this point, with the stark distinction between Old Spain and New Spain, particularly because that binary opposition fails to do justice to the new New Spain – to the ways, that is, in which neoliberalism has taken hold in Spain. The new New Spain is, at this point, one of the most gay-friendly locations in the world. Not only is an openly gay filmmaker one of the country's most recognizable, globally-disseminated commodities, but 70% of the population supported gay marriage at the time of its ratification in 2004 (when *Bad Education* premiered), representations of 'tolerance' or acceptance of homosexuality abound, and Madrid, Barcelona, Sitges, and other locations

---

7 | "Old Spain" would be the repressive fascist dictatorship of Francisco Franco, which lasted from 1939 until Franco's death in 1975. The period following the dictatorship was characterized both by a greater openness and also a wariness about the ways in which repression lingered on or took new forms. Spain has been dominated by two parties since the dictatorship, the conservative Partido Popular and the centrist Socialist Democrats. Almodóvar is making films in the "New Spain," but specters of repression linger on, regardless of the desire to move beyond the country's dark history.

are major gay tourist sites marketed to gay-identified consumers everywhere. The San Francisco gay travel magazine *Passport* announces, for instance, "Few cities in Europe boast the kind of frenetic fun people can experience in Madrid [...]. A few may be coy about their sexuality outside the gay quarters or at work, but once they get to Chuecea [Madrid's most famous gay neighborhood] – well, you'll have to see it with your own eyes" (cited in Giorgio 60). In this context, I argue, 'Old Spain,' even as it does persist in spectral forms, is at times a bit of a straw target. I also contend that neoliberal tolerance or even celebration of gay people is more complicated than it at first appears and that those complications are legible in a film like *Bad Education*.

Gabriel Giorgio, in his essay "Madrid *en Tránsito*: Travelers, Visibility, and Gay Identity," argues that "in a democracy that still needs to demonstrate its strength and its resemblance to the older, so-called advanced democracies of the United States and northern Europe, gay visibility [in Spain] stands out as a symbol, a token of social tolerance and achieved freedom" (61). To borrow a line from a courtroom scene in another Spanish film of 2004, Alejandro Amenábar's *Mar adentro* (*The Sea Inside*), where lawyers are attempting to make precisely this sharp distinction between a dark past and a bright present: "We are a civilized nation." If, in the New Spain gender and sexual difference marked 'freedom' and 'liberation' in opposition to the 'repression' of the fascist past, in the new New Spain, gay bodies now mark civilization and tolerance as opposed to barbarism and irrationality. Gay identity (indeed, identity in general) is, I argue, disciplined in this new, neoliberal formation. Giorgio insists that gayness "sets in motion a narrative that locates bodies in a geopolitical order, making them visible in some ways and determining their visibility under different conditions" (73). For Giorgio, a legible gay identity in Spain now marketed globally to gay and non-gay consumers (decidedly different conditions from the immediate post-Franco years) ghosts larger economic and cultural processes. For Giorgio in his essay, the new New Spain is 'open' and 'tolerant' in relation to gay identity, but this tolerance can mask other forms of exploitation, such as the exploitation of immigrant labor and immigrant bodies.

Bad Education, in my reading, can be interpreted as exposing or disordering this neoliberal pedagogy. Tellingly, Almodóvar gives us, in the film (this would be, in fact, a nutshell summary of the film), a gay filmmaker (Enrique) caught up in processes or histories much larger than himself. And, indeed, outside the film, Almodóvar likewise cannot fully control the uses to which his own body and identity are put – as one of Spain's most recognizable commodities, he is inescapably a character in the new gay-friendly story about a tolerant, civilized, cosmopolitan Spain. *Bad Education*, however, seduces you with gay and transgender identities that you learn to tolerate or even love, and then strikes *back* against that compulsory affect, pulling the rug out from under you and giving you a figure that is almost impossible to love, a figure that has no future in the new social order, a disorderly and drug-addicted crip who fails spectacularly even as she types the unfinished sentence "Enrique, I think I have succeeded..." (and remember here what I said earlier about no unequivocal achievements or successes in modernity).

Since I invoked *The Sea Inside* a moment ago, one might conclude that disability in general functions somewhat differently from sex and gender in the new New Spain. *The Sea Inside* arguably puts forward quite negative views of disability, because it is a film about a quadriplegic, Ramón Sampedro (Javier Bardem), who feels his life has no value and who thus petitions the state for the right to end that life. The award-winning film (it won the Oscar for best foreign film in 2004) both represents the seemingly 'rational' desire of a quadriplegic to kill himself and schools you in how 'we' should respond (in an orderly fashion): "We are a civilized nation," Ramón Sampedro's lawyers argue in court as they advocate for his death. One might conclude from the invocation of *The Sea Inside*, in other words, that even as some gay bodies are now tolerated or 'included,' disabled bodies are still 'excluded' in expected ways and that a disabled life is necessarily perceived as intolerable. Yet as I said at the beginning, my concern is the disability movement in a moment of danger (our own, neoliberal moment) and – as Michel Foucault famously recognized, arguing "not that everything is bad, but that everything is dangerous" (231-232) – moments of danger always present a range of possible responses or outcomes. As it narrates for itself a story of civilization and tolerance, then, the new New Spain can, without question, in a very familiar (although I would call it residual) move, position recognizably disabled bodies like Sampedro's as expendable. But recognizably disabled bodies can *also* be disciplined in ways not unlike recognizably gay bodies, and this, I would say, represents a more emergent neoliberal discourse in Spain (and elsewhere) today, a discourse again organized around identity and again ghosting much larger and exploitative cultural and economic processes: As Jesús Hernández, accessibility director of Spain's ONCE Foundation (Spain's largest disability organization) insists, in relation to the new disabled tourism, "No te preocupes de mis derechos, preocúpate de mi cartera" – "don't overly concern yourself about my rights, pay attention to my wallet!" ("Preocúpate").

Bad Education is a crip film because it paradoxically keeps alive the notion that there is no future for crips even as it critically disorders or critiques the futures we are inheriting (and 'critique' is necessarily futural, so my point here is that the film – simultaneously futural and antifutural – hands us a logical contradiction that exceeds Edelman's over-simplified embrace of queer negativity). The real Ignacio dies, in the film, imbibing a substance that she herself needs but cannot biologically 'tolerate.' Similarly, at another level, through figurations that cannot be tolerated or re-membered to fit the new social order but that also can never be entirely forgotten, Almodóvar presents us with impossible bodies engaged in disorderly conduct – with (put differently) disorderly specters that we, in the interest of always-expanding notions of crip justice, must attend to.

REFERENCES

Almodóvar, Pedro. *La Mala Educación*. El Deseo, TVE, Canal+, 2004. Film.

Amenábar, Alejandro. *Mar adentro*. Fine Line Features, 2004. Film.

Baynton, Douglas. "Disability and the Justification of Inequality in American History." *The New Disability History: American Perspectives*. Eds. Paul K. Longmore and Lauri Umansky. New York: New York University Press, 2001. 33-57. Print.

Campbell, Fiona Kumari. "Re-cognising Disability: Cross-Examining Social Inclusion through the Prism of Queer Anti-Sociality." *Jindal Global Law Review* 4.2 (2013): 209-238. Print.

D'Lugo, Marvin. *Pedro Almodóvar*. Urbana: University of Illinois Press, 2006. Print.

Edelman, Lee. *No Future: Queer Theory and the Death Drive*. Durham: Duke University Press, 2004. Print.

Foucault, Michel. "On the Genealogy of Ethics: An Overview of Work in Progress." *Michel Foucault: Beyond Structuralism and Hermeneutics*. 2nd ed. Eds. Herbert L Dreyfus and Paul Rabinow. Chicago: University of Chicago Press, 1983. 253-280. Print.

Giorgio, Gabriel. "Madrid *en Tránsito*: Travelers, Visibility, and Gay Identity." *GLQ: A Journal of Lesbian and Gay Studies* 8.1-2 (2002): 57-80. Print.

Halberstam, Judith. *In a Queer Time and Place: Transgender Bodies, Subcultural Lives*. New York: NYU Press, 2006. Print.

Hanhardt, Christina. *Safe Space: Gay Neighborhood History and the Politics of Violence*. Durham: Duke UP, 2013. Print.

Markotić, Nicole and Robert McRuer. "Leading with Your Head: On the Borders of Disability, Sexuality, and the Nation." *Sex and Disability*. Eds. Robert McRuer and Anna Mollow. Durham: Duke University Press, 2012. 165-182. Print.

McRuer, Robert. "Afterword: The Future of Critical Intersex." *Critical Intersex*. Ed. Morgan Holmes. Surrey: Ashgate, 2009. 245-250. Print.

—. *Crip Theory: Cultural Signs of Queerness and Disability*. New York: New York University Press, 2006. Print.

—. "Fuck the Disabled: The Prequel." *Shakesqueer: A Queer Companion to the Complete Works of Shakespeare*. Ed. Madhavi Menon. Durham: Duke University Press, 2011. 294-301. Print.

McRuer, Robert and Anna Mollow. "Introduction." *Sex and Disablity*. Ed. Robert McRuer and Anna Mollow. Durham: Duke University Press, 2012. 1-34. Print.

Mitchell, David T. and Sharon L. Snyder. *Narrative Prosthesis: Disability and the Dependencies of Discourse*. Ann Arbor: University of Michigan Press, 2000. Print.

Mollow, Anna. "Is Sex Disability? Queer Theory and the Disability Drive." *Sex and Disability*. Eds. Robert McRuer and Anna Mollow. Durham: Duke University Press, 2012. 285-312. Print.

"Preocúpate de mi cartera, no de mis derechos." *LaVozDigital.es* November 3, 2007. Web. 15 April 2015. <http://www.lavozdigital.es/cadiz/20071103/turismo/preocupate-cartera-derechos-20071103.html>.

Schweik, Susan. "Lomax's Matrix: Disability, Solidarity, and the Black Power of 504." *Disability Studies Quarterly* 31.1 (2011). Web. <http://dsq-sds.org/article/view/1371/1539>.

Shapiro, Joseph P. *No Pity: People with Disabilities Forging a New Civil Rights Movement*. New York: Random House, 1993. Print.

Spivak, Gayatri Chakravorty. *In Other Worlds: Essays in Cultural Politics*. New York: Routledge, 1988. Print.

Spurgas, Alyson K. "(Un)Queering Identity: The Biosocial Production of Intersex/DSD." *Critical Intersex*. Ed. Morgan Holmes. Surrey: Ashgate, 2009. 97-122. Print.

Encountering ...

Dis/entangling Critical Disability Studies[1]

Dan Goodley

INTRODUCTION

If late-twentieth-century disability studies was associated with establishing the factors that led to the structural, economic and cultural exclusion of people with sensory, physical and cognitive impairments, then disability studies in the current century might be seen as a time of developing nuanced theoretical responses to these factors. The politicization of disabled people is at the heart of these developments. Disability activisms have brought about a host of national and pan-national responses, including the UN Convention on the Rights of Persons with Disabilities. The potency of Disabled People's International is testimony to the growing interconnectedness of the politics of disability across the globe. On the ground, disability studies have entered a host of training and educational contexts, social policies, legislative discourses and professional practices. Furthermore, disability studies have dallied with many theoretical ideas. Contemporary disability studies occupy and agitate for what Carol Thomas defines in her book *Sociologies of Disability and Illness* as a transdisciplinary space breaking boundaries between disciplines, deconstructing professional/ lay distinctions and decolonizing traditional medicalized views of disability with socio-cultural conceptions of disablism. Thomas defines *disablism* as "a form of social oppression involving the social imposition of restrictions of activity on people with impairments and the socially engendered undermining of their psycho-emotional well being" (*Sociologies* 73). This definition sits alongside other forms of oppression including hetero/sexism and racism. Indeed, as explained below, the intersectional character of disability is one of a number of reasons why we might conceptualize the contemporary state of the field as *critical* disability studies.

---

1 | A previous version of this essay has been published as "Dis/entangling Critical Disability Studies" in *Disability & Society* 28.5 (2013): 631-644. It is reprinted with the kind permission of Routledge Taylor and Francis Group.

Critical disability studies start with disability but never end with it: Disability is *the* space from which to think through a host of political, theoretical and practical issues that are relevant to all (see Goodley 157). The emergence of a critical approach to the analysis of disability may be put down to a number of recent developments. According to Helen Meekosha and Russell Shuttleworth these include a shift in theorizing beyond the social model; the influence of disciplines previously on the outskirts, such as psychology, entering the field; attempts to challenge the dogmatic tendencies of some theories and theorists through reference to eclecticism; and the merging of Marxist accounts with those from feminism, queer and post-colonial studies. The word 'critical' denotes a sense of self-appraisal; re-assessing where we have come from, where we are at and where we might be going. For Margrit Shildrick critical disability studies rethink the conventions, assumptions and aspirations of research, theory and activism in an age of postmodernity (see "Critical"). Disability studies, at least in Britain, were conceived as a modern day project to challenge capitalist conditions of alienation. Critical disability studies build upon these insights but acknowledge that we are living in a time of complex identity politics, of huge debates around the ethics of care, political and theoretical appeals to the significance of the body, in a climate of economic downturn that is leading yet again to reformulations of what counts as disabled. These contemporary events pose critical questions about the usefulness of dominant theories of disability. In short, are ideas developed in the 1990s or before still relevant to our current late capitalist or postmodernist times? This paper builds on the work of Meekosha, Shuttleworth, Shildrick and others to offer an inevitably personal and therefore selective account of a number of emerging analytical insights from critical disability studies.

Theorizing through Materialism

It is an imperative to recognize and celebrate Marxism's contribution to disability studies. Critical disability studies owe a debt to the many activists and scholars that unearthed the structural foundations of oppression faced by disabled people. In Britain, the materialist social model of disability might be now viewed as a product of the twentieth century: a modernist response to the socio-economic exclusion of disabled people from everyday life. Key writers such as Mike Oliver, Colin Barnes and Vic Finkelstein unashamedly drew on neo-Marxist and Gramscian analyses of material barriers to work, education and community living experienced in everyday, often mundane, ways by disabled people. In contexts where anti-discriminatory legislation was still only a dream, their analyses were a clarion call to activists and academics alike to overturn the material conditions of disablement. Rather than changing attitudes or pushing for the mainstreaming of disability issues, materialist social modellists, as Carol Thomas defines them (see *Sociologies*), politicized disability and sought to address material needs via increased socio-political participation (see Oliver *Politics*). Vic Finkelstein's influential analysis – summarized in Goodley (61-62) – maintained that while early capitalism offered some inclusion in the community through disabled people's involvement in small-scale cottage industries, the rapid growth of manufacturing and machinery supplanted their contribution to a growing labour force. The middle phase of capitalist development saw manufacturing industries such as coal and steel expanding. Mass migration from rural to urban areas increased exponentially. Industrialization deskilled and impoverished disabled people who had previously worked in agrarian communities. Many disabled people, deemed incapable of offering labour, quickly joined the unemployed in the cities. Industrialization demanded fit workers. Factories exposed uncompetitive workers. Institutionalization provided a means of controlling non-viable workers and, in contrast, developed new forms of labour for those working in them. Later forms of capitalism, marked by the growth of the human service industry, offered more opportunities for consumer groups and disabled people's organizations to challenge their exclusion from mainstream life. There is no doubt that disability would have lacked recognition as a political phenomenon without this materialist rationale.

Critical disability studies emerged, in part, according to Meekosha and Shuttleworth, in reaction to the dominance of this materialist stance. For some, such as Tom Shakespeare (see *Disability Rights*), the social model had become a shibboleth; a dogmatic totalizing epistemology against which all disability research was expected to judge itself. Any deviation from the materialist social model risked being dismissed for watering down the politics of disability (see Oliver "Hammer;" Barnes). It is no surprise that materialist disability studies found homes in sociology and social policy departments. Yet, as the end of the twentieth century approached, it was very clear that critical disability studies were being developed in other social science disciplines including psychology, social work, education and the humanities. Materialism appeared to explain only so much for researchers working in these disciplines. Scholars from critical and community psychology, for example, whilst sharing a view of disablism as fundamentally a socio-economic problem (and in some cases identifying themselves as Marxists), also recognized that marginalization is a relational concept, emerging in the routines of (and interactions between) non-disabled and disabled people, often experienced in deeply psychological ways (see Marks; Parker; Kagan et al.). For researchers from the humanities, trained in post-Marxist theories such as poststructuralism and post-colonialism, materialist social model theories were deemed old-fashioned and out of tune with the ever more complex nature of disablism. David Mitchell and Sharon Snyder, for example, recognized the need to develop an analysis of the cultural locations of disability that evoked sites of violence, restriction, confinement and absence of liberty for disabled people. While attentive to the lessons learnt from materialism, these cultural modellists (see Goodley) developed analyses of the ways in which representations of disability and impairment are manufactured by charities, science and popular culture in ways that *dis*-locate disabled people (Snyder and Mitchell, *Locations* 19). An overview of the cultural turn is provided by Rosemarie Garland-Thomson ("Integrating" 2). She posits that disability is a cultural trope and historical community that raises questions about the materiality of the body and the social formulations that are used to interpret bodily and cognitive differences. Affiliated scholars "rejected a firm distinction between impairment and disability because they viewed biology and culture as impinging upon one another" (Goodley 14). Looking back over the last decade it is possible to recognize the emergence of critical disability studies that are less centred around the materialist imperative and open to a host of theoretical developments including post-conventionist (Shildrick *Dangerous*); postmodernist (Corker and Shakespeare) and poststructuralist (Tremain). Each of these persuasions emphasizes the cultural, discursive and relational undergirdings of the disability experience. The variegated nature of critical disability studies theory led Lennard Davis to confidently define the contemporary field as *dismodernist*: where disability links together other identities as *the* moment of reflection. For Davis, disabled people are *the* ultimate intersectional subject, the universal image, the important modality through which we can understand exclusion and resistance. Indeed, the fact that disability absorbs the fetishized and projected insecurities of the precariously 'able-bodied' suggests that disability studies scholars are in a key position to challenge a host of oppressive practices associated with dominant hegemony of able society. A point we will return to later.

Bodies that Matter

One of the initial contributions of twentieth-century disability studies was to sever the causal link between the body and disability. As a direct riposte to medicalized and psychologized hegemonies of disability – that sited disability as a personal tragedy, biological deficiency and psychical trauma – disability studies relocated disability to social, cultural, economic and political registers. Having an impaired body did not equate with disability. In contrast, disability was a problem of society. While a strong sociological analysis of disability became ever more accepted in disability circles, questions still abounded about the absent presence of the impaired body. While disabled feminists such as Sally French, Liz Crow, Mairian Corker, Carol Thomas and Donna Reeve had made a strong case for the inclusion of discussions about impairment, Tom Shakespeare's book *Disability Rights and Wrongs* was perhaps the most concerted and controversial attempt to address the question: what about impairment? For Shakespeare the body had been denied in disability studies because the (materialist) social model had bracketed impairment by means similar to the ways in which biological difference had been denied by some feminists in the 1970s (see Goodley 28). He argued that impairments are important because some are static, others episodic, some degenerative and others terminal. Hence, a social model can only explain so much before we need to return to the experiential realities of 'impairment' as object(s) independent of knowledge (see Shakespeare 54). Impairment *is* a predicament and *can* be tragic. This critical realist conception of the body has been taken up by Tobin Siebers and is well represented in the collection by Kristiana Kristiansen, Simo Vehmas, and Tom Shakespeare. These interventions publicized many long-standing private misgivings about the lack of consideration given to the biological within disability studies circles. Realists have left an indelible mark on the field addressing what might be termed the somatophobic tendencies of disability studies.

While the realist turn has been powerful – allowing the body to resurface as a significant element of the disability experience – other critical disability studies theorists have addressed the corporeality of disability in order to emphasize the impaired body as social body. It is quite clear that when we start to scrutinize the disabled or impaired body, its reality soon breaks down (see Campbell *Contours*). For Anita Ghai (*Forms* 147), disabled bodies risk becoming dis-embodied because of constructions around them that threaten to create a total invisibility of the disabled individual. At the same time, however, as Anne McGuire argues: "disability marks the body in ambiguous ways – it appears and disappears, is noticed and is hidden – as we move through different physical and social spaces, and as we find ourselves in different political and historical moments" (n. pag.). The work of Margrit Shildrick extends this idea of the fluid social body. Shildrick's post-conventionalist approach to embodiment refutes any simple biological/social division and, instead, recasts the body as a complex site of cultural and corporeal production. Owing much to the work of Judith Butler and Gilles Deleuze, Shildrick demands us to think about the ways in which non-normative bodies are performative entities illuminating but also potentially refuting corporeal standards. Disabled bodies challenge normative ideas of able bodies. This can be productive. Indeed impaired embodiment demands new, inclusive and potentially exciting forms of response from others.

Disability as possibility (see McKenzie) has been taken further by phe-nomenological disability studies (e.g. Michalko; Titchkosky). Phenomenologists attend to the capacities of the body to be a source of self and society. The work of Bill Hughes and Kevin Paterson has been particularly significant in reinserting the body back into sociologies of disability. A "carnal sociology" has emerged, theorizing the body as *the* place where self and society interact (Goodley 56).

Bodies do matter for critical disability studies. The question, however, is how do bodies matter or, perhaps more accurately, how do they become materialized: that is, made to matter? An answer to this question is provided by Rod Michalko in his book *The Two-in-One: Walking with Smokie, Walking with Blindness*. The partnership with his dog Smokie allows Michalko to rethink conventional essentialist understandings of blindness (as individually deficient, lacking sight and therefore inevitably disabled). In contrast, his blindness becomes revised through his relationship with Smokie as an intimate, sustained and in-depth experience of walking through blindness with a companion guide dog. Hence, his embodiment and that of Smokie's become deeply connected and blurred to the extent that the phenomenology of blindness is significantly reshaped and refashioned. Bodies are lived in; but in the social settings that they inhabit. Michalko supports this argument when he writes:

"Smokie and I move through our world *alone together*; focusing on one another in the midst of the plurality of our world and its many blindnesses. Smokie keeps me company in this estranged familiarity of opinion. I experience my blindness *together* with Smokie in this plurality. My focus is on Smokie and on myself. The world we generate springs from our communication in the midst of the world and from our movements through it." (186)

Michalko's phenomenological account is one in which sense, connection and community are necessarily entangled. A further exploration of the tangled nature of bodies is provided by poststructuralist critical disability studies scholars (see Tremain; Shildrick *Dangerous*). In *Bodies That Matter: On the Discursive Limits of Sex*, Judith Butler asked a number of questions of bodies (see 243), which we can appropriate in reference to disability:

"How are non-disabled bodies made more seemingly viable and desirable than non-disabled bodies? How do societal practices uphold the precarious higher status of non-disabled people through the abjection (rejection) of disabled people? In what ways do disabled bodies rearticulate what qualifies as a body that matters?" (Goodley 159)

The body is, for the poststructuralist feminist Rosi Braidotti, neither a biological nor sociological category (see Braidotti 44). Instead, she conceptualizes it as an interface, a threshold, a field where intersecting material and symbolic forces converge; a surface where multiple codes of sex, class, age, race, and so forth, are inscribed. The normative body is understood as being fashioned and materialized through cultural, political and social conditions ranging from surgery to self-help. The non-normative body – a body that appears as an object of fear and curiosity – is therefore considered an opportunity to think through values, ethics and politics that congregate around such bodies. In this sense, any intimate bodily function is also a function of a body within given standards of embodiment. A body that sticks out – that challenges conventions and standards – permits a moment of disruption and a chance to ask, what counts as a valued body? Through these reflections, non-normative bodies are recast as unique embodied entities through which we can consider how bodies should and *could* be lived (see Overboe). This entanglement is advanced by our next theme of critical disability studies.

Inter/Trans-sectionality

There is no doubt that disability studies have struggled for recognition from other transformative arenas such as feminism, critical race, Marxist and queer theory. The absence of disability issues led Maureen Olkin to ask 'When will disabled people be allowed to board the diversity train?' (see 136). Rather than waiting for the good intentions of others, critical disability studies is characterized by an unwillingness to be ignored by potential theoretical and political allies and a proactive drive to connect and influence these allies. This has led to a number of intersectional engagements. For Gerard Goggin this inter-sectionality is hardly surprising when one considers the ways in which disability is directly wrapped up with other categories of difference, experiences of marginality and forms of political activism (n. pag.). Disability studies have a long history of engaging with other minority groups as demonstrated by Paul Hunt:

"What I am rejecting is society's tendency to set up rigid standards of what is right and proper, to force the individual into a mould. Our constant experience of this pressure towards unthinking conformity in some way relates us to other obvious deviants [*sic*] and outcasts like the Jew in a gentile world, a negro [*sic*] in a white world, homosexuals, the mentally handicapped [*sic*]; and also to more voluntary rebels in every sphere – artists, philosophers, prophets, who are essentially subversive elements in our society." (151)

Intersectionality is not simply about bringing together these markers but to consider how each supports or unsettles the constitution of one another. Intersectionality seeks to explore convergence and divergence of multiple markers. This involves difficult conversations across socio-cultural categories and forms of interpellation to ask how, for example, disability, gender, race, sexuality and class constitute or contradict one another. Historically, following Goodley (35), disability and femininity have been coupled, as mad, bad and ill women's bodies are categorized through conditions such as premenstrual tension, hysteria, post-natal depression and Munchausen's syndrome by proxy (see Campbell, *Contours* 100). At the same time, we know that men's criminality is distinguished as bad rather than mad, thus separating amorality from an essentialist diagnosis. Disability is constructed through direct recourse to these gendered norms and sexist practices (see Goodley 36). To think of dis/ability we need also to be cognisant of fe/male. This has led Garland-Thomson to argue that a cross-referencing of feminist and critical disability studies perspectives elicits new insights or *reimaginings* for feminists and disability activists alike, "because prevailing narratives constrict disability's complexities they not only restrict the lives and govern the bodies of people we think of as disabled, but they limit the imaginations of those who think of themselves as non-disabled" ("Feminist" 1567). These limits on the imagination – experienced by disabled and non-disabled alike – are taken further by Fiona Kumari Campbell in her grounding-breaking work on ableism.

Campbell's *Contours of Ableism* has had far-reaching influence on the field of critical disability studies, perhaps because her work is an elegant example of intersectional analysis. Her work shifts attention away from the problems of disablism ('the Other') to the problems of ableism ('the same' or 'the dominant'). As soon as disability emerges as a site of otherness and marginality, then so too do 'Other' identities, performances and processes. Ethnicity, class, gender, sexuality and pan-national identities converge around the problems of disability as a consequence of attempts to maintain what Campbell terms ableist normativity (see *Contours*). Disabled people, women, children, queer, people of colour and poor people share an Other space to that of the dominant same that is founded upon ableist, heteronormative, adult, white European and North American, high-income nation's values. For McGuire, "disability marks different bodies in different and relational ways; systems of ableism come into contact with racialized bodies, queer bodies, classed bodies, gendered bodies, bodies that already have been touched by other (and perhaps multiple) systems of oppression" (n. pag.). One of the key tasks of critical disability studies, following Campbell in *Contours of Ableism*, is to explain how these conditions of dominance crisscross in ways that promote values and, simultaneously, justify forms of oppression such as disablism, racism, homophobia and orientalism that negate the existence of Others.

One fruitful arena of work to emerge out of intersectional analysis can be found at the merging of queer and disability studies. Mark Sherry asks: How is queerness evoked in the construction of disability? How is disability evoked in the construction of queerness? These questions, alongside others, have been addressed by Robert McRuer through his development of "crip theory." Drawing largely on ideas from queer theory, McRuer explores the ways in which forms of 'compulsory' hetero-normativity and ablebodiedness merge at sites of domination such as the family, the school and the workplace. McRuer adapts Adrienne Rich's concept of 'compulsory heterosexuality' to develop the notion of 'compulsory able-bodiedness:' an imbricated system interwoven with the system of compulsory heterosexuality. Following Goodley, the most successful heterosexual subject is one whose sexuality is not compromised by the 'disability' of being queer and the most successful able-bodied subject is the one whose ability is not compromised by the 'queerness' of disability (see 41). Compulsory ablebodiedness functions by covering over, with the appearance of choice, a system in which there is actually no choice (ibid.). Yet while conditions of domination are exposed, crip theory re-emphasizes the potentiality of a queer reading of disability. The disabled body, then, is not only a site of oppression but (like all forms of oppression) always contradictory and therefore full of the promise of potentiality. Disabled people occupy *cripping* positions of subversion, connection and reappraisal precisely because they embody Other positions to those demanded by ableist cultures. A crip position has been advanced by Jim Overboe in his discussion of his own disabled body as a crip body. His account of his body rejects the stereotypical disabled body as deficient, and refigures it as a place of becoming, reflection and production (see Goodley 158). Overboe describes his spasms (normatively and medically understood as a sign of the negative affliction of his Cerebral Palsy) as creative elements of his embodiment (queerly understood as productive, creative, physical attributes). Similarly, Amy Vidali's reappropriation of the term "spastic colon" as an alternative to irritable bowel syndrome recasts her normatively understood deficient body as a body that crips how we understand reasonable, appropriate, contained bodies of contemporary life (n. pag.). This draws us into a very specific embodied arena associated with 'odour poetics;' the rhetorics of bodily control associated with 'the politics of shit' (see ibid.). Her spastic colon demands others to think again about the kinds of constraints and expectations ableism demands of its reasonable bodies. Overboe and Vidali powerfully extend what we might term a *trans-sectional* engagement with ableism; articulating what it might mean to embody the counter-hegemonic of crip lives. Trans-sectionality, following Robert Kulpa, captures the disruptive, boundary-breaking, paradigm shifting nature of the crip/queer body and identity; recasting it as a place of possibility. This position fits with Franz Fanon's call for "agents provocateurs and counter subversion" (*Skins* 108-109) because "we only become what we are by the radical and deep-seated refusal of that which others have made us" (Sartre, preface to Fanon's *Wretched* 15).

'Global' Disability Studies

Much of the work I have cited has been written in the minority-world, Global North, Western European and North American high-income nations. Yet critical disability studies have become ever more sensitized to – and to some extents, representational of – disability theory emerging from the Global South. Helen Meekosha, for example, combines anglocentric social model analyses of class with North American cultural studies of colonial settler communities but finding neither suitable for explaining disability in indigenous Australian Aboriginal people and Torres Strait Islanders communities. Countries at the periphery of the English speaking world, such as India, South Africa and Asia-Pacific rim nations, require analyses of disability that reflect their own specific colonial-settler histories (Meekosha, "Drifting" 725). Meekosha questions the implicit values of Northern hemisphere disability studies, including claims to universality (what happens in the Global North should happen in the South); a reading from the metropole (a methodological projection of ideas from the centre into the periphery); emphasis on the importance of northern feudal/capitalist modes of production (with an accompanying ignorance and grand erasure of indigenous/traditional modes of living of the South); a colonialism of psychic, cultural and geographical life of the South by the North; and ignorance of the resistant-subaltern positions of 'Global Southerners' (see Meekosha, "Contextualizing" n.pag.).

Shaun Grech seeks to challenge the shortcomings implicit in the assumptions of Global North disability studies by contextualizing a consideration of a Global South concerns. He reminds us that, for example in Latin America, we need to be mindful of the oppression of indigenous people; the decolonization and formation of new nation-states with the ensuing exploitation and exclusion of minority workers; violent struggles that have increased the movement of refugees and racialized conflicts that have increased the difficult position of these new migrant workers. Consequently, the goal for many Global South disability activists has been basic survival (see Ghai). Concerns associated with educational inclusion, human rights and the development of positive disability cultures might be of less importance to people who are living a hand to mouth existence (Goodley 37).

That said, the complex interweaving of disabled and post-colonized identities has been captured in very nuanced ways. Jude McKenzie, writing from a South African context, and Anita Ghai writing from an Indian perspective, have each demonstrated the hybridized nature of culture, economics and politics and its impact upon the lives of disabled people. Ghai's work is an exemplary account of tradition, history, (post)colonization and (post)modernity on the Indian psyche of disabled and non-disabled people. While mindful of the realities of poverty, colonization and caste/class in India, as a critical psychologist, Ghai is interested in the varying ways in which the subjectivities are constituted through culture. Impairment, she argues, is a "material-semiotic phenomenon dependent upon one's relationships with others and their relationship with you" (*Forms* 128). She goes on:

"The internalisation that I carried in such a cultural milieu [India] accustomed me to seeing my disability as a personal quest and tragedy to be borne alone. [...] I learnt to cope with the limitations, imposed by my impairment. The recurring anxiety was placed in the realm of what Freud so aptly termed as the 'unconscious.'" (*Forms* 14-15)

A global critical disability studies must be ever mindful of connecting across nation-states that recognize specific socio-historical conditions of oppression alongside wider considerations of the globalization of disablism.

The Self and the Other

A key site of the oppression of disabled people pertains to those moments when they are judged to fail to match up to the ideal individual. Susanne Mintz makes the point that social discourses around disability are not about disability at all (see 162). Rather, they relate to the need to guarantee the privileged status of the non-disabled individual; "a need that, in its turn, emerges from fears about the fragility and unpredictability of embodied identity" (ibid.). Similarly, Deb Marks observes that disabled people constitute a huge problem for non-disabled society precisely because they disrupt the normative individual: The person that dribbles, Marks comments, disrupts a culture that emphasises bodily control and associated cultural norms around manners, convention and bodily comportment (see *Controversial*). An individual whose speech is difficult to understand is assumed to have a problem because they challenge a colonising stance of certainty about how people should speak. People who do not walk are understood as tragic because they do not embody the idealised mobility of the autonomous walker (see Oliver "Politics"). People with learning difficulties, who fail to meet developmentalist stages, are discarded from mainstream educational systems because of their lack of fit with educational prerogatives. Individuals who depend on – or require connections with – others to live are not individuals at all. They are burdens (see Goodley 79).

The disabled individual queers – or crips – the normative pitch of the autonomous citizen. For Braidotti our cultural landscape is split between 'his self and his many Others,' with the self of embodied man assumed to be masculine, white urbanized, speaking a standard language, heterosexually inscribed in a reproductive unit and a full citizen of a recognized polity (see 55). This is the dominant self against which we are all expected to judge our own selves. Just as the dominant self 'for the black man is the white man' (see Fanon, *Skins* 97), for the disabled person this is the non-disabled or able self (see Campbell "Exploring").

Campbell suggests that critical disability studies shift attention away from 'the disabled' onto 'the abled.' Ableist processes create a corporeal standard, which presumes ablebodiedness, inaugurates the norm and purifies the ableist ideal. When disabled people (and non-disabled people for that matter) ask 'Who am I?,' they risk being hit with the mirror of the abled self. This self looks back at the disabled Other knowing "disabled people in deficient ways. Disabled people are their impairment. *They* are broken individuals. *They* lack development. *They* cannot do. *They* do not have the abilities to lead an independent life" (Goodley 80). This dominant self threatens to create epistemic invalidation: to make disabled people not know themselves, to become Other (for further discussion, see Wendell; Marks, "Dimensions"). The dominant ableist self is ready and willing to bring disabled people back into the norm (re/habilitate, educate) or banish them (cure, segregate) from its ghostly centre. But, following Goodley, while disabled people undoubtedly suffer the psychologization of ableism, the individual remains a key site of everyday life, oppression and perhaps resistance for *everyone* (see 81). The fashioning of our selves takes place in relation to that which we are not: other people. Moreover, as Couse Venn notes, the multiple objects of otherness allow us to cobble together an ontological sense of who we are. Hence, (disabled) people will find objects within the dominant cultural self through which to fashion their selves. Indeed, the disabled people's movement has built a strong case around human rights and human capital, in which they demand to be part of a wider more inclusive realm of independent living.

Although the disabled self sits uneasily with the narrow construction of the abled self in contemporary society, so too do many other members of society, who are judged against equally pernicious standards of worth associated with the fully functioning self of contemporary society. Indeed, we are *all* engaged in the constitution of ourselves every minute of everyday day, through our relationship with others (see Goodley 81). Our task then is, as Fanon would have it, to recapture the self from its position as Other (see *Black Skin*).

Conclusion: Dangers/Possibilities of Critical Disability Studies

If one was to compare the contemporary state of critical disability studies with disability studies from the last century, one would have to conclude that much has changed – not least – in terms of the growing theoretical confidence of this transdisciplinary community. Some scholars mourn the passing of time and suggest that, while theoretical avenues have been widened, the field has lost touch with the real material problems of disabled people's lives. A preoccupation with theory over politics seems at odds with the very real global economic crisis that threatens to place more and more disabled people in vulnerable and devalued societal positions across the world (see Barnes). Others worry that disability studies are becoming ever more comfortably settled into the academic world so that disability becomes a field of study – rather than a phenomenon around which to collectively campaign – so domesticating the previously radical origins of disability studies (see Shakespeare "Debate"). Furthermore, the moves towards postmodern and queer theories of the 'crip experience' – while celebrating the ever-morphing potential of disability – also threaten to make disability difficult to pin down, identify with and mobilize around (see Swain). The suggestion here is that theory gets in the way of understanding the realities of disablism (see Watson). Indeed, a suggestion from one of the reviewers of this paper is that critical disability studies are in danger of becoming a new uncritical orthodoxy – one distanced from empirical evidence and often only internally critiqued. Also, if disability studies perspectives are no longer exclusively related to the discourses of the disabled people's movement – no longer associated with one strong orthodoxy or model – then one wonders whether disability studies has lost its anchoring.

In contrast, a move towards critical disability studies might be viewed as the logical consequence of disabled people and their allies unpacking and illuminating the complex nature of disability. This is not simply about academic curiosity (although some might ask what the problem is with curiosity). The themes I present above offer, I would suggest, spaces for the development of praxis: the inter-twining of activism and theory. A new generation of scholars and activists are populating these spaces utilizing cyber worlds, plugged into rhizomatic networks of relationships with others, spurning traditional fixed identity categories and realizing community membership through rich diverse connections, and have no time for static modernist theories. Critical disability studies, then, capture some of the sophisticated ways in which bodies, knowledge, and technology merge. Critical disability studies might be viewed then, following Scott Lash, as a lifted-out space: a platform or plateau through which to think through, act, resist, relate, communicate, engage with one another against the hybridized forms of oppression and discrimination that so often do not speak singularly of disability. Discrimination is an increasingly complicated entanglement of disability, gender, sexuality, nation, ethnicity, age and class. Critical disability studies have not developed simply to capture the theoretical interests of scholars, but have developed theories that are in concert with contemporary lives, the complexities of alienation and rich hopes of resistance.

Acknowledgements

The author would like to thank Rebecca Lawthom, Helen Meekosha, Shaun Grech, Donna Reeve, Katherine Runswick Cole and the three anonymous reviewers who have provided thought-provoking feedback on the foci of this paper.

REFERENCES

Barnes, Colin. "Understanding the Social Model of Disability: Past, Present and Future." *Routledge Handbook of Disability Studies*. Print.

Braidotti, Rosi. "Becoming Woman, or Sexual Difference Revisited. *Theory, Culture & Society* 20.3 (2003): 43-64. Print.

Butler, Judith. *Bodies That Matter: On the Discursive Limits of Sex*. London: Routledge, 1993. Print.

—. "Bodies that matter." *Feminist Theory and the Body*. Eds. Janet Price and Margrit Shildrick. Edinburgh: Edinburgh University Press, 1999. 235-245. Print.

Campbell, Fiona Kumari. "Exploring Internalized Ableism Using Critical Race Theory." *Disability & Society* 23.2 (2008): 151-162. Print.

—. *Contours of Ableism: Territories, Objects, Disability and Desire*. London: Palgrave Macmillan, 2009. Print.

—. "Refusing Able(ness): A Preliminary Conversation about Ableism. *M/C – Media and Culture* 11.3 (2008). Web. 7 Sept. 2012. <http://journal.media-culture.org.au/index.php/mcjournal/article/viewArticle/46/>.

Corker, Mairian. *Deaf and Disabled or Deafness Disabled*. Buckingham: Open University Press, 1998. Print.

Corker, Mairian and Tom Shakespeare, eds. *Disability/Postmodernity: Embodying Disability Theory*. London: Continuum, 2002. Print.

Crow, Liz. "Including All of Our Lives: Renewing the Social Model of Disability." *Exploring the Divide*. Eds. Colin Barnes and Geoff Mercer. Leeds: The Disability Press, 1996. 55-72. Print.

Davis, Lennard. *Bending over Backwards: Disability, Dismodernism and other Difficult Positions*. New York: New York University Press, 2002. Print.

Fanon, Frantz. *The Wretched of the Earth*. Trans. C. Farrington. London: Penguin, 1976. Print.

—. *Black Skins, White Masks*. 3rd ed. London: Pluto Press, 1993. Print.

Finkelstein, Vic. "Disability and the Helper/Helped Relationship: An Historical View." *Handicap in a Social World*. Eds. Ann Brechin, Pam Liddiard and John Swain. London: Hodder and Stoughton, 1981. 12-22. Print.

French, Sally. "Can You See the Rainbow?." *Disabling Barriers – Enabling Environments*. Eds. John Swain, Vic Finkelstein et al. London: Sage, 1993. 69-77. Print.

Garland-Thomson, Rosemarie. "Integrating Disability, Transforming Feminist Theory." *National Women's Studies Association Journal* 14.2 (2002): 1-32. Print.

—. "Feminist Disability Studies." *Signs: Journal of Women in Culture and Society* 30.2 (2005): 1557-1587. Print.

Ghai, Anita. "Disabled Women: An Excluded Agenda for Indian Feminism." *Hypatia: A Journal of Feminist Philosophy* 17.3. (2002): 49-66. Print.

—. *(Dis)embodied forms: Issues of Disabled Women.* Delhi: Shakti Books, 2006. Print.

Goggin, Gerard. "Innovation and disability." *M/C Journal* 11.3 (2008). Web. 22 Mar. 2012. <http://dev.mediaculture.ci.qut.edu.au/ojs/index.php/mcjournal/article/viewArticle/56>.

Goodley, Dan. *Disability Studies: An Interdisciplinary Introduction.* London: Sage, 2011. Print.

Grech, Shaun. "Disability, Poverty and Development: Critical Reflections on the Majority World Debate. *Disability & Society* 24.6 (2009): 771-784. Print.

Hughes, Bill. "Medicine and the Aesthetic Invalidation of Disabled People." *Disability & Society* 15.3 (2000): 555-568. Print.

—. "Disability and the Body." *Disability Studies Today.* Eds. Colin Barnes, Len Barton and Mike Oliver. Cambridge: Polity Press, 2002: 58-76. Print.

—. "Invalidated Strangers: Impairment and the Cultures of Modernity and Postmodernity." *Disability & Society.* 17.5 (2002): 571-584. Print.

—. "Disability and the body." *Disabling Barriers – Enabling Environments.* Eds. John Swain, Vic Finkelstein et al. London: Sage, 2004. 63-68. Print.

Hughes, Bill and Kevin Paterson. "The Social Model of Disability and the Disappearing Body: Towards a Sociology of 'Impairment.'" *Disability & Society* 12.3 (1997): 325-340. Print.

Hunt, Paul. "A Critical Condition." *Stigma: The Experience of Disability.* Ed. Paul Hunt. London: Geoffrey Chapman, 1966. 145-149. Print.

Kagan, Carolyn, et al. *Critical Community Psychology.* Oxford: Wiley-Blackwell, 2011. Print.

Kristiansen, Kristiana, et al. *Arguing About Disability: Philosophical Perspectives.* Abingdon: Routledge, 2009. Print.

Kulpa, Robert. *Personal Homepage.* Web. 12 Mar. 2012. <robertkulpa.com>.

Lash, Scott. "Technological Forms of Life." *Theory, Culture and Society* 18.1 (2001): 105-120. Print.

Marks, Deb. *Disability: Controversial Debates and Psychosocial Perspectives.* London: Routledge, 1999. Print.

—. "Dimensions of Oppression: Theorizing the Embodied Subject." *Disability & Society* 14.5 (1999): 611-626. Print.

McGuire, Anne. "Disability, Non-Disability and the Politics of Mourning: Re-conceiving the 'We.'" *Disability Studies Quarterly* 30.3/4 (2010). Web. 22 Mar. 2012. <http://www.dsq-sds.org/article/view/1282/1309>.

McKenzie, Jude. "Constructing the Intellectually Disabled Person as a Subject of Education: A Discourse Analysis Using Q-Methodology." Diss. Rhodes University, South Africa, 2009. Print.

McRuer, Robert. *Crip theory: Cultural signs of queerness and disability*, New York: New York University Press, 2006. Print.

Meekosha, Helen. "Drifting Down the Gulf Stream: Navigating the Cultures of Disability Studies." *Disability & Society* 19.7 (2004): 721-733. Print.

—. "Contextualizing Disability: Developing Southern Theory." Fourth Disability Studies Association Conference. University of Lancaster, Lancaster, UK. 2-4 Sept. 2008. Keynote Address.

Meekosha, Helen and Russell Shuttlewort. "What's so 'Critical' About Critical Disability Studies?." *Australian Journal of Human Rights* 15.1 (2009): 47-76. Print.

Michalko, Rod. *The Two-in-One: Walking with Smokie, Walking with Blindness.* Philadelphia, PA: Temple University Press, 1999. Print.

—. *The Difference that Disability Makes.* Philadelphia, PA: Temple University Press, 2002. Print.

Mintz, Susanne. "Invisible disability: Georgina Kleege's *Sight Unseen.*" *Feminist Disability Studies.* Ed. Kay Hall. Special issue of *National Women's Studies Association Journal* 14.3 (2002). 155-77. Print.

Mitchell, David T. and Sharon L. Snyder. "Narrative Prosthesis and the Materiality of Metaphor." *The Disability Studies Reader.* 2nd ed. Ed. Lennard Davis. New York: Routledge, 2006. 205-216. Print.

Oliver, Mike. *The Politics of Disablement.* Basingstoke: Macmillan, 1990. Print.

—. "If I Had a Hammer: The Social Model in Action." *The Social Model of Disability: Theory and Research.* Ed. Colin Barnes. Leeds: The Disability Press, 2004. 18-31. Print.

Olkin, Rhona. "Could You Hold the Door for Me?: Including Disability in Diversity." *Cultural Diversity & Ethnic Minority Psychology* 8.2 (2002): 130-137. Print.

Overboe, Jim. "Disability and Genetics: Affirming the Bare Life (The State of Exception)." *Canadian Review of Sociology* 44.2 (2007). Special Issue. Genes and Society: Looking Back on the Future. 219-235. Print.

Parker, Ian. *Revolution in Psychology: Alienation to Emancipation.* London: Pluto Press, 2007. Print.

Reeve, Donna. "Negotiating Psycho-Emotional Dimensions of Disability and their Influence on Identity Constructions." *Disability & Society* 17.5 (2002): 493-508. Print.

—. "Negotiating Disability in Everyday Life: The Experience of Psycho-Emotional Disablism." Diss. University of Lancaster, UK, 2008. Print.

Rich, Adrienne. "Compulsory Heterosexuality and Lesbian Existence." *Signs* 5.4 (1980): 631-660. Print.

Sartre, Jean-Paul. Preface. *The Wretched of the Earth.* By Frantz Fanon. Trans. C. Farrington. London: Penguin, 1976. Print.

Shakespeare, Tom. *Disability Rights and Wrongs*. London: Routledge, 2006. Print.

—. "Disability Studies Debate." University of Tokyo. 24 Oct. 2010. Keynote Address.

Sherry, Mark. "Overlaps and Contradictions between Queer Theory and Disability Studies." *Disability & Society* 19.7 (2004): 769-783. Print.

Shildrick, Margrit. *Dangerous Discourses of Disability, Subjectivity and Sexuality*. London: Palgrave Macmillan, 2009. Print.

—. "Critical Disability Studies: Rethinking the Conventions for the Age of Postmodernity." *Routledge Handbook of Disability Studies*. Eds. Nick Watson, Alan Roulstone and Carol Thomas. London: Routledge, 2012. 30-41. Print.

Siebers, Tobin. *Disability Theory*. Ann Arbor: University of Michigan Press, 2008. Print.

Snyder, Sharon L. and David T. Mitchell. *Cultural Locations of Disability*. Chicago: University of Chicago Press, 2006. Print.

Swain, John. Rev. of *Disability Studies: An Interdisciplinary Introduction*, by Dan Goodley. *Disability & Society* 26.4 (2011): 503-505. Print.

Thomas, Carol. "The Body and Society: Some Reflections on the Concepts 'Disability' and 'Impairment.'" *Reframing the Body*. Eds. Nick Watson and Sarah Cunningham-Burley. London: Palgrave, 2001. 47-62. Print.

—. *Sociologies of Disability and Illness: Contested Ideas in Disability Studies and Medical Sociology*. London: Palgrave, 2007. Print.

Titchkosky, Tanya. *Disability, Self and Society*. Toronto: University of Toronto Press, 2003. Print.

—. "I Got Trouble with my Reading: An Emerging Literacy." *Disability and the International Politics of Education*. Eds. Susan Gabel and Scott Danforth. New York: Peter Lang Publisher, 2006. 337-352. Print.

Tremain, Shelley, ed. *Foucault and the Government of Disability*. Ann Arbor: University of Michigan Press, 2005. Print.

Venn, Couse. *Occidentalism: Modernity and Subjectivity*. London: Sage, 2001. Print.

Vidali, Amy. "Out of Control: The Rhetoric of Gastrointestinal Disorders." *Disability Studies* 30.3/4 (2010). Web. 22 Mar. 2012. <http://www.dsq-sds.org/article/view/1287/1313>.

Responses to Dan Goodley

Konstantin Butz

THE PROMISE OF POTENTIALITY

My response to Dan Goodley's paper cannot but be extremely shallow. First, because I am far from being an expert concerning the matter at hand and, second, because it seems to be impossible to adequately summarize, let alone comment on, all of the aspects that are so convincingly laid out in his text. In order to mask the superficiality of my remarks, I have opted for a rather pragmatist solution and decided to concentrate on or rather *zoom into* only a few aspects raised in Goodley's broad account of disability studies past and present. I can thus reduce the risk of getting lost in the extensive complexities that necessarily characterize the topic, while simultaneously preparing for an argument that seeks to underscore the importance of infinitesimally small phenomena which require a focused and concentrated approach.

I would like to take my cue from Goodley's remarks concerning the importance of intersectionality as a constitutive characteristic for what I read as his call for a *critical* disability studies. Referencing Carol Thomas's definition of *disablism* and drawing on Fiona Kumari Campbell's concept of *ableism*, he advances the argument that disability can be positioned "alongside other forms of oppression including hetero/sexism and racism" (Goodley 81), thus establishing the field as *in fact* intersectional and thus "relevant to all" (82). Picking up on this argument, I will offer a way in which we might employ intersectionality as a 'tool' in preparing for what could ideally turn into a 'revolutionary response' or at least a point of departure for "rich hopes of resistance," as Goodley states in concluding his article (93).

"What exactly *is* intersectionality?," we might ask, before delving into its theoretical and practical implementations. The importance of this seemingly trivial question cannot be overestimated, as it inevitably leads us to the origins of what is much more than 'just' a theoretical concept.

Intersectionality mainly developed from the African-American feminist movement originating in the 1960s (and before). In its initial setting, intersectionality uncovers in what ways working class African-American women suffer from the ramifications of different axes of differentiation that identify them according to attributes of race, class, and gender. It reveals to what extent the struggle of these women – and other women who are discursively rendered as 'non-white' – is different from that of, say, white middle-class feminists. For reasons of space, I will not go into the details of the groundbreaking works of feminist scholars and activists such as bell hooks, Patricia Hill Collins, the women of the Combahee River Collective, or Kimberlé Crenshaw who coined the term *intersectionality theory* in 1989. However, at this point it can be stated that intersectionality as a concept is deeply rooted in social resistance, activism, and *black feminist thought* (as the book with the same title by Patricia Hill Collins implies).

In other words, intersectionality theory did not develop from purely academic interests, but from the real-life struggles of non-white women who had to cope with the discursive and material grip of white supremacy. It prevents what Judith Butler might call "epistemological imperialism" (18) – i.e. the assumption that one could grasp every vector of power in a single work of theoretical writing – by practically concentrating on aspects of differentiation that affect people in the setting of a white patriarchal society. In short, intersectionality neither developed from theoretical or epistemological curiosity nor from the purely intellectual aspiration to analyze complexity, but instead it arose from actual, conflictual experience and, consequently, from political necessity.

This undeniable necessity is what makes intersectionality an almost in-evitable 'ally' in the development of a *critical* disability studies, as we find similar situations of political urgency at the outset of what is much more than simply an academic endeavor. As Goodley remarks in his introduction, "the politicization of disabled people is at the heart" of the developments that have led to the disciplinary formation of the field discussed in this book (81). One aspect of this formation, according to Goodley, is an approach to critical disability studies that acknowledges the complexities of postmodern conditions, among other aspects, and maybe most importantly the complexities of identity politics.

Intersectionality, I argue, can be very helpful in disentangling the highly affective vectors of differentiation that are crucial in the creation of what we perceive as our own or other people's identities, which includes the identifying attributions of 'disabled' and 'abled.' These attributions, among others, set the standard of what we perceive as normal and acceptable. If we take a closer look at how such standardizations are implemented in the realm of corporeal living, we acquire insight into the way they diminish free, or personal developments, and, most importantly, developments that are *different* from social norms. We might ask ourselves how these standards could be challenged, how they could be changed. Goodley explains that "any intimate bodily function is also a function of a body within given standards of embodiment" (87). Consequently, I propose that it is from the "intimate bodily function" that a challenging of "given standards" could be generated. But how can we evaluate these functions? How could we form an idea of their potentiality to generate new and non-standard ways of embodiment?

This is the point where intersectionality becomes practicable, as it can accompany us on a phenomenological journey towards the intimate bodily functions that provide a corporeal interface characterized by its convergence of material and symbolic forces, as described by Goodley with reference to feminist philosopher Rosi Braidotti. An intersectional analysis first and foremost uncovers differentiating categories that are used to discursively render everybody, i.e. literally *every body*, identifiable according to attributes of race, class, gender, sexuality, ethnicity, age, ability, and so on. As I pointed out, such an analysis is politically informed and thus reveals precisely those axes of differentiation that have either oppressive or privileging effects for the body and its associated identity. We can thus use intersectional analyses to uncover and momentarily bracket these discursive (more precisely: symbolic) differentiations and approach the purely material forces that characterize bodily functions. These functions, even if infinitesimal, always include moments of corporeal movement, be it only the blood cells running through our veins.

This movement, I argue, offers the chance to resist intersectional ascriptions as, by definition, it escapes the notion of fixity and thus of fixed meaning, of fixed identity. It is within ephemeral moments of movement that we enter fluid modes of becoming or, to reference Goodley's reference to the works of Margrit Shildrick, it is in these moments that we inhabit a "fluid social body" which potentially refutes "corporeal standards" (85).

Let me use an example to elucidate the importance of such moments: In *The Interpretation of Cultures*, Clifford Geertz introduces the potential of what he calls a "thick description" by referring to Gilbert Ryle's account of "two boys rapidly contracting the eyelids of their right eyes" (6). It is certainly not merely by chance that Geertz emphasizes the boys' actions as "movements" (of the eyelids), which only by reading them through "a public code" can be differentiated as either "twitch" or "wink" (ibid.). He thus reintegrates the importance of movement into any analysis of human being (and becoming). As apparently identical movements, the "'phenomenalistic' observation of them alone" would not reveal the significance of one movement as a mere contraction and the other one as a purposeful wink. It is only in "a public code [that the contraction of eyelids] counts as a conspiratorial sign" (ibid.). Either way, the factual physicality of *movement* pervades the situation as a matter of presence, which is subsequently, and maybe even simultaneously, enhanced (or could we say: constrained?) through a cultural interpretation in the form of a thick description. Geertz summarizes: "That's all there is to it: a speck of behavior, a fleck of culture, and *voilà!*—a gesture" (ibid.).

It is this notion of a *gesture* (and the "fleck of culture" it embodies) that is important for our discussion. Just as with the "public code" that turns a "twitch" into a "wink" and thus a gesture, it seems to be the discursive power of the differentiating categories of intersectionality that classifies people's corporeal movements within notions of ability and disability. (Corporeal) movements always happen within a cultural matrix and are interpreted, read, and coded according to normative standards. They are, one could say, always read as gestures.

Let us take a look at a few of the examples that Goodley invokes in his paper: The "person that dribbles," an "individual whose speech is difficult to understand," "people who do not walk," he points out, all disrupt "a culture that emphasises bodily control" and thus, in the broadest sense they deviate from the culturally standardized norms of movement (91). But what if we – at least momentarily – stop to read these movements as gestures? What if we push aside the intersectional differentiations providing the public code through which we read corporeal living? What if we refuse to read a twitch as a wink and, for a moment, remain with the purely 'phenomenalistic observation' of movement that constitutes its material base? The answer to these questions, I think, might help to generate a moment of potentiality, a moment that presents movement in its fluid and contingent state of becoming, of becoming something new, something different, something that is and cannot be fixed, a moment that would illuminate what Goodley calls "the promise of potentiality" (89), which, in fact, characterizes any kind of bodily movement. This could be precisely one of those moments Goodley refers to for its potential to "consider how bodies should and *could* be lived" (87). An intersectional analysis could help us to disentangle discursively imposed vectors of differentiations and offer an unbiased insight into a corporeal life that is full of potentiality and not (yet) restricted and evaluated by standardizing distinction.

Of course, this uncovering of entirely free material movement is so far based on a purely theoretical conceptualization. It is from the coziness of the academic armchair that I push aside the intersectional categories encapsulating all movements and turning them into a coded gesture within dominant discourse. I implied that an intersectional analysis might help to reveal the potentiality of pure movement by following a top down approach that works through layers of intersecting differentiations. It would be the challenge for further enquiries to develop a bottom-up approach that not only zooms into the infinitesimal movements that take place under layers of discursive inscription, but that in fact *departs* from these material and corporeal realities; an approach departing from a twitch (to remain with the Geertzian example) in order to evaluate a single moment of movement and its potential to create something new, different, and unprecedented, something that is not filtered through the gatekeepers of intersectional differentiation but which factually generates the potential to alter our conception of what is normal. Such an approach might indeed bracket the "prevailing narratives [which] constrict disability's complexities" that Goodley mentions in quoting Rosemarie Garland-Thomson, and it could thus broaden what she calls "the imaginations of those who think of themselves as non-disabled" (cited in Goodley 88).

Intersectionality theory, I would like to think, will help us to produce and make way for such imaginings and *re-imaginings* as it deconstructs the coded barriers that hinder our imagination's free-floating development. Intersectionality's rootedness in direct political action thereby underscores Goodley's anticipation of spaces that offer "the inter-twining of activism and theory" (93). His essay shows how the field of critical disability studies promises to support a substantial challenge to a world that needs both a theoretical reflection on the normative discourses that render its realities meaningful *and* the activist response, resistance, reimagination, reorganization, and realization of its material and corporeal potential.

References

Butler, Judith. *Bodies that Matter*. New York: Routledge, 1993. Print.

Collins, Patricia Hill. *Black Feminist Thought*. New York: Routledge, 2000. Print.

Crenshaw, Kimberlé. "Demarginalizing the Intersection of Race and Sex: A Black Feminist Critique of Antidiscrimination Doctrine, Feminist Theory and Antiracist Politics." *University of Chicago Legal Forum* (1989): 139-167. Print.

Geertz, Clifford. *The Interpretation of Cultures*. New York: Basic Books, 1973. Print.

Goodley, Dan. "Dis/entangling Critical Disability Studies." This volume. 81-97. Print.

Rouven Schlegel

BEYOND JUDGMENT: TOWARDS CRITICAL DISABILITY STUDIES

What does 'critical disability studies' mean? Which particular importance does the adjective *critical* receive in a disability studies context? While being emancipatory, are these studies not critical *per se*? Why is this accentuation necessary, and which discursive function does it fulfill? These questions relate to Dan Goodley's essay on critical disability studies, which I will use as an opportunity to define the term 'critique' and situate it in the context of critical theory, as well as an occasion to deconstruct the notion of impairment. In doing so, I intend to demonstrate both the conditions and opportunities of a critical perspective on disability.

What Is Critique?

Generally and etymologically speaking, the French loanword *critique* derives from the Greek *kritikós* and its infinitive *krínein*, which means to differ, to distinguish, or to divide (Bittner 134). With reference to Michel Foucault, one could also ask the philosophical question: "What is critique?" According to this French thinker, critique exists only in relation to something other than itself, "it is an instrument, a means for a future or a truth that it will not know nor happen to be [...]. All this means that it is a function which is subordinated in relation to what philosophy, science, politics, ethics, law, literature, etc., positively constitute" (Foucault 42). Hence critique is to be understood as a political attitude, it is the counterpart to the "arts of governing" (44). In this context, Foucault claims that critique is "the art of not being governed quite so much" (45). Starting with a decision of resisting being governed 'quite so much,' critique must reverse and release the "coercion characteristics" (66) which lead to specific knowledge within a concrete strategic field.

Following Foucault, we should differentiate between the practice of criticism, which refers to any valuing or judging statement, and critique as a general attitude of analysis of the effective complexes of power-knowledge. The latter leads me to Critical Theory, a well-known German social philosophy. Founded in the 1930s in Frankfurt by Max Horkheimer (541 et seq.) and others, this school of thought was oriented towards critiquing and changing society as a whole by applying knowledge from the social sciences and humanities. The approach of Critical Theory is fundamentally different from traditional theory, since it reflects its own socio-cultural and historico-political contexts rather than adhering to an empiristic-scientific positivism. In other words, traditional theory is orientated to understanding or to explaining society 'the way it is,' whereas Critical Theory seeks to develop new ways of thinking that help to liberate human beings "from the circumstances that enslave them" (Horkheimer 578; translation by author).

Judith Butler posits a combination of Foucault's notion of critique and the Frankfurt School's criticizing impetus. For her, the two approaches can be understood based on the difference between judgment and critique: "Judgments operate for both [Foucault and Critical Theory] as ways to subsume a particular under an already constituted category, whereas critique asks after the occlusive constitution of the field of categories themselves" ("Critique" n. pag.). So, according to Butler, judgments depend on a given categorical structure, whereas critique points to those conditions and circumstances which are constitutive for all evaluated and constructed categories. Thus, Butler's conception allows for the possibility of thinking any key categories of any critical theory "beyond judgment" (ibid).

In the following, this framework provides the basis for addressing critical disability studies and it enables a distinction between critical und general disability studies. If disability studies wish to become *critical*, they must not only be understood as an appraising perspective which judges different conceptions of disability. Rather, critical disability studies must question its own major categories, constitutive conditions, and concrete relationships. Last but not least, it should reflect on its relationship to and functioning within general disability studies. Hereafter, I will focus on the issue of impairment. Based on a critical disability studies perspective, we need to first ask, 'What is impairment and how is it related to disability?' and furthermore: 'What kind of category is impairment and how is it used?'

Impairment

In all models of disability, impairment is a main point of reference even though it is understood and used in different ways. This is not at all surprising, since impairment unites the contingent array of disability. According to Bill Hughes and Kevin Paterson, "[i]mpairment is consequently entrenched in the biomedical and reduced to its dysfunctional anatomo-physiological correlates" (329). Within German disability studies, the debate about impairment is more or less neglected, whereas in Anglo-American publications the discussion is more controversial. In a nutshell, two lines of the hermeneutics of impairment, which are mostly regarded as contrary, can be named.

The so-called social model of disability tends to adhere to a scientific-biological framework: It strictly separates disability from impairment, and while it postulates disability as a social effect of exclusion, it considers impairment as a medical fact. By contrast, from a post-structuralist point of view and the perspective of a cultural model of disability, the "subject of impairment" (Tremain) is conceptualized as discursively constructed as a materialization in a historico-political complex of power-knowledge (see Hughes and Paterson 333; Waldschmidt "Macht").[2]

Both approaches leave unanswered questions concerning the relationship between impairment and disability, such as: Which impairment leads to disability and which does not? When does it do so and at what point does it not? Why does it (not) do so and what are the constitutive conditions of both constructed categories? A decidedly *critical* perspective inevitably has to consider, first, that impairment as a category is neither static nor arbitrary. Secondly, this perspective must focus on the historico-cultural transformations which generate a contemporary "integrated field" (Link 179; translation by author) of impairment and disability.

Finally, Hughes and Peterson's conception of a 'sociology of impairment' rightly indicates that the debate about impairment tends to neglect the lived experiences of disabled persons. Referring to Maurice Merleau-Ponty's phenomenological concept of a lived body's being in the 'world,' they consider that "impairment is more than a medical issue. It is both an experience and a discursive construction. It has phenomenological parameters, and it can be analysed as an effect of discourse and language" (335). Furthermore, they add, that "most importantly, the (impaired) body is not just experienced: It is also the very basic of experience" (ibid).

In my opinion, Hughes and Paterson raise important aspects which a critical discussion of impairment – and thus of disability – must deal with if it does not assume that disability is merely an effect or indication of oppression (see for a similar argument Schneider and Waldschmidt 67).

Deconstruction

A deconstructionist point of view will make this position more evident. According to Jacques Derrida, deconstruction is not a method but rather a critical perspective, for it allows a fundamental criticism of all descriptive terms, because their significance is no longer regarded as inherent (see Quadflieg 106; Kimmerle 27 et seq.). Following Derrida, a signifier does not refer to an ideally signified 'thing,' but rather to other signifiers. Each and every signified is always in the signifier's position (see Derrida, *Grammatologie* 129). Meaning and signification are not immanent or even transcendent, but rather result from the sign's differences.

To summarize Derrida, differences emerge in a process of repetition. They are not certain, rather they are *in becoming*. Thus, meaning depends on time and space; it can only be expressed ex post, in a lag, a deferral, a delay. Furthermore,

2 | About the cultural model and its relation to the social model see Schneider and Waldschmidt.

repetition and motion have a spatial structure, such as intervals or distance. The French verb *différer* has two meanings and can be used transitively (to delay or to postpone) as well as intransitively (to differ or to be different) (see Hill 15). Derrida's neologism *différance* denotes this ambiguity, because it combines spatial as well as temporal parameters. The spatial parameter concerns the aspect of differentiating one element from another (binary opposition), while the latter emphasizes the necessity to postpone temporarily one interpretation for another. In short, meaning is an effect that is entangled in a network of references and produced in and by *différance*. Hence, for a deconstructive point of view it is necessary to analyze the effects of differentiations (meanings) according to their spacing and temporalization – and to analyze them critically.

To approach impairment from this point of view, I would like to refer to body theory as a complement to my argument. Drawing on Butler, Dan Goodley points out that in disability studies bodies also matter. Within a socio-cultural model disability is basically to be considered as a corporeal, embodied difference, so it is necessary to focus on the body. But here I would like to ask: 'Which bodies matter?'

According to Robert Gugutzer, the body is both product and producer of culture and society, and both the docile body (*Körper*) and the phenomenological lived body (*Leib*) are to be understood as a unit rather than as a duality (see Gugutzer 6). Furthermore, as 'Leib,' the lived body, features self-will, it is a living body: Rather than being simply a medium, the body *acts* pre-reflexively and on its own (see Jäger 54). This self-will can be unruly, it contains a "subversive potential" (Gugutzer and Schneider 43; translation by author), and thus also the possibility for resistance.[3] However, this unruliness is not to be mistaken for impairment: Whether and how a certain body practice counts as rebellious or as impairment depends on its temporalization, spacing,[4] and performative utterance.

Deconstructing Impairment

A body's specifications, descriptions, expressions, perceptions, characteristics, in short, all bodily signs, can be conceptualized as traces. In short and in keeping with Derrida's conception of *différance* with its spatial and temporal parameters, a trace is the always contingent term for the absence implied by a sign's presence. As such, traces hint at past signs which define them.[5] To

---

3 | Gugutzer and Schneider give the example of laughing out loud unintentionally in situations commonly regarded as cheerless, e.g. a funeral.

4 | See Schillmeier about the importance of time and space for the negotiation of disability.

5 | See Kimmerle (43) about Derrida's conception of trace.

assume a structure of reference which allows one to 'read' and 'understand' bodily signs, implies that bodies, and thus impairments, depend on context. Both the power perspective as well as the phenomenological approach and the acceptance of a body's self-will support this conclusion. Thus, both the body as well as impairment refer to 'nature' as well as to 'culture' (power), but not necessarily to one *or* the other; instead they are concomitant with each other. This conception therefore indicates that both the body and impairment should be thought of as interdependent categories.

The example of 'obstructive sleep apnea' (OSA)[6] provides an illustration. Whether and how we sleep and breathe is (usually) controllable only to a limited extent by persons themselves; in particular breathing while sleeping is hardly a matter of conscious control. Nevertheless, the medical definition defines OSA as "abnormal breathing during sleep" (Lurie 3). So from this medical point of view, breathing can be categorized according to a normalizing scale, and consequently problems of breathing while asleep are regarded as impairment. Instead, I would like to argue for an understanding of both (temporarily not) breathing and sleeping as a body's own practices, as essential corporeal actions. Following Merleau-Ponty, experiences of tiredness, wakefulness, pain, etc., are unique and constitutive of one's accession to the world: A specific corporeality generates specific insights. Thus, embodied experiences are more than 'just' sensations or, phenomenologically speaking, points of origin: They matter.

Therefore, the example of OSA illustrates a threefold taxonomy of the body as described above with reference to Gugutzer: the docile body (power), the lived body (phenomenology), and the autonomous body (self-will). The medical classification of OSA as impairment includes aspects of power, whereas sleep-related experiences belong to the lived body. Finally, the practice of (temporarily not) breathing can be understood as expressing a body's self-will. Thus, with this example in mind, from a critical and deconstructive point of view impairment is no longer conceptualized as a distinct sign, neither a natural nor a cultural one. Rather, it consists of signs and refers to other signs. Some of them may be described, others may be experienced, they may be encoded, their context may be medical, individual, social, cultural, etc. Whether and how the meaning of any so-called impairment operates, depends on repetition, spacing, and temporalization. In other words, impairment is an effect as well as effective.

---

6 | Obstructive sleep apnea is characterized by "repetitive episodes of complete or partial obstructions of the upper airway during sleep" and its diagnosis requires "the objective demonstration of abnormal breathing during sleep" (Lurie 3).

Conclusion

In this essay I argue that we should overcome essentialist conceptions of impairment and begin to deconstruct the binary dichotomy of nature and culture, to re-think the main issues of disability from a critical angle. To use Butler's words:

"The critical task is [...] to locate strategies of subversive repetition enabled by those constructions, to affirm the local possibilities of intervention through participating in precisely those practices of repetition that constitute identity and, therefore, present the immanent possibility of contesting them." (*Gender* 188)

Finally, to come full circle, embedding this perspective into general disability studies would help to overcome judging conceptions of disability guided by a general supposition of repression. Coming back to Foucault, this approach would offer the possibility of not being governed quite so much. It would, last but not least, offer a space within general disability studies where a perspective of *critical* disability studies would be possible.

References

Bittner, Rüdiger. "Kritik, und wie es besser wäre." *Was ist Kritik?* Eds. Rahel Jaeggi and Tilo Wesche. Frankfurt a.M.: Suhrkamp, 2008. 134-149. Print.

Butler, Judith. *Gender Trouble: Feminism and the Subversion of Identity.* New York: Routledge, 1990. Print.

—. "What is Critique? An Essay on Foucault's Virtue." *Transversal – Eipcp Multilingual Webjournal.* European Institute for Progressive Cultural Policies. (2001). Web. 03 Sept. 2013. <http://eipcp.net/transversal/0806/butler/en>.

Derrida, Jacques. *Grammatologie.* Frankfurt a.M.: Suhrkamp, 1974. Print.

—. "Die Différance." *Postmoderne und Dekonstruktion. Texte französischer Philosophen der Gegenwart.* Stuttgart: Reclam, 1997. 76-113. Print.

Foucault, Michel. "What is Critique?." *The Politics of Truth.* Los Angeles: Semiotext(e), 2007. 41-82. Print.

Goodley, Dan. *Disability Studies: An Interdisciplinary Introduction.* Los Angeles: SAGE, 2011. Print.

Gugutzer, Robert and Werner Schneider. "Der 'behinderte' Körper in den Disability Studies. Eine körpersoziologische Grundlegung." *Disability Studies, Kultursoziologie und Soziologie der Behinderung. Erkundungen in einem neuen Forschungsfeld.* Eds. Anne Waldschmidt and Werner Schneider. Bielefeld: transcript, 2007. 31-53. Print.

Gugutzer, Robert. *Soziologie des Körpers.* Bielefeld: transcript, 2004. Print.

Hill, Leslie. *The Cambridge Introduction to Jacques Derrida*. Cambridge: Cambridge University Press, 2007. Print.

Horkheimer, Max. "Traditionelle und Kritische Theorie." *Kritische Theorie*. Frankfurt a.M.: S. Fischer, 1977. 521-575. Print.

Hughes, Bill and Kevin Paterson. "The Social Model of Disability and the Disappearing Body: Towards a Sociology of Impairment." *Disability & Society* 12.3 (1997): 325-340. Print.

Jäger, Ulle. *Der Körper, der Leib und die Soziologie: Entwurf einer Theorie der Inkorporierung*. Königstein: Helmer, 2004. Print.

Kimmerle, Heinz. *Jaques Derrida zur Einführung*. Hamburg: Junius, 2000. Print.

Link, Jürgen. "Erzählen, wie man in andere Zustände kommt. Mentale Denormalisierung in der Literatur (mit einem Blick auf Zola und Musil)." *Andere Bilder. Zur Produktion von Behinderung in der visuellen Kultur*. Eds. Beate Ochsner and Anna Grebe. Bielefeld: transcript, 2013. 179-194. Print.

Lurie, Alain. *Obstructive Sleep Apnea in Adults: Relationship with Cardiovascular and Metabolic Disorders*. Basel: Karger, 2011. Print.

Quadflieg, Dirk. "Sprache und Diskurs. Von der Struktur zur Différance." *Poststrukturalistische Sozialwissenschaften*. Eds. Stephan Moebius and Andreas Reckwitz. Frankfurt a.M.: Suhrkamp, 2008. 93-107. Print.

Schillmeier, Michael. "Time-Spaces of In/dependence and Disability." *Time & Society* 17.2/3 (2003): 215-31. Print.

Schneider, Werner and Anne Waldschmidt. "Disability Studies." *Kultur. Von den Cultural Studies zu den Visual Studies. Eine Einführung*. Ed. Stephan Moebius. Bielefeld: transcript, 2013. 128-50. Print.

Tremain, Shelley. "On the Subject of Impairment." *Disability/Postmodernity. Embodying Disability Theory*. Eds. Mairian Corker and Tom Shakespeare. London: Continuum, 2002. 32-47. Print.

Waldschmidt, Anne. "Disability Studies: Individuelles, Soziales und/oder Kulturelles Modell von Behinderung?." *Psychologie & Gesellschaft* 1 (2005): 9-31. Print.

—. "Macht – Wissen – Körper. Anschlüsse an Michel Foucault in den Disability Studies." *Disability Studies, Kultursoziologie und Soziologie der Behinderung. Erkundungen in einem neuen Forschungsfeld*. Eds. Anne Waldschmidt and Werner Schneider. Bielefeld: transcript, 2007. 56-77. Print.

Disability, Pain, and the Politics of Minority Identity[1]

Tobin Siebers

1.

What is the trouble with minority identity? Minority identity is supposedly about pain.[2] Produced by coercion, clung to by subjects because the pain of coercion is hard to forget, minority identity is twice disabling. First, one is subjected; then the subject internalizes its suffering and lays claim to its own subordination. Pain serves as the glue that laminates the outside and inside of minority identity, ensuring that the violence enacted by society against individuals remains embedded in their psyche.

Such is the everyday experience of minority identity, according to many contemporary cultural theorists, but the trouble with minority identity grows worse when it is politicized. Identity politics apparently steeps the subject in pain by privileging the defective and weak identities produced by historical injustices like sexism and racism and by asking individuals to dwell on their suffering to produce political capital for themselves.[3] People given to identity

---

1 | This essay was originally published in *Foundations of Disability Studies* (eds. Matthew Wappett and Katrina Arndt. New York: Palgrave Macmillan, 2013. 17-28). It is reprinted with the kind permission of Palgrave Macmillan.

2 | This essay, along with my "Disability Trouble" and "Tender Organs," form part one of a two-pronged analysis of the representation of pain on the contemporary theoretical scene. Part one offers a counterargument to the pervasive belief that pain disables the ability of minority people to participate in politics. Part two, "In the Name of Pain," analyzes and takes issue with the use of pain in court decisions and legislation to justify unequal treatment of and violence against disabled people. The three essays together contribute to my ongoing correction of social constructionism by arguing that it ignores disabled bodies and their contribution to the knowledge base of society.

3 | For more on the notion that minority identity is supposedly injured or disabled in itself, and so inadequate for coalition building, see my *Disability Theory*, 34-95.

politics, according to Judith Butler, internalize the injurious names given to them by history and accept subordination to heal themselves, but the result is greater disability, not health or political power.[4] Either minority groups end up blaming themselves for their status as victims, which solidifies the sense of historical failure inherent in their minority status, or they avenge their pain by making scapegoats of others, which produces a morality of the powerless and resentful. Identity-based politics, Wendy Brown claims, thrives on "wounded attachments" (Brown 52 et seq.), and these affiliations, because linked to suffering, offer no alternative to subordination: "What kinds of political recognition can identity-based claims seek [...] that will not resubordinate a subject itself historically subordinated through identity?" (55). Pain apparently disables the ability of identity politics to form alliances based on self-affirmation, emancipation, and empowerment, producing instead a desire for recognition that "breeds a politics of paralysis and suffering" (55). "Politicized identity thus enunciates itself, makes claims for itself," Brown concludes, "only by entrenching, restating, dramatizing, and inscribing its pain in politics; it can hold out no future – for itself or others – that triumphs over this pain" (74). Friedrich Nietzsche, who is Brown's mentor in the theory of wounded attachments, uses stronger language to portray the identities created when oppressed people form political coalitions. He complains about being "condemned to the repellent sight of the ill-constituted, dwarfed, atrophied, and poisoned" (43).

The use of disability identity as a prop to denigrate minority politics has a long and pernicious history on the right, although it is bewildering to find the usage alive and well in Butler, Brown, and other cultural critics on the left.[5] (This surprising agreement between the right and left gives one small clue to the tenacious hold that ability as an ideology exercises over political thinking today.[6]) Indeed, the idea that the political claims made by people of color and women are illegitimate because their identities are disabled would be outrageous

---

4 | As Butler explains in *The Psychic Life of Power*, once "called by an injurious name" and "a certain narcissism takes hold of any term that confers existence, I am led to embrace the terms that injure me because they constitute me socially" (Butler 104).

5 | In "Disability Trouble," I trace the disagreement about minority identity during the last twenty-five years between the right and the left. On the right, I chart the continuum from Allan Bloom to Walter Benn Michaels. On the left worth mentioning are Brown, Butler, *Gender Trouble*, and Fraser.

6 | The ideology of ability establishes ability as the measure of human status, determining whether individuals are allowed to participate in a broad range of activities. Most important, in the context of politics, the degree of ability decides whether one is a rights-bearing person. Racism, sexism, classism, and other prejudices find justification in the argument that individuals lack ability, thereby establishing their inferiority and

if it were not such a familiar and successful ploy. Historical opponents of political and social equality for women, Douglas Baynton shows, cite their supposed physical, intellectual, and psychological flaws, stressing irrationality, excessive emotions, and physical weakness, while similar arguments for racial inequality and immigration restrictions involving particular races and ethnic groups invoke their apparent susceptibility to feeble-mindedness, mental illness, deafness, blindness, and other disabilities (see Baynton 33). Moreover, disability remains today, Baynton explains, an acceptable reason for unequal treatment, even as other justifications for discrimination, based on race, ethnicity, sex, and gender, have begun to fall away. It is no longer considered permissible to treat minority people as inferior citizens, although it happens all the time, unless that inferiority is tied to disability.

As long as minority identities are thought disabled, there is little hope for the political and social equality of either persons with these identities or disabled people, for there will always be one last justification for inferior treatment. There will always be the possibility of proving the inferiority of any given human being at any given moment as long as inferiority is tied to physical and mental difference. Moreover, that pain in itself leads to inferior identities, ones given to greater self-recrimination or frequent victimizing of others, relies on a fallacious psychological scenario prejudiced inherently against disability.[7] Once touching a person, pain is apparently transformative, to all intents and purposes serving as an organic and natural cause whose psychological formation evolves with little variation according to the internal logic of the psyche. First, the psychology of pain links mental and physical suffering inextricably, and, second, it names pain, opposed to all other causes, as transformative of individuals, compelling them to withdraw into selfish, narcissistic, and anti-social behavior. Any attempt to sketch a political theory, especially of minority identity, based on this misleading psychology will produce the same predictable and deplorable results.

Pain and disability are not equivalent, although prejudices against disabled people often reduce disability to pain, but both supposedly individualize the concept of identity. Disability is often misinterpreted as a personal misfortune, as inherently individual, and in a manner similar to pain. A major obstacle to the political organization of disabled people is the belief in the individuality

---

excusing discrimination against them. For an extended definition of the ideology of ability, see my *Disability Theory*, 7-11.

7 | It would be worth writing a history of this misguided psychology, if only to understand one of the strongest cultural biases against disability. My contribution to this project concentrates on Sigmund Freud, although Nietzsche precedes him in the idea that pain and disability play defining roles in the constitution of individual psychology. See my "Tender Organs" and the expanded argument in *Disability Theory*.

of disability itself. What does a woman with a head trauma share with a male wheelchair user? On what basis, since their disabilities are so different, do they form a political alliance that speaks to their unique and different needs? While disabled people confront the same concerns as other minority groups about the authenticity of their experiences, an added problem supposedly arises because of the individualization of disability. It is often argued that women alone understand feminine experience or African-Americans black experience, and that only they should be allowed to represent the political concerns of their respective groups, but disabled people are required to represent the experience of disability in general and the experience of different disabilities in particular. The question posed to the disability community is not only how to design a unified political coalition for disabled people but how to determine whether a deaf person, for example, can represent a blind person in a political debate.

Such demands would arise less often if pain and disability did not serve as differentials in the creation of identity, if they were not thought to set off a mysterious organic and psychological mechanism that renders the individual person defective as a social and political agent. Pain does not spring from and differentiate the individual. It does not belong to one person alone. It is a social invention, external to people, that marks them as individual. The dominant social representation of pain in the West is the individual alone in pain, and it is difficult to find alternative representations, especially those that reveal pain's social origins.

2.

Although pain seems in most accounts on the right and the left to define minority identity, little attention has in fact been paid to what minorities experience as pain. The assumption seems to be that their pain is debilitating and all consuming, that pain prevents minorities from pursuing independent actions, and when they do manage to act, that pain brings out the worst in them, twisting their actions in the direction of selfishness, anger, and revenge. The model for defining minority pain is severe physical pain – its effects determined according to the dubious psychological scenario examined above – the very kind of pain supposedly exemplified by the disability community.

How accurate is this view? And what does the experience of the disability community tell us about minority pain? Now it is certainly the case that some disabled people experience severe pain on an hourly basis. This kind of pain deserves attention, but here I have set aside this focus to trace two ideas with enormous political weight on the current scene. First is the idea already examined above that critics of minority identity use disability to imagine minority pain. Second, I explore what pain means to the disability community.

Now, despite the fact that chronic pain is a plague upon disabled people, there exists relatively few accounts of organic pain in disability life writing. Rather, we discover accounts of another experience of pain, one that can be called with justice not organic but political and epistemological pain, that is, a feeling of suffering derived from the collision between two different worldviews, the worldviews of the nondisabled and the disabled. These accounts of pain stress a vision of the disability experience in which individuals derive new knowledge and self-understandings from the limitations placed on them by nondisabled society, while at the same time embodying in their interactions with other disabled individuals an alternative society in which people with disabilities feel at home.[8]

The array of disability life writings is now vast, as are the types of disabilities represented by them.[9] I will focus on only one narrative here, but I want to claim that it is exemplary in its vivid insistence on social location as epistemology. This narrative by Cheryl Davis focuses on the pain experienced because of her mobility impairment. She catalogues for the most part obstacles in the built environment and their impact on her everyday life. The story insists – like the majority of disability narratives – that disability confines affected individuals in social locations that carry negative meanings beyond those that the individuals are themselves capable of generating.[10] Because disabled people do not cause the meanings attached to them, their confinement in particular social locations is often arbitrary, experienced as violent and existentially absurd but also as a spur to awaken new perceptions about society.

Davis confesses that "Disability and the Experience of Architecture" was painful to write, and yet the essay is not about how much pain strikes her body. In fact, we know very little about the physical pain that she experiences on a daily basis. The central focus of the essay is the subjective experience of pain caused her by society. What makes Davis suffer is the clash between what she sees and what the rest of the world sees:

---

8 | Of course, not all disabled people self-identify as disabled; nor are all disabled people politicized. I am speaking here and elsewhere in the essay about disabled people who have acquired an awareness of and desire to participate in movement politics. In *Disability Theory*, I trace the process of becoming a politically aware minority (see 11-22).

9 | Thomas Couser provides an introduction to the broad range of issues covered in disability memoirs.

10 | Sharon Snyder and David Mitchell make the case that the disabled are not excluded from society but held in specific "cultural locations" whose meanings both rely on disabled people and define them.

"I could tell you the objective facts of my life, but they would tell you little about me; to truly know me you must try imaginatively to enter the realm of my subjective experience. For example, in the objective mode you would learn that I went to a special school; in the subjective mode you would learn how I felt every morning as the bus drove into the schoolyard, past a sign that read School for Crippled and Deformed Children. That sign stabbed me to the core five days a week. It meant that society labeled me as different – Other – that able-bodied people did not consider me a child but a *deformed child*, and that I should be 'happier with my own kind.'" (Davis 19-20)

Davis concentrates on the minutia of everyday life, mapping the topography of society and cataloguing her emotions and those of the people around her – all detailed from her location as a disabled young woman living in a lower middle class family in Milton, Massachusetts. More significant than her observations, however, is Davis' understanding of her subjective experience as a contribution to the knowledge of her society. Davis claims "the value of the subjective mode, best entered through the analysis of experience, as a tool for understanding the interactive effects of society and the environment on the development of physically disabled individuals" (20). The value of Davis' experience is not complaint, energized by resentment, but the ability to expand the knowledge base of society, both for nondisabled and disabled people alike.

Here is the goal, then, for the best disability life writing, at least the variety that wants to claim its own distinctive point of view. Davis pursues this goal by recounting her own experiences, transmuting them into tools for measuring a different reality, one whose objectivity relies not on the subtraction of subjective experience but on the addition of one subjective experience to another. Davis records concrete details, specific conversations, and sequences of events, binding them into an epistemology shared by other disabled people. She is a determined cartographer of the social locations in which people with disabilities are represented as inferior, defective, contagious, and in physical pain.

One of Davis' stories explores what it means to occupy an inferior social location and to want to escape from it. The story recounts an experience at the visiting Moscow Circus where Davis dares to sit with her able-bodied friends in nondisabled seating. The account is long and builds slowly, accumulating details essential to understanding Davis' worldview, why it clashes with the worldview of the people assaulting her, and why the conflict is valuable as a contribution to knowledge:

"My friends were shown their seats, which were several feet beneath the level of the aisle, while I remained in my wheelchair, since a transfer to the regular seat below was too difficult for me. With their heads at the same level as my footrests, conversation was awkward, but at least we were together. The aisle, more than six feet wide, left plenty of room for people to pass me as long as I sat sideways. (My chair was less than twenty-three inches wide.) The arrangement offered uncomfortable viewing, but I was willing to put up with it. The management, unfortunately, was less willing to put up with me. The young usher, who sported a rather self-important air, advised me that 'wheelchairs are supposed to sit over there,' indicating a spot only slightly closer than Siberia.

'That's fine,' I said, 'but I'm with two friends who walk; they haven't brought their own chairs.'

'You have to move. You're a fire hazard,' he said.

'I'll move if you'll put folding chairs down there for my friends.' I thought that sounded reasonable, and Marsha and Kent seemed agreeable.

'Impossible!' he snapped. 'I have other things to do.'

'Then I'm afraid I can't move.' I replied.

'Well,' said the usher, 'I'll let you stay, but the Chief Usher will be along soon. If you refuse to move for him, he'll throw you out.' ...

Inevitably, the Chief Usher materialized, a red-nosed, pudgy man of about sixty. ...

'You'll have to move,' he fairly barked at me. ...

'No,' I quavered in a small voice.

The veins in his forehead popped out. His face was purely purple. He shouted. 'I'm gonna get a policeman to throw you out,' and left. I sat there shaking. My friends were angry yet calm, but I was intensely upset. They urged me to hold my ground and not permit him to bully me. ...

While the Chief Usher summoned the law, I performed my own circus act in the stands. Dropping from my wheelchair to the floor, I crawled beneath the barrier, swung from it, and clambered up into a regular seat. Then I folded the wheelchair and brought it flush against the barrier. It now took up less than a foot of aisle space. ...

No sooner had I settled in than a policeman appeared. ...

'Ma'am,' he said softly, 'I'm afraid you'll have to move the chair, or leave. ...'

'Do you see all those people sitting in the aisles?' I asked. He did. 'Well, if you make me move, without making all of them move, that's discrimination.' Puffing out his cheeks, he lifted the bill of his cap, then expelled the air. Cheeks deflated, he looked depressed. 'I'm sure not going to be the one to make you move,' he said as he walked away.

The Chief Usher returned just then. ...The old man began to hector and bully me afresh. I had resisted all efforts to move for nearly an hour. The circus had been going on for half an hour and I hadn't seen any of it. I was tired, angry, and humiliated. Suddenly all I wanted to do was leave. ...

As we rose from our seats, a little girl in a wheelchair entered, escorted by her mother and a girlfriend. She was crying, and from her mother's words, it was clear that she too had been told that she had to 'sit with the wheelchairs,' apart from her mother and friend." (27-30)

It is important to note that Davis is not resentful, envious, or angry – at least not in the way that minorities are typically represented as being in the various attacks on identity politics. She does not want to limit her friends' freedom to enjoy the circus. She does not resent the ease with which other people move through the aisles and choose their seats. She is angry not because other people are permitted to break the rules that she is compelled to obey. She is angry because the people surrounding her do not recognize her as a human being. To claim that Davis is angry because people do not recognize her as a human being may seem an extreme statement, but it is a crucial formulation to keep in mind. It exposes the fact that denying participation in everyday activities such as going to the circus, entering and leaving a restaurant, or choosing whether to sit in the front or back of a bus is an attack on human status more effective and serious than the insignificance of the activities suggest. For it is in everyday life that we win or lose our right to be recognized as a human being. The point is that Davis understands exactly why her disability limits her participation in the social world. It limits her participation not specifically because she is physically unable to participate and not because the built environment is inaccessible, although it is. Her disability limits her participation because other people do not welcome her presence sufficiently to make it possible for her to live among them.

Once Davis begins to use a wheelchair, her identity merges in the public mind with it. In fact, she literally becomes a 'wheelchair' – a social location that erases any trace of her identity as a person living among other persons. A social location is in this case a set of specific spatial coordinates – the space reserved for handicapped seating – but this social location, positioned among the array of other social locations comprising any given society, also represents a class of disqualified people. Among the many characteristics of the people in this social location are these modifiers: defective, unfit, inferior, diseased, contagious, pained, unsociable, angry, resentful, envious, selfish, etc. All wheelchairs must occupy this social location, one by which their inferiority is maintained, isolated, and exhibited, and any attempt to escape provokes a strong and violent reaction. It is almost as if Davis' desire to move out of her location causes the social edifice surrounding her to wobble on its foundation, setting off alarms to summon rescuers and police. That a tiny woman in a wheelchair represents a danger to society seems a comic proposition, but this is what the authorities tell her. The police and ushers call Davis a 'fire hazard' who must be isolated and confined for other people's protection. This official reaction draws its authority, meaning, and incentive from Davis' identity as a disabled person because her social location is stigmatized as inferior and undesirable. Supporting the organization of society is an architectural version of apartheid, a built environment that methodically excludes people with disabilities, and when a disabled person trespasses on able-bodied space, the social organization is threatened. The value of Davis' story derives from her discovery of this painful truth and from her ability to express it in a form recognizable as a contribution to knowledge.

3.

If current arguments among cultural critics are to be believed, minority identity is born, not made – born in the nest of pain. Pain as a natural cause, unfolding according to an unbending and unvaried psychology, supposedly takes control of minority individuals and dictates their behavior in and responses to the social world. Politicizing their identities only exacerbates the negative and painful experiences of minority people, endangering group cohesion and political action by giving power to individuals whose pain renders them too isolated and self-preoccupied to make responsible contributions to society. It is as if their nature makes minority people unfit for politics – that is, if we accept the current arguments. These arguments fail when we realize that the lack of political fitness ascribed to minority people depends on an analogy to disabled people and on the false belief that disabled people are biologically inferior.

The main trends of disability studies reject the idea that disability identity derives from biological pain or individual bodily properties. Disability identity is not based on impairment similarity but on social experience that includes a shared encounter with oppression, discrimination, and medicalization, on the negative side, and a shared knowledge of survival strategies, healthcare policy, and environmental conditions, on the positive side. According to Carol Gill, "disability culture" includes an emerging sense of its own history, art, humor, evolving symbols, and a "remarkably unified worldview" (Gill n. pag.). The woman with a head trauma shares with the male wheelchair user the knowledge of both the negative and positive sides of disability experience. A deaf person may speak for a blind person in a political debate because both people understand the social location of disability, including the fact that their disabilities represent sources of oppression and social knowledge not experienced by most people. The medical approach to disability treats each and every disabled person as unique, as an individual patient whose distinct pathology requires a treatment designed specifically for it. Disability studies exposes the fact that this difference between patients is a product of medicalization, and it need not form an unbridgeable political gap between disabled people. We are not naturally unfit for politics because we are disabled. In fact, our experience of and resistance to the medicalization of disability may make it easier for us to understand that people are never fit or unfit for political participation.[11]

Disability studies embraces the social construction of minority identity, not as a negative with which to dispense with identities as inauthentic, but

---

11 | This is a trick statement in that it invites the reader to think of arguments to deny participation based on disability, thereby demonstrating the degree to which disability represents the last frontier of unquestioned human inferiority.

as a mode of social integration that carries with it specific knowledge based on social location. Here the conclusion that an identity, because it is a social construction, is not an authentic identity on which to base political rights is a dubious proposition, because only an argument based on epistemology can demonstrate the value or lack of value of an identity claim. It may appear as if disability identity is based on natural or biological categories, but it is based in reality on an epistemology – a new knowledge about, and understanding of, what it means to be 'disabled.' This new knowledge lies at the heart of the disability rights movement, and it is what we have to offer to other political movements, whether they represent minorities or not.

REFERENCES

Baynton, Douglas C. "Disability and the Justification of Inequality in American History." *The New Disability History: American Perspectives.* Eds. Paul K. Longmore and Lauri Umansky. New York: NYU Press, 2001, 33-57. Print.

Bloom, Allan. *The Closing of the American Mind: How Higher Education Has Failed Democracy and Impoverished the Souls of Today's Students.* New York: Simon and Schuster, 1987. Print.

Brown, Wendy. *States of Injury: Power and Freedom in Late Modernity.* Princeton, NJ: Princeton University Press, 1995. Print.

Butler, Judith. *Gender Trouble: Feminism and the Subversion of Identity.* New York: Routledge, 1990; reprint 1999. Print.

—. *The Psychic Life of Power: Theories in Subjection.* Stanford: Stanford University Press, 1997. Print.

Couser, G. Thomas. *Signifying Bodies: Disability in Contemporary Life Writing.* Ann Arbor: University of Michigan Press, 2009. Print.

Davis, Cheryl. "Disability and the Experience of Architecture." *Rethinking Architecture: Design Students and Physically Disabled People.* Ed. Raymond Lifchez. Berkeley: University of California Press, 1987, 19-33. Print.

Fraser, Nancy. "Rethinking Recognition." *New Left Review* 3 (2000): 107-20. Print.

Gill, Carol J. "A Psychological View of Disability Culture." *Disability Studies Quarterly* 15.4 (1995). 16-19. Print.

Michaels, Walter Benn. *The Trouble with Diversity: How We Learned to Love Identity and Ignore Inequality.* New York: Metropolitan Books, 2007. Print.

Nietzsche, Friedrich. *On the Genealogy of Morals* and *Ecce Homo.* Ed. Walter Kaufmann. New York: Vintage, 1967. Print.

Siebers, Tobin. *Disability Theory.* Ann Arbor: University of Michigan Press, 2008. Print.

—. "Disability Trouble." *Civil Disabilities*. Ed. Nancy Hirschmann. Philadelphia: University of Pennsylvania Press, 2015. 223-236. Print.

—. "In the Name of Pain." *Against Health: How Health Became the New Morality*. Eds. Anna Kirkland and Jonathan Metzl. New York: New York University Press, 2010, 183-94. Print.

—. "Tender Organs, Narcissism, and Identity Politics." *Disability Studies: Enabling the Humanities*. Eds. Brenda Jo Brueggemann, Sharon L. Snyder and Rosemarie Garland-Thomson. New York: PMLA, 2002. 40-55. Print.

Snyder, Sharon L. and David T. Mitchell. *Cultural Locations of Disability*. Chicago: University of Chicago Press, 2006. Print.

Responses to Tobin Siebers

Andreas Sturm
THE EXPERIENCE OF PAIN, DISABILITY IDENTITY AND THE DISABILITY RIGHTS MOVEMENT

Introduction

With regard to political mobilisation, Richard K. Scotch reasons that identification as a disabled person is not an automatic process, but rather that political involvement relies on whether the individual accepts or rejects this role (162). His deduction sheds light on a paradox that is linked to the so-called 'reification argument:' Refusal to identify as a person with disabilities prevents an individual from being politically involved, while accepting this identity implies possibly acknowledging "its handicapping connotations of dependency and thus also avoiding political involvement" (ibid.). Scotch's response to this dilemma is to strategically address disability as social oppression without adopting its negative connotations (162-63). Another option is to develop positive ideas that can become part of one's identity, for instance by rejecting negative stereotypes or challenging conventional ideas of normality. One classic example of this strategy is 'disability pride' which discovers "merit in the atypical, beauty in the uncommon, and value in the unusual" (Sherry 907).

Upon reading Tobin Siebers' essay, my impression is that his way of thinking is in line with these approaches. However, he tries to substantiate the argument by taking into account personal experiences of pain. Using a body theory and the concept of pain, as Siebers suggests, implies that the full range of (bodily) experiences shaping personal and political identities can be considered. By making use of disabled persons' biographical narratives, he describes how experiences of pain may lead to a political consciousness which forms the basis for political participation and activism. In responding to Siebers' essay my intention is, by applying a sociological perspective, to elucidate his approach and comment on its implications for disability identity and identity politics as prerequisites for the formation and proliferation of disability rights movements.

First, this response will explore different meanings of pain. Implicit in this exploration is the question of how a conceptualisation of pain can function as a point of reference when it comes to the identity politics of disability rights movements. Second, I will take into account the theoretical context of minority identity studies, which Siebers draws on in his study on pain, to investigate the pros and cons of collective identity politics that explicitly relate to the status of belonging to a socially oppressed minority. Third, this response will touch upon the relation between identity politics and recent developments in disability politics directly affecting the disability rights movement.

Pain – Linking the Individual and the Political

Siebers' approach is closely linked to the ongoing critical discussion of the social model of disability which has been of relevance for international disability rights movements since the 1970s. The idea that the social model of disability "perpetuates a *disembodied* notion of disability" (Beckett 735) and therefore is to be criticized can be found in many publications (see for example Schneider and Waldschmidt 138-43). At the same time, however, reintroducing the body into a social theory of disability runs the risk of opening up the discourse for naturalist and essentialist, medical and individualist perspectives on disability and identity (Hughes 684). Against this background, reflecting on the notion of pain in its full complexity is essential but somewhat problematic.

Pain is a broad term used not only in science but also in everyday language and implies various connotations that may favour political mobilisation but also transports negative stereotypes that may possibly hinder political or emancipatory struggles. As a first step, one needs to consider that everybody seems to know what pain means. In everyday situations, a person who experiences pain resembles a suffering victim deserving pity from 'others,' who usually regard this individual in need of medical treatment or as restricted in her or his abilities.

In the medical realm, pain is a bodily signal that is interpreted as a marker of an illness or disease. The International Association for the Study of Pain defines pain as "unpleasant sensory and emotional experience associated with actual or potential tissue damage, or described in terms of such damage" ("Iasp Taxonomy;" see also Glucklich 11). Typically, when making a diagnosis medical practitioners locate pain in a specific body part or organ and also qualify and assess pain, for instance its intensity and duration, in order to identify appropriate treatment. Understanding pain as described above implies considering pain as an individual condition that has to be overcome, a burden which makes the person dependent on medical treatment and the help of others. At the same time, the medical perspective makes us aware that feeling no pain can also be dangerous, as it is the case with diseases involving sensory deficiencies.

However, in other life situations pain can also be viewed positively, for instance as a tool in religious rituals or a means for personal development and a kind of moral compass (Glucklich 34). Moreover, under certain conditions pain can be a solution instead of a problem (12): Experiences of pain are able to evoke new insights, decisions, and actions. There are more complex and paradoxical implications, such as in sadomasochistic practices or in the queer/crip art of Bob Flanagan and Sheree Rose, in which pain becomes a liberating tool to challenge notions of suffering and normalcy. These practices reveal that sensations of pain can be perceived as joyful or pleasurable, as well as enabling alternative ways of identifying as a disabled person (Kolářová 44).

There are also academic discussions with regard to pain in sociology, cultural studies and disability studies. In his text *The Culture of Pain*, David B. Morris refers to the "myth of two pains:" "You feel physical pain if your arm breaks, and you feel mental pain if your heart breaks. Between these two different events we seem to imagine a gulf so wide and deep that it might as well be filled by a sea that is impossible to navigate" (Morris 9). This differentiation is reminiscent of Helmuth Plessner's well known approach of criticising the 'crude' dichotomy between nature and culture, corresponding to the problematisation of the Cartesian division between the body and the mind in disability studies (see Gugutzer and Schneider 34-35; Hughes and Paterson 326).

As mentioned earlier, the social model of disability has been developed to overcome the individualisation and medicalisation of disability in favour of a perspective that allows for the definition of disability as an effect of a disabling environment. While this approach has proven capable of boosting the political activism of disabled persons, it fails to address the stereotype that disabled persons are suffering from pain, as Irving Kenneth Zola points out: "Similarly, the terms 'suffering from,' 'afflicted with' are projections and evaluations of an outside world. No person with a disability is automatically 'suffering' or 'afflicted' except in specific situations where they do indeed 'hurt,' are 'in pain' or 'feel victimized'" (170). Similar to impairment, pain is not theorised by the social model, and it is to Siebers' credit that he problematizes this weakness.

On the one hand, both pain and disability are easily reduced to bio-medical human conditions and may provide the basis for victimisation and (self-) blaming, despite the fact that pain and impairment are universal human experiences. On the other hand, disability, impairment and pain can also be used strategically to shape (self-)perceptions and identities. Concerning the latter, Siebers stresses its potential to unify diverse groups of persons (with disabilities) on the basis of shared personal experiences. In this view, pain becomes the vanishing point of unwanted or painful living conditions at precisely the moment when a social group shares the experience of the same 'social' pain.

Pain and Minority Identity

Siebers employs the concept of 'pain' within the context of disability and minority conscious of the fact that terms and labels have the potential to either unite or divide minority groups fighting for political change. To understand why this author engages in a concept of pain with regard to minority identity, it is necessary to shed light on his theoretical background.

Siebers belongs to a group of minority studies scholars who pursue a post-positivist realist approach to conceptualise identity and identity politics. In the volume *Identity Politics Reconsidered*, Linda Martin Alcoff and her colleagues explicate this perspective by arguing that identities are neither an essence nor fictional, instead the complexity of "identity-based political struggles and the subjective experiences on which these struggles draw" must be considered (6). Furthermore, while according to Mary Bernstein most approaches to identity politics assume an essential core of identity[12] (Bernstein 49-56), for minority studies scholars identities resemble "social embodied facts about ourselves in our world" that may function as "*causal explanations* of our social locations in a world that is shaped by such locations, by the way they are distributed and hierarchically organized" (Alcoff et al. 6).

Against this conceptual background, Siebers confronts the idea that social minority groups such as persons with disabilities are unable to participate politically, since pain – if regarded as a 'natural' cause of inferiority – would prevent them from doing so. He shows that this so-called inferiority needs to be traced back to the internalisation of 'natural' pain as a part of self-perceptions and self-definitions which undermine the actual development of self-efficacy. Countering prevailing stereotypes, Siebers focuses on the concept of pain as a strategy of resistance. Precisely because pain is often used to victimise persons with disabilities and minorities in general, he reassesses this phenomenon from a critical disability studies perspective.

With this approach, Siebers also implicitly pursues a critical line on the social model of disability. While this model focalises disablement caused by

---

12 | This argument relates to Erving Goffman's ground-breaking study on stigma and 'spoiled' identity, as it focuses on the interactions between disabled persons and 'normal' people with respect to identity management (Goffman 1963). However, according to Waldschmidt, Goffman assumes a naturalistic core of identity as he does not question prevailing (body) norms, but perceives visible (bodily) defects as phenomena necessarily leading to stigma management, implying that the body is a natural source and basis for social interactions (5803).

society, it leaves out the question of how to locate or assess the actual disabling barriers. Siebers' approach, in contrast, highlights this question, thus not turning away from the (impaired) body in favour of a (socially constructed) disability, but rather avoiding labels of inability and inferiority for the benefit of a notion of pain inflicted on minorities by society and, at the same time, subjectively experienced. Such a perspective suggests that the political act of creating one's identity, searching for allies, and identifying as a socially oppressed person is closely linked to sharing 'pain' as a common experience with other disabled persons, an experience that enables one to address not only collectively but also very personally disabling barriers, discrimination, and the lack of rights. Siebers' argument also opens up the opportunity to refer to specific experiences of 'being in pain' (for instance, as a disabled person with learning difficulties).

Identity Politics and the Disability Rights Movement

In order to be able to understand the position from which Siebers conceptualises the relations between disability identity, minority identity and pain, it is also crucial to discuss which notion of identity *politics* he uses, in particular as a political practice employed by activists, groups, networks and organisations of the disability rights movement.

Reflecting on this notion of politics, the work of Erving Goffman comes to mind. Implying that identities can be managed and are part of social interactions, Goffman introduces the term "politics of identity" with regard to group alignments, and argues that the stigmatised person is identified "as a member of the wider group, which means he is a normal human being, but that he is also 'different' in some degree, and that it would be foolish to deny this difference" (123). The individual, in reaction, manages societal perceptions and expectations in relation to the group she or he belongs to and also with respect to the wider society. Drawing on Goffman's work, Renée R. Anspach defines identity politics as an act of "forging an image or conception of self and propagating this self to attentive publics" (66). Mary Bernstein also argues that identity politics is to be conceptualised in relation to "experience, culture, politics and power" (48).

While Siebers would certainly agree with these definitions, in his article "Tender Organs, Narcissism, and Identity Politics" he states that "identity politics is no different from any other form of political representation, since it is defined by ideological, historical, geographic, or temporal borders" (Siebers 42). In his view, the distinctive features of identity politics in comparison to other forms of political representation are, first, the goal of self-identification, second, the deduction of an identity "from a singular subjectivity," and third, possibly highlighting oneself as distinctively and/or individually suffering. The last feature marks the focus of Siebers' critique, as identity politics centring on suffering runs the risk of provoking accusations of narcissism (ibid.).

Such disparagement can, in Siebers' terms, be avoided by transferring "the reality of disability into the public imagination," by "tell[ing] stories in a way that allows people without disabilities to recognize our reality and theirs is a common one" (51). He further elaborates that this would require a specific "symbolism," so "private emotions and thoughts are made compelling to the public imagination" (ibid.). Implicit in this approach is, in my understanding, the assumption that telling the larger public about experiences of 'social pain' needs to be done in a manner that overcomes the divide between the 'general public' and 'persons with disabilities.'

While it should be admitted that pain, just as suffering, carries connotations that might refer to 'deficient' subjects, Siebers might be right when he advocates for a 'symbolism' that enables the larger society to recognise the experiences of disabled persons as part of its own social reality, just as any other social group that makes effective use of identity politics. Thus, pain might be a metaphor which stresses the necessity of narrating or framing experiences of individuals or groups of (disabled) persons in ways that relate to universal human experiences, including the aspects of social oppression, discrimination, inequality, and lack of recognition.

Conclusion

This essay has attempted to provide a critical analysis of Siebers' approach to disability identity (politics) and pain. But there is one open question: Which lessons can be learnt from this concept for current disability rights activism?

At present, the United Nations Convention on the Rights of Persons with Disabilities (CRPD) is shaping disability policies across the world. It is, to a large extent, the result of political struggles, owing its main ideas and principles to the international disability rights movement. In future decades, the CRPD will play a crucial role in framing disability as a political concept and as a human rights issue, and it is not difficult to predict that it will also inform the identity politics and self-identification of persons with disabilities and their representative organisations. The CRPD appears to be a useful tool to frame personal experiences such as discrimination and to legitimise the removal of barriers that many disabled persons face every day around the globe.

However, this human rights Convention does not emphasise per se subjective experiences of social oppression in the way Siebers calls for. It tolerates the notion, but does not regard it as particularly relevant to tell personal narratives of painful experiences to catch the attention of societies and thus raise public awareness. Instead, the CRPD's value lies in drawing attention to the objective environmental conditions, adaptations and opportunities in a given society. While it allows for an open-ended, processual definition of disability by describing it as an evolving concept, the Convention, as Karen Soldatic and Shaun Grech highlight, largely avoids the term "impairment" apart from the Preamble and Article 1. These disability studies scholars argue that as a result impairment cannot be discussed as a political issue and tends to be ignored within the human rights discourse. Against this background, Siebers' approach of using personal experiences (of pain) as a means to identify with the minority group of disabled persons could provide a stimulus for future disability rights activism, and even more so when the current human rights convention is reviewed and revised.

References

Alcoff, Linda Martín, et al., eds. *Identity Politics Reconsidered*. New York, Houndmills, Basingstoke, Hampshire: Palgrave Macmillan, 2006. Print.

Anspach, Renée R. "From Stigma to Identity Politics: Political Activism among the Physically Disabled and Former Mental Patients." *Social Science and Medicine* 13A (1979): 765-73. Print.

Beckett, Angharad E. "Understanding Social Movements: Theorising the Disability Movement in Conditions of Late Modernity." *The Sociological Review* 54.4 (2006): 734-52. Print.

Bernstein, Mary. "Identity Politics." *Annual Review of Sociology* 31 (2005): 47-74. Print.

Glucklich, Ariel. *Sacred Pain. Hurting the Body for the Sake of the Soul*. Oxford, New York and others: Oxford University Press, 2001. Print.

Goffman, Erving. *Stigma. Notes on the Management of Spoiled Identity*. New York, London, Toronto: Simon & Schuster, 1963. Print.

Gugutzer, Robert and Werner Schneider. "Der 'behinderte' Körper in den Disability Studies: Eine körpersoziologische Grundlegung." *Disability Studies, Kultursoziologie und Soziologie der Behinderung. Erkundungen in einem neuen Forschungsfeld*. Eds. Anne Waldschmidt and Werner Schneider. Bielefeld: transcript, 2007. 31-53. Print.

Hughes, Bill. "Disability Activisms: Social Model Stalwarts and Biological Citizens." *Disability and Society* 24.6 (2009): 677-88. Print.

Hughes, Bill and Kevin Paterson. "The Social Model of Disability and the Disappearing Body: Towards a Sociology of Impairment." *Disability & Society* 12.3 (1997): 325-40. Print.

International Association for the Study of Pain. "Iasp Taxonomy". Web. 26 Nov. 2015. <http://www.iasp-pain.org/Education/Content.aspx?ItemNumber=1698&&navItemNumber=576>.

Kolářová, Kateřina. "Performing the Pain: Opening the (Crip) Body for (Queer) Pleasures." *Review of Disability Studies: An International Journal* 6.3 (2010): 44-52. Print.

Morris, David B. *The Culture of Pain*. Los Angeles, London: University of California Press, 1993. Print.

Plessner, Helmuth. *Die Stufen des Organischen und der Mensch*. Berlin, New York: de Gruyter, 1975. Print.

Schneider, Werner and Anne Waldschmidt. "Disability Studies: (Nicht-) Behinderung anders denken." *Kultur: Von den Cultural Studies bis zu den Visual Studies. Eine Einführung*. Ed. Stephan Moebius. Bielefeld: transcript, 2012. 128-50. Print.

Scotch, Richard K. "Disability as the Basis for a Social Movement: Advocacy and the Politics of Definition." *Journal of Social Issues* 44.1 (1988): 159-72. Print.

Sherry, Mark. "Identity." *Encyclopedia of Disability*. Ed. Gary Albrecht. Vol. 2. Thousand Oaks, London, New Delhi: Sage Publications, 2006. 906-13. Print.

Siebers, Tobin. "Disability, Pain, and the Politics of Minority Identity." This volume. 111-121. Print.

—. "Tender Organs, Narcissism, and Identity Politics." *Disability Studies: Enabling the Humanities*. Eds. Sharon L. Snyder, Brenda Jo Brueggemann and Rosemarie Garland-Thomson. New York: The Modern Language Association of America, 2002. 40-55. Print.

Soldatic, Karen and Shaun Grech. "Transnationalising Disability Studies: Rights, Justice and Impairment." *Disability Studies Quarterly*. 34.2 (2014). Web. 30-11-2015. <http://dsq-sds.org/article/view/4249/3588>.

Waldschmidt, Anne. "'Wir Normalen' – 'die Behinderten'?: Erving Goffman meets Michel Foucault." *Die Natur der Gesellschaft: Verhandlungen des 33. Kongresses der Deutschen Gesellschaft für Soziologie in Kassel 2006*. Eds. Karl Siegbert Rehberg and Deutsche Gesellschaft für Soziologie (DGS). Frankfurt a.M.: Campus, 2008. 5799-5809. Print.

Zola, Irving Kenneth. "Self, Identity and the Naming Question: Reflections on the Language of Disability." *Social Science and Medicine* 36.2 (1993): 167-73. Print.

Arta Karāne

BOB FLANAGAN: FROM THE PAIN OF DISABILITY TO THE PAIN OF PENIS TORTURING

Along with the concepts of the minority group and identity politics, one of the key categories that Tobin Siebers analyzes in his article "Disability, Pain, and the Politics of Minority Identity" is pain. Siebers criticizes the existing standpoint of many cultural researchers who believe that minority identity is founded on pain; because pain is enclosed within one's psyche, it is considered psychological and organic. When minorities enter the political realm their identities are supposed to become even more troublesome, for their political capital is based on projecting the suffering of historically imprinted injustices such as racism or sexism. Furthermore, precisely because minority group behavior in the social world is determined by this historically entrenched suffering, they are supposed to reproduce this pain in their political claims. This means that for the majority of cultural researchers, a member of a minority group is considered passive and subjected to pain; it is assumed that the only interaction he or she can have with his or her own suffering is to reproduce it. A final assumption is that pain is disabling. Pain leads a person of a minority group to inferiority, resulting either in greater self-victimization or accusation of others for their pain.

To deflate these arguments, the author compares the pain of minority groups to that of people with disabilities by discussing the pain experience of Cheryl Davis, a person with "mobility impairment" (Siebers, "Pain" 115). Analyzing her case study, Siebers concludes that what binds both disabled and minority people's identities and can serve as a basis for creating a political platform for a minority identity is the common epistemological experience of pain – that is, a shared social knowledge of both the positive and the negative everyday experiences of a person living with 'disabilities.'

Siebers interestingly shows the social nature of pain, yet, it occurs to me that the epistemological pain argument does not counteract all previously mentioned assumptions about pain. The Davis case does not answer whether, or how, a disabled person can avoid the reproduction of pain or escape the inferior position to which he or she is subjugated by society. Furthermore, Siebers' epistemological argument about pain opens questions that his paper does not touch on: What about the internal, bodily experience of pain as experienced by disabled people? How does such pain interact not so much in a political but in a cultural space? Can pain only be reproduced, or can it also be transformed into a resource, for instance, of sexual pleasure? Does pain simply disable and victimize a person or can it perhaps become a tool to challenge culturally constructed categories of normalcy and disability? After all, can a disabled person play an active role in transcending his or her own pain?

Siebers' argument focuses on the representation of the pain of disabled people in political space. I would like to echo yet also extend Siebers' discussion of pain and bring in another counter-argument to the previously mentioned assumptions about pain. My aim is to address the pain of disabled people as an expression within cultural space and to show how the experience of an active living with pain caused by disability can challenge the social construction of disability itself. In order to do so, I will focus on Bob Flanagan, an exceptional American performance artist whose physical pain and disability was at the centre of his life and art performances.

Bob Flanagan (1952-1996) was an American performance artist whose life centred around a physical impairment, cystic fibrosis[13] (see Hladki 269). Because of this incurable genetic illness, Flanagan's daily life was dominated by physical pain and suffering (see Jones 573). His disease caused constant coughing, weight loss, and regular breathing and digestion problems; it kept him under extreme pain and required constant medical treatment (see Kauffman 20; Hladki 269). In medical terms Flanagan had a physical impairment, in a cultural context his disease became a source of disability, in accordance with the social construction model of disability, which, furthermore, defines the normative body as invulnerable in its "wholeness, independence and integrity" (see Shildrick 757). Bodies different from it are subdued and excluded from the 'healthy' "social body" (see Shildrick 759), rendered as "not yet the 'subject'" (see Siebers *Theory* 56), and thus disabled.

Flanagan's disability occurs by failing the normative standards of sexuality and masculinity.[14] Following the dominant able-bodied normalcy discourse, sexuality is valid only for healthy, physically fit, heterosexual people and is assumed to involve sexual pleasure (see Cheng 114; Brodwin and Frederick 37). Perceived as 'the Other' of the cultural norm of able-bodiedness, disabled

---

13 | Cystic fibrosis is a fatal and incurable genetic disease that mostly affects the lungs, which overproduce mucus. The secretion settles deep in the lungs in that way creating a great environment for viruses and dangerous lung infections (see Juno and Vale 11). Although the medical technologies and treatment such as gene therapy of cystic fibrosis has advanced and thus improved life expectancy and quality of patients, in Flanagan's lifetime they were yet to be developed. Therefore, cystic fibrosis was treated mainly with the medicine that would dilute mucus and the therapy that would pump the overproduced secretion out (see Juno and Vale 10). The disease often led to the death of a patient who literally drowned in mucus or got a life-threatening lung infection. Unlike the majority of patients, who often died in their infancy or early adulthood, Flanagan became one of the oldest survivors of the disease in his lifetime. He died at age 43 on January 4th, 1996 (see Sandahl 97).

14 | For a lucid discussion of Bob Flanagan's art and life at the nexus of disability and queer studies see Robert McRuer's *Crip Theory* (181-198).

people are subject to myths about their sexuality and are most commonly even considered as asexual bodies, bodies that lack sexual desire and pleasure (see Brodwin and Frederick 37-38).

Intertwined with sexuality is also the phenomenon of gender performance, in this case masculinity. Theories of hegemonic masculinity (see Flood 391) presume that masculinity as a symbolic power of male gender is based on particular bodily manifestations such as strength, invulnerability, self-reliance, and excellent sexual performance (see Butler and Parr 169; Shakespeare 56; Brodwin and Frederick 39). Precisely because masculinity is viewed as embedded within a man's body, physical impairment emasculates a man. It is associated with medicalization, lack of sexuality, and an overall loss of power (see Shakespeare 56-57; Sandahl 97; Brodwin and Frederick 38-39). Physically sick, medicalized, and infertile because of cystic fibrosis, Flanagan fell into the disabled category as an asexual, sexually desireless, and therefore emasculated person: feminine, impotent, castrated, someone too weak to perform the 'accurate' gender (see Brodwin and Frederick 38; Bredenkamp 57; Shakespeare 56-57). And yet, although Flanagan did not fit into the norm of able-bodied sexuality and gender performance, he did not remain a passive victim of pain and disability. On the contrary, he consciously took his pain into his own hands and transformed it into a source of sexual pleasure.[15] To overcome the physical pain of disease, he began in his early childhood to experiment with torturing his own body, in particular his penis. Not only did this practice ease the pain, it also gave him sexual excitement and became a regular practice in his adult life both in private and in public art performances.

In Flanagan's rich and vivid performance art there were countless episodes of torture; inflicting pain by, for instance, tying, stretching, or nailing his penis, hanging heavy weights on it, piercing it and sewing it back up, etc. For the purpose of demonstrating the intensity of the pain Flanagan inflicted on himself and showing how he was able to transform this pain into a source of sexual pleasure, I would like to discuss three of his most well-known penis torturing acts. The first act that he often performed in front of audiences was sewing up his scrotum. In one such performance in San Francisco, he "pushed the penis head into the shaft of the penis and sewed the loose skin around it so it looked like it was totally cut off" (see Juno and Vale 63). Then the rest was sewed up in the scrotum (see Juno and Vale 63). The second act, called "Nailed", has been referred to by many authors as one of the most well-known examples of Flanagan's performance art. The movie *Sick: Life and Death of Bob Flanagan*,

---

15 | Flanagan in an interview for the volume *Bob-Flanagan: Super-Masochist* elaborates on how he could not control the cystic fibrosis, yet how he learned to organize and control his pain and transform it into sadomasochistic experience that led him to sexual excitement. For further reading see Juno.

Supermasochist offers the opportunity to follow one such performance. The spectator sees the close-up of a wooden board with Flanagan's penis placed on top of it. A nail teeters on the edge of his genitals until, with a few quick movements, it is hammered in. Seconds pass, then the nail is pulled out of the board, revealing a view of the penis pierced by a metal nail. In the final part of the episode Flanagan slowly pulls the nail out, which results in an outpour of blood filling the screen. As a third example, the "Butterfly Penis" performance displays Flanagan's penis literally stretched over a board in the shape of a butterfly. Placed in the hole of a board, the penis is stretched to all sides and fixed with pins while the scrotum is also spiked with medical pins.

Although these examples of genital mutilation might seem like extremely painful acts, Flanagan claimed and demonstrated through his frequent performances that penis torture was a way of transcending his physical pain to the point where it became a source of sexual satisfaction. For instance, Flanagan described the act of sewing the penis into the scrotum as "auto-eroticism" (cited in Juno and Vale 62), or during one performance of "Nailed" accidentally missing the nail and hitting the head of his penis as sexual excitement: "[E]verything was cleaned up and I started getting hard. I [...] started masturbating against the sheets in a real frenzy; now I was really turned on by what had just happened to me! I had a really good orgasm" (cited in Juno and Vale 22). While he affirmed that piercing his penis was a painful process, his sexual sensations performing "Butterfly Penis" surpassed the pain. As he says:

"[...] I play Cupid to my stupid love-sick dick, each fiery pinprick another shot of adrenalin coursing through the veins of my porcupine pal, thick and purple, bobbing in front of me like a festive party balloon just begging to be popped." (Cited in Juno and Vale 59)

Flanagan's testimony contradicts the notion of pain as something that an individual must simply accept and remain passive toward. Instead of subjection to pain, Flanagan's sexual pleasure while nailing the penis shows that he can stay actively involved with his pain, controlling and transforming it into a resource of another bodily experience. The body is not only physical but also has a "social skin" (see Schildkrout 321), even more in disability art where the body turns into "self-representation" and "autobiography" (Garland-Thomson 334), which incorporates both visual and narrative layers. The disabled body is more than a medium – it becomes the "content of performance" (ibid) that can counteract "cultural images of disabled people" and "social construction of disability identity" (335). Displaying the transformation of the pain of disability into a pain of bodily torture in his public performances, Flanagan lives out his disability (see Sandahl 98); his body becomes a statement that challenges his own disability by calling preconceived categories of able-bodied sexuality and masculinity into question.

Although he does not fit into the normative social constructs of sexuality and masculinity, Flanagan's penis torture deflates the notion of disabled people as asexual and emasculated. On the contrary, the penis torturing acts display Flanagan as sexually functioning, actively involved in sexual exploration and intensively receiving sexual pleasure. Similarly, Flanagan challenges dominant notions of masculinity through phallic torture. If the 'penis' is a symbolic carrier of phallic masculinity,[16] i.e., the notion of masculine power by show of dominance, strength and sexual performance, then this masculinity is precisely what Flanagan embodies during his penis torturing acts. He does not simply nail, sew up or pierce his penis, but he embodies phallic power. All three examples of penis torture reveal Flanagan's ability to go beyond and interrogate normative gender performance. For instance, in the sewing performance Flanagan consciously enacts sex inversion and gains "temporary castration" (see Anderson), which serves as a way to deconstruct gender (see Juno and Vale 63) and to ridicule it (see Kauffman 26). Similarly, he exerts control over the pain of his disability and exceeds its limits. Spectators are inevitably forced to ask, "Why does Flanagan do that?" "Could I be able to do that?", "How does that feel?" (see Kuppers 89), thereby challenging individual limits of corporeal knowledge of pain as something one cannot control and would never want to inflict on oneself. Flanagan not only exceeds pain but he, moreover, turns it into sexual experience. Flanagan's masculine strength is recreated through this ability to surpass the limits of pain. His dominance occurs through control over his own gender category, symbolically embodied in the penis. By living out the pain and confusing the normalcy categories of sexuality and masculinity, Flanagan shows that pain is not disabling and victimizing. Rather, he disables the pain and gains power and superiority over his disability.

In his article, Siebers has initiated a discussion about the category of *pain*. He opposes current arguments among cultural researchers who approach pain of minorities mainly as organic and psychological, as something that subjugates and exposes those who feel it to inferiority and victimization. What can serve as the basis for minorities to build their identity in politics, Siebers claims, is an epistemological knowledge of pain. In order to refute these

---

16 | Psychoanalysis, Sigmund Freud's and Jacques Lacan's work in particular, has influenced the prevailing notion of 'phallic masculinity.' They view the phallus as a symbolic signifier and the penis can be its physical dimension. A man during childhood adopts and learns the phallic and paternal law, thus the Freudian 'Father-in-the-head' or Lacanian 'Name-of-the-Father' stands for the masculine power of the man in culture. Thereby, the notion of the phallus from childhood transferred to adulthood embodies masculinity (see Bredenkamp 62) and functions as the symbol of "power, authority and fertility" (see Flood 475). The phallus goes beyond its corporal physicality and represents male superiority, intellectual, political and cultural authority (see Tuana 7).

current assumptions that Siebers is critical of, I attempted to extend his pain argument further. Shifting the perspective from the political to the cultural field, I focused on the exceptional case of Bob Flanagan, whose disability and experience with penis torture provides a new and alternative perspective on understanding pain. Flanagan's performance acts allow us to read pain not simply as something psychological and externally constructed or as something that subjugates and can only be reproduced. On the contrary, his case shows a person with a disability who can take agency over physical pain and thereby transform his experience into something different, even into a source of pleasure. For Flanagan and for us, this transformation of pain and living it out publicly is a form of power, a manifestation that challenges constructed categories of sexuality, masculinity, and disability.

References

Anderson, Don. "The Force that Through the Wall Drives the Penis: The Becomings and Desiring-Machines of Glory Hole Sex." *Rhizomes: Cultural Studies in Emerging Knowledge* 11.12 (2005/2006). Web. 20 Sept. 2013. <http://www.rhizomes.net/issue11/anderson/index.html>.

Bredenkamp, Susannah. "Gesturing Towards Definition: Thought on Lack and the Phallus." *Left History* 11.2 (2006). 47-74. Print.

Brodwin, Martin G. and Pauline Cheryl Frederick. "Sexuality and Societal Beliefs Regarding Persons Living with Disabilities." *Journal of Rehabilitation* 76.4 (2010). 37-41. Print.

Butler, Ruth and Hester Parr. *Mind and Body Spaces: Geographies of Illness, Impairment and Disability*. London and New York: Routledge, 1999. Print.

Cheng, Ryu P. "Sociological Theories of Disability, Gender and Sexuality: A Review of the Literature." *Journal of Human Behavior in the Social Environment* 19.1 (2009). 112-122. Print.

Flood, Michael. *International Encyclopedia of Men and Masculinities*. London and New York: Routledge, 2007. Print.

Garland-Thomson, Rosemarie. "Staring Back: Self-Representation of Disabled Performance Artists." *American Quarterly*, 52.2 (2000). 334-338. Print.

Hladki, Janice. "Threshold of the Flesh: Disability and Dis-ease and Producing 'Ability Trouble.'" *The Review of Education, Pedagogy and Cultural Studies* 27.3 (2005). 265-285. Print.

Jones, Amelia. "Dis/playing the Phallus: Male Artists Perform Their Masculinities." *Art History*. 17.4 (1994). 546-584. Print.

Juno, Andrea and V. Vale. *Bob Flanagan: Supermasochist*. Hong Kong: Re/Search Publications, 1993. Print.

Kauffman, Linda S. *Bad Girls and Sick Boys: Fantasies in Contemporary Art and Culture.* London and Los Angeles: University of California Press, 1998. Print.

Kuppers, Petra. *The Scar of Visibility, Medical Performances and Contemporary Art.* Minneapolis and London: University of Minnesota Press, 2007. Print.

McRuer, Robert. *Crip Theory: Cultural Signs of Queerness and Disability.* New York: New York University Press, 2006. Print.

Sandahl, Carrie. "Bob Flanagan: Taking It Like a Man." *Journal of Dramatic Theory and Criticism* 15.1 (2000). 97-106. Print.

Schildkrout, Enid. "Inscribing the Body." *Annual Review of Anthropology* 22 (2004). 319-344. Print.

Shakespeare, Tom. "The Sexual Politics of Disabled Masculinity." *Sexuality and Disability* 17.1 (1999). 53-64. Print.

Shildrick, Margrit. "The Disabled Body, Genealogy and Undecidability." *Cultural Studies.* 19.6 (2005). 755-770. Print.

Siebers, Tobin. "Disability, Pain, and the Politics of Minority Identity." This volume. 111-121. Print.

—. *Disability Theory.* Ann Arbor: The University of Michigan Press, 2008. Print.

Sick: The Life and Death of Bob Flanagan, Supermasochist. Dir. and prod. Kirby Dick, Perf. Bob Flanagan, Sheree Rose, Kirby Dick, Kathe Burkhart and Rita Valencia. Lion Gate Films, 2007. DVD.

Tuana, Nancy. *Revealing Male Bodies.* Bloomington: Indiana University Press, 2002. Print.

Border Crossings

The Technologies of Disability and Desire[1]

Margrit Shildrick

When conventional disability studies encounters cultural theory, it generates what is now usually referred to as critical disability studies (CDS). Unlike the social model, which focuses on the structural inequalities of Western societies that are seen to produce disability, or at least cement it, CDS is a diverse entity that encompasses both material and discursive underpinnings, the psycho-cultural imaginary as much as law and social policy, and the phenomenology of the individual embodied subject as well as any identification with a sociological category. Critical disability studies is, in my view, inherently interdisciplinary in its scope and significance and must engage with the full range of what cultural studies – among other areas – has to offer rather than limiting itself to the narrower range of socio-political concerns. In this it moves away from the more familiar focus on rights, entitlements, and autonomy to encompass a complex analytic approach that goes well beyond mere description of how it is to be disabled. At the same time, cultural studies – like feminism before it – will benefit enormously from recognising that disability just is one of those intersectional modalities that cannot be separated out for discrete study as though its implications were fully contained within the material condition of those with anomalous embodiment. These are not just contact zones, but border crossings where bodies of knowledge inflect and disturb one another in what we can understand as highly productive ways. Within such a context, and as a body theorist, I shall focus especially on what is at stake in some aspects of human corporeality in the era of postmodern biotechnologies, technologies, that is, which have the capacity to not simply reorder morphological forms but to transform them.

---

1 | This essay draws on previous work in *Dangerous Discourses of Disability, Subjectivity and Sexuality*, chap. 6 (Palgrave Macmillian, 2009) and part of "Re-imagining Embodiment: Prostheses, Supplements and Boundaries" (*Somatechnics* 3.2, 2013).

In Western modernity, the reassuring, and yet fundamentally illusory, image of the Cartesian body as the unified, unchanging material base of continuing existence has long held sway, but is now radically challenged, not only by postconventional models of theoretical enquiry which are the concern of the few, but more materially and disturbingly by a range of contemporary bioscientific developments that pervade cultural understanding at every level. At precisely this juncture, the disabled body can raise acute questions about the always ambivalent relationship between embodied subjects, culture and biotechnology. While for nearly all of us, our bodily engagement in everyday life is always already technologically inflected, for many people with disabilities the relationship is an inescapable dimension of practical embodiment, not least in the use of prosthetic supports. But where in conventional usage the term prosthesis has intended some material object that compensated for a perceived lack or failure in embodiment, the emphasis now has turned to enhancement and supplement. Regardless of whether prostheses operate externally as conventional 'replacements' for missing limbs, or internally as with pacemakers or even transplanted organs, in all cases the endeavour to restore the clean and proper body paradoxically undermines our faith in an intrinsic corporeal integrity. In exposing instead the inherent plasticity of the body and its multiple possibilities of transcorporeality, and in incorporating non-self matter, such modes of morphological transformation can comprehensively undo the conventional limits of the corporeal self. Taking initially a phenomenological approach to the lived experience of prostheticized life, I shall move by way of Jacques Derrida's insights into prosthetic supplementarity and his re-imagination of corporeal boundaries to the Deleuzian understanding of embodiment as necessarily entailing assemblage. For Gilles Deleuze, assemblages mobilise an expanded notion of desire which inevitably queers not just sexuality but conventional models of embodiment in general. They speak to border crossings not as the passage from one realm to another but as the criss-crossing imbrication that productively disrupts all meanings. More importantly, in their respective work, both Derrida and Deleuze understand the dis-organisation of traditional bodily being as a matter not of nostalgia for lost certainties, but as the occasion for a potentially celebratory re-imagining of the multiple possibilities of corporeal extensiveness.

The current academic concern with the notion of prostheses builds on a lay fascination – not least on show during the Paralympics of 2012 – with the ubiquity and availability of technological interventions that seem to indicate new ways of being human. But before suggesting that such a move would demand radical reconfigurations of the concept of 'human' itself, let me first contextualise the word 'prosthesis' in its historical emergence. Clearly the use of mechanical aids to enhance bodily functionality or appearance extends right back to the Classical world, but the term itself (derived from the homologous

Greek word meaning 'addition') first appeared in English in early eighteenth century medical texts, where it was used to denote the "replacement of a missing part of the body with an artificial one" (Wills 215). As so often, the initial significant developments were driven by military issues, particularly following the rehabilitative treatment of mass casualties in the American Civil War and the two world wars. As David Serlin ("Engineering") makes clear, prosthetics in the Second World War were used to re-normalise the disabled male body, and he positions prosthetic practice as operating within "the fiercely heterosexual culture of rehabilitation medicine, especially its orthodox zeal to preserve the masculine status of disabled veterans" (Serlin, "Crippling" 170).[2] Similarly, the success of mid-century civilian prosthetics was often measured in professional literature by the extent to which they enabled the wearer to engage in normal gender activities like dating, dancing and ultimately marriage (see Ott). At those levels, the use of prostheses can be understood as therapeutic in both a medical and cultural sense, but the sense of enhancement – the crossing of the boundaries of the normative body – was never entirely absent. As early as the inter-war period in Europe, the emergence in Germany of the New Man took off from the rehabilitative goal of 'recovered' veterans, but introduced the notion of prostheses as offering something superior to the natural body (see Biro; Neumann).

More recently, contemporary critical cultural and body theory has de-constructed the initial definition of prostheses as functional replacements to evoke a sense in which the interface of biology and technology is a matter not of instrumental expediency but of a deep ambiguity. Prostheses are at once material artifacts and scaffolds of semiotic meaning where – in both the original, uncomplicated sense, and in the complex discursive notion – the infinite confusion of contact zones between the human, animal and machine plays itself out most tellingly. Like Donna Haraway's cyborg which once pushed the limits of embodiment in its imaginative daring, the prosthetic body troubles the binaries of the organic and inorganic, the natural and artificial, therapeutic and enhancement, male and female, and ultimately self and other. Speaking of the 'illegitimate fusions of animal and machine,' Haraway writes: "These are the couplings which make Man and Woman so problematic, subverting the structure of desire, the force imagined to generate language and gender, and so subverting the structure and modes of reproduction of 'Western' identity" (Haraway, "Manifesto" 176). Though Haraway has long since abandoned the cyborg as such, she indicates how the human/machine interface that conventional biomedical prostheses inevitably speak to can be pushed much further in both scope and meaning. Contemporary

---

2 | See also Serlin ("Crippling") for the surprisingly counter-normative possibilities of masculine prosthetic performativity.

critical cultural scholarship plays with the idea that we are all always already prosthetic. As disability theorists David Mitchell and Sharon Snyder put it, "the prostheticized body is the rule, not the exception" (Mitchell and Snyder 7). The significance of this insight for either embodied individuals or the body politic is yet to be decided, but what cannot be denied is the recognition that human corporeality is never given but can be manipulated, supplemented or substituted to the extent that normative embodiment becomes increasingly a term without meaning. Whether prostheses reference the cumbersome and heavy artificial legs functioning as replacement limbs in the aftermath of the Civil War, the transfer of a 'live' organ from one body to another, or the swivel chair that allows me to sit comfortably at my computer, it is clear that 'natural' self-complete and singular embodiment is an illusion. To give a less literal meaning to the term prosthesis and to engage with an expanded understanding of the 'prosthetic impulse' (see Smith and Morra) would open the field to a nexus of unexpected but constitutive assemblages that disorder the very idea of normative corporeality.

Both contemporary biotechnologies, which multiply the possibilities of embodiment, and postmodernist body theory make clear that embodiment, far from being fundamentally stable over time, is highly complex and indeterminate. Nonetheless, the Western psycho-social imaginary privileges corporeal wholeness and integrity and thus devalues disability. The point, then, of conventional prosthetic use has been to recover and rehabilitate the 'failing' body to better fit with that imaginary, albeit at the expense of an inevitable transformation in the imaginary. What I mean is that from a phenomenological perspective, it is apparent that the use of a prosthesis goes beyond a simple reliance on an exterior technology that leaves the self unchanged, but is a matter of becoming embodied as hybrid. In an auto-ethnographical account, Vivian Sobchack – whose left leg was amputated several years ago – reflects on how her experience of using a prosthetic limb entails an unsettling contestation not only of her relations to others, but of her understanding of the subjective self. She outlines the lived experience of her body in which she is acutely aware of the way in which both the phantom affects of amputation – which are very common following excision of a limb – and the biomedical prosthesis itself profoundly unsettle the usual binaries that map the clean and proper body of the psycho-social imaginary. For Sobchack, the either/or of real/ artificial, objective/subjective, material/imaginary lose their distinctions and prove inadequate to what she understands of her own embodied experience. Instead she is simultaneously aware of an originary 'wholebodied' corporeality, the absent presence of her phantom limb, and the solid materiality of her prosthesis. Those diverse felt experiences are not easily reconciled nor open to any fixed meaning or significance to the self. Even as she consciously strives for a sense of a *whole* body, Sobchack's endeavour is constantly thwarted, not by the diminution associated with amputation, but by the uncannily extended boundaries of her embodiment.

The slippery spectre of incorporation, evident in Sobchack's account, moves centre stage when we consider the transplantation of organs and tissue from one body to another. The translocation of human organic material, which encompasses not only things like heart and kidney transplants but also hands, corneas or skin, may raise acute problems for recipients insofar as the material incorporation of living parts from the body of another deeply complicates notions of an integrated self (see Shildrick et al. "Troubling;" Poole et al.). Where lay understanding of the transplant procedure might be expected to generate unsettling thoughts with regard to the co-constitution of the embodied self post-transplant, that potential disturbance to the psycho-social imaginary is widely negotiated by a determined separation of the supposedly singular materiality of individual embodiment from intimations of intercorporeality. Some recipients hold fast to a similar model, but the majority do in fact experience a range of affects that speak directly to the transformatory effects of biotechnical interventions (see Shildrick "Imagining"). What is at stake is that donated organs and tissue in particular open up the problematic of how such effectively prosthetic interventions into the interiority of human corporeality contest the body's supposed wholeness and unity. In positivist representations of biomedicine, organ transplantation is rightly presented as a therapeutic, often life-saving, procedure, but as with the disabled users of mechanical prostheses, the well-Being (and I mean here much more than simple health) of recipients themselves is driven by their capacity to tolerate the hybridity that any embodied prosthesis introduces. The question of organic transplantation, nor its as yet unacceptable variant of xenotransplantation, will not be pursued further here, but what is emerging is that all prostheses, whether mechanical or organic, implicitly contest the normative attributions of human being.

What can be taken, then, from the imbrication of a developing theoretical framework and the specific biotechnologies is the urgent need to problematise the notion of prostheses as simply replacements or functional substitutes for 'missing' parts of bodies that appear less than whole. In everyday understanding, prostheses are subsidiary additions to a given, but flawed, body and their value lies in their reparative effect. Yet the designation of them as *supplementary* calls to mind Derrida's 'logic of the supplement' (see Derrida *Speech and Phenomenon*; *Of Grammatology*), which operates as one of many idioms through which he signals the fluidity of categorical boundaries. What Derrida emphasises instead is the familiar nexus central to his work of deferral, ambiguity, undecidability, and the ultimate impossibility of completion. And, he argues (*The Truth in Painting*), the very possibility of (prosthetic) augmentation shows that there is no originary wholeness to restore. Whatever the object – paradigmatically here the body – it has never been self-sufficient. In effect, the supplement is essential in constituting the object as such and in exposing the undecidable nature of categorical distinctions between self/other, natural/artificial and so on that are usually taken for granted. In other words, prostheses cannot be seen as merely instrumental but construct that which they purport to enhance. As he puts it, "technology has not simply added itself, from the outside [...]. [T]his foreign or dangerous supplement is 'originarily' at work and in place in the supposedly ideal interiority of the 'body and soul'" (*Points...Interviews* 244). And in a further complication to unproblematised accounts of prosthetic usage, Derrida's insistence on the paradox of supplementarity – it implies both the augmentation or making whole of an object *and* the substitution for or replacement of aspects of that object – indicates that a prosthesis may equally increase functionality *and* radically subvert specifically human agency as such. Any supplement may be both compensatory and "something that substitutes, violates and usurps" (Kamuf 139). The ideal of concordant reparation – the making 'whole' of the disabled person, or the restoration of normative life for the transplant recipient – cannot be satisfied. Whatever their form then, prostheses contest the illusion of an originary unified and singular body, exposing instead the fluidity of categorical boundaries, and they raise fundamental questions about the hybrid nature of intercorporeality.

Where Derrida uncovers the mechanics of the Western logos – and by derivation its coincident socio-cultural imaginary – I wonder whether rethinking the whole nexus of the relation between self and other need end with the notion of intercorporeality. Given the material and ambiguous experience of prosthetic limbs or donated organs, which both put into question the singularity of the embodied self, might not the idea of assemblages be more appropriate? Though useful, the term intercorporeality still speaks to solid bodies and a certain stability that belies the fluidity of the multiple and often provisional permutations and combinations that construct and deconstruct what is usually designated as 'human' life. In enabling us to read prostheses in the mode of supplementarity, Derrida opens up an important step in the reconfiguration of corporeal boundaries, but I would suggest that the Deleuzian notion of assemblage might provide further insights into our ongoing re-imagination of the nature of the body. It is apposite that in the loosely labelled new materialism that has come to the fore in recent feminist work, one major focus has been on the immersion of the singular human 'I' in its environmental context of multiple complex relations. Although the emphasis is often on our interconnections with other organisms and species as constitutive of life (see Braidotti; Haraway, *Companion Species*; Rossini), it is as important to provide an account of the part played by inorganic technologies in materializing the putatively human. In that respect, a turn to Deleuze might be highly appropriate in our attempts to reconfigure the terrain.

In the work of Deleuze and Félix Guattari (*Anti-Oedipus*; *A Thousand Plateaus*) the embodied self – rather than being goal-driven and singular as it would be in a modernist model – becomes a network of flows, energies and capacities that are always open to transformation, and that figure what they call desire. Desire, then, is not sexual as such, but denotes a dynamic, indeterminate and productive force, excessive to the embodied self. As Guattari explains: "desire is everything that exists before the opposition between subject and object [...]. It's everything whereby the world and affects constitute us outside ourselves [...]. It's everything that overflows from us" (Guattari 46). And rather than grounding the conventional ideal of autonomous action, separation and self-sufficiency, Deleuzian embodiment emerges from the capacity to make connections, both organic and inorganic, and to constitute new assemblages – 'desiring machines' as Deleuze and Guattari call them – which are in turn disassembled. In place of the normative organisation of the body, Deleuze and Guattari propose "a body populated by multiplicities" (*Plateaus* 30) in which the process of becoming is the process of desire (see 301). In effect, what they promote is a deconstruction, a queering, of *all* bodies to the extent that borders and boundaries no longer function as limits (see Shildrick, *Discourses* 132).

What then is the relevance to disability? Taking off from Deleuzian ideas, which start with the body one has in all its possible variations, makes clear that to think specifically of the disabled body in this context is not to single it out in its difference (there are after all only differences), still less to position it as incomplete or inadequate. Rather the materiality of such a body is a productive site of possibility where anomalous forms, 'missing' parts, and prostheses are enablers of new channels of desiring production that are unconstrained by conventional organisation. In effect – and this clarifies again why cultural studies has much to gain from an engagement with critical disability work – the explicitly anomalous nature of disability demonstrates the promise of an immanent desire that embraces the strange and opens up to new linkages and provisional incorporations. It speaks of multiple connectors that leave behind the normative distinctions between the human and animal, between organic and inorganic, or between an originary body and a prosthesis. Like all of us in varying ways, but perhaps more overtly, people with disabilities come into being through such provisional assemblages: there are human-machine assemblages enmeshing flesh and blood with prosthetic limbs, ventilators, pacemakers, wheelchairs; human-human assemblages with family or assistants, or the incorporation of transplant organs; and human-animal assemblages that rely on service animals such as helper dogs and monkeys, or therapeutic encounters with cats and horses. All of these are forms of prostheses, far exceeding superficial functionality, engaging with the production of new forms of embodiment and desire, and mobilising a particular performativity of the embodied self.

Crucially, Deleuze and Guattari show that the embodied self is already prosthetic and on the way to becoming an assemblage. Although there is nothing to imply that prostheses are especial to disability, nevertheless, disabled people may be made more conscious of the extension, substitution, or supplementation of their bodies both through practical instances and insofar as those modes are taken to speak to the desire to recuperate the body in the face of some kind of *lack* not experienced by the normative majority. The conventional distinction between a positive and negative grounding for prosthetic use is made clear if we compare two recent images. When the non-disabled performance artist Stelarc creates a virtual robotic and interactive arm, that is seen as an amplification of bodily possibilities and critique of biological limitations, whereas the amputee man who uses two arm prostheses is understood to be countering a functional failure of embodiment. Clearly one example is far more technologically advanced than the other, but it is a difference in degree not in kind. What this illustrates is the illusory distinction between the development of prostheses as part of human enhancement technologies (HET) and their use in relation to disability where they are usually intended to replicate normative function and appearance.[3] It might even be argued that human enhancement technologies directed towards disability are the ground zero of deeply ambiguous future developments that will render the notion of disability obsolete. Beyond any Foucauldian sense of the technological disciplining and regulation of the body, nonetheless, all such technological modes are supplementary, excessive to the body, and figure a form of assemblage.

My point is that insofar as they are able to take up the potential of prostheses, disabled people are already well-placed to experience the transformative nature of transcorporeality across both organic and inorganic elements, the assembly and disassembly of surprising and innovative connections, and even the productive troubling of intentionality. As with minoritarian thought and practices more generally, the necessity of breaking through the supposed limits of the resources to hand can both intensify the decomposition of binaries – body/machine; active/passive; natural/artificial; biology/technology – and multiply the erotics of connection (see Shildrick *Discourses*). As Deleuze and Guattari note: "[d]esire constantly couples continuous flows and partial objects that are by nature fragmentary and fragmented. Desire causes the current to flow" (*Anti-Oedipus* 5). The move that Deleuze and Guattari make is to ask not what a body *is* but what a body can *do*. And once the conventional focus on the disabled body as lacking has changed, it becomes clear that the experience of a dis-unified or prosthetic body demands a degree of inventiveness that most

---

3 | The trope of enhancement does, however, extend to many disabled sportsmen and women who are increasingly using highly technical prostheses that are seen to not just restore functionality but to bestow certain advantages over normative bodies.

people are rarely open to. For Deleuze and Guattari, that connectedness of the body is at the heart of creativity, superseding the prohibition, repression and disavowal of disabled people's forms of vitality with a desire that is expansive, fluid, and connective. On that level, desire itself is liberated not simply from the bounds of genital sexuality, but more generally transcends the restricted parameters of what is usually defined as *sexual*. Above all, what mobilises or stalls the multifarious nature of desire is the extent to which the diverse connective elements escape organised patterns. In shifting the emphasis from the integrity and co-ordination of the whole body to the provisional imbrication of disparate parts, it is no longer appropriate to think of bodies as either whole or broken, able-bodied or disabled. Embodiment is simply a provisional manifestation in a process of becoming driven by the circulation of desire. For Deleuze and Guattari, such flows of energy extend embodiment beyond the merely human. It is not that there is no distinction to be made between one corporeal element and the next, but rather that becoming inherently transgresses borders and turns away from dominant notions of autonomous and strictly human agency. It speaks to bodies – organic and inorganic alike – whose interconnected fluidity and energies mobilise mutual transformations.

At just this point, then, the potential to reclaim disability from its conventional association with lack and to reposition it at the forefront of the circulation of desire is strong. Given a stress on the multiple possibilities of interconnection, anomalous bodies escape their status as a site of repression and disavowal, and instead hold out the promise of productive new becomings.[4] For Deleuze and Guattari the take up of a positive model of desire, limited neither to those already satisfying certain fixed corporeal criteria, nor to the modernist privileging of autonomous agency, underpins a move from the givenness of being to the fluidity of becoming. In place of the limits that the ideal of independence imposes, the emphasis is on connectivity and linkage such that a reliance on prosthetic devices – the crossings between human, animal, and machine – figures not as evidence of inadequacies but of transformative possibilities of becoming other along multiple lines of flight. In tracing how this might have practical implications for disabled people who – because of their perceived lack of self-reliance and oftentimes recourse to prosthetic devices – are usually characterised as dependent and beyond a full experience of pleasure and desire, I want to look briefly at a couple of empirical studies undertaken by a scholar of physical therapy, Barbara Gibson, whose

---

4 | It is worth noting that where the ideas developed by Deleuze and Guattari with regard to the connectivity and implications of desiring machines have struggled for understanding, the similar and almost cotemporaneous - albeit partially ironic - imaginings of Haraway in "A Cyborg Manifesto" - originally a 1983 conference paper - have become, for feminist and queer theorists at least, seminal fare.

critical work theorises the practical day to day functioning and lived experience of people with severe disabilities.

In one study of young men with Duchenne's disease – who all required long-term use of ventilators – Gibson recognises that the conventional goal of physical therapy to achieve some form of 'independence' bears little relation to what the men actually experience in their own lives. In her perception that her subjects are "both confined to individual bodies and simultaneously connected, overlapping with other bodies, nature and machines" (Gibson, "Disability" 189), Gibson finds greater adequacy in Deleuze and Guattari's rejection of individual autonomy and in their promotion of active becoming as that which breaks through the bounded limits of the singular self. Referring to one disabled man whose life is intertwined with, and made possible by, a series of prostheses (a wheelchair, a ventilator, a gastronomy tube and a voice synthesizer), Gibson remarks not his dependency, but the multiple connections and exchanges of energy: "He is a fluid body [...] a conglomeration of energies. He has replaceable parts [...]. He is an excitation, a point of contact, a relay on a power grid" (191-192). And in a recent study that even more deeply problematises the therapeutic drive, Gibson follows Mimi, a severely disabled 12 year old girl, to show not only how Mimi and her mother are interdependent, but, more profoundly,

"their selves connect and merge into assemblages and later disconnect and reconnect with others to form different assemblages. Within these assemblages there are no clear distinction between persons or between persons and technologies." (Gibson et al., "Reimagining" 1895)

From her Deleuzian perspective, Gibson offers a radical suggestion of how therapy might be rethought as the task of "facilitating creative assemblages rather than (only) independence. The goal becomes helping persons to live well through making and breaking connections" (1898).

While the accounts outlined here are specific to particular embodiments, the Deleuzian mechanisms that Gibson demonstrates figure both an individual moment of becoming through connection and a modality of existence common to every one of us. The intrinsic vulnerability of embodiment – that we all share – need not be read in terms of weakness and negativity, but opens up the possibility of desiring production through the intensity of multiple connections that are not limited to the human alone. This is what Gibson calls "transgressive connectivity" (Gibson, "Disability" 191). It suggests, at the very least, that the bodily transgressions associated with disabled embodiment are a powerful step towards a re-imagining of 'disability;' and at a wider level it demands that we rethink the significance of such immersive encounters in all areas of life. Whatever the starting place, the dynamic and always unfinished processes of assemblage point to the unlimited potential of becoming. There is no doubt that the concept of desiring machines enables us to think the experiences of embodiment in a different plane that is as receptive to disabled people as to any others. It may even be more so given that disabled people may have less identification with sovereign subjectivity, or have been compelled to let go of such illusions. It is not, however, that I want to advocate a romanticised view of disability in which desire – in its Deleuzian sense – is always able to circulate as an unimpeded positivity. Clearly, there are some physical and cognitive constraints, some specific corporeal differences and discontinuities that continue to obstruct the flow of energies and frustrate intentionality. It is not easy to let go of the image of a controlling self, even when the body itself demands otherwise. But the reimagining that I am outlining here has no place for the characteristically modernist notions of self-determined choice or for the putative liberty to pursue every possibility. Rather, it offers an alternative way forward that does not rely on the illusion of a coherent subject with fixed and organised desires, and turns instead to the libidinal intensities of what I have called an erotics of connection. It figures desire as a movement of realignment and reorganisation of the body's affects and structures that disperses the subject as such. What matters is the transformative potential of the process such that any existing exclusion from the parameters of normativity must lessen resistance. Those who are anomalously embodied or disabled may find unexpected value in their very location as outsiders.

That is not to say that people with disabilities already exemplify a Deleuzian imaginary. In any case, when Deleuze and Guattari refer to becoming-minoritarian, they are not privileging any given category, but referring to processes that engage in radical forms of border crossing, the capacity to enter into disparate machinic connections, and to the emergence of provisional assemblages. Such channels are *open to all*. Already existent and substantive minorities, like people who are disabled, must – from a Deleuzo-Guattarian perspective – also enter into those processes of becoming, which inherently disperse the relations of power that define desire within limited sexual parameters and position it only within normative borders. It is clear that in the face of an irreducible connectivity as a condition of becoming and the productive play of desire, the privileging of autonomous agency and the conventional forms of embodiment that circumscribe the normative subject would lose their power to set up hierarchies of value. The significance of such an approach is that it offers a fundamental critique of the way in which the dominant discourse of disability activism, and indeed of much standard disability theory, is typically organised. Where the emphasis is currently shaped by the liberal demand for rights, choice, and self-determination – all of which echo modernist principles and speak to a goal of sameness rather than a celebration of differences – a more productive model, and the one taken up by critical disability studies, proposes a revaluation of the qualities of those already living at the margins. Once the extraordinary plasticity of the body is acknowledged rather than disavowed, then the circulation of desire and the dis-organised and partial satisfactions of pleasure would be a matter of differential exploration, innovation and experimentation, rather than the discredited sites of suppression or shame.

My claim, then, is that were the notion of the technologised body focussed not on individual agency, but on the *emergence* of a sense of self through an erotics of connection, it could transform our understanding of disability and desire. The specific corporeal differences of disability not only contest the very separation of self and other, but in many ways they are already queer in the sense of fulfilling Eve Sedgwick's original delineation of queer as denoting an "open mesh of possibilities, gaps, overlaps, dissonances and resonances, lapses and excesses of meaning [...]" (Sedgwick 8). "A lot of the most exciting work around 'queer,'" she points out, "spins the term outward along dimensions that can't be subsumed under gender and sexuality" (8-9).[5] As I have stressed throughout, it is not that disability is unique, but that its forms of embodiment, and its embrace of prosthetic technologies, serve to exemplify the fragility, instability and provisionality of corporeality in general. This intends nothing negative as it would in modernist discourse, but speaks to the postmodernist insistence that all bodies – normative and non-normative alike – are constantly open to reconfiguration and to the potential of becoming hybrid, nomadic, machinic assemblages. Such radical transformation looks risky and uneasy, but so long as acceptable embodiment remains constituted by the repressive parameters of the modernist imaginary, certain bodies – disabled bodies – will never matter. The mobilisation of desire, which Rosi Braidotti figures as "the ontological drive to become [that] seduces us into going on living" (Braidotti 134), is one answer to that danger. As such, the promise of a Deleuzian-inspired re-imagination may be both necessary and life-enhancing.

The interchange and intersectionality of critical cultural studies and critical disability studies strongly promotes the understanding that it is no longer possible to speak of the body in any unproblematised way, nor as a self-contained unit that might be fitted to a category. The conventional attachment to the fixity of corporeal boundaries and the singularity of the embodied self must give way to an embrace of the criss-crossings of multiple and fluid forms of embodiment. As the plasticity of all our bodies and the capacity of disparate parts to constitute hybrid assemblages become increasingly apparent,

---

5 | Disability theorists have approached the notion of 'queer' in both more and less radical ways, but most would concur with Michael Warner that queer is defined "against the norm rather than the heterosexual" (Warner xxvi). See in particular work by Robert McRuer, McRuer and Abby Wilkerson, as well as several other articles focusing on the intersections between disability and queer in an issue of GLQ: A Journal of Lesbian and Gay Studies 9.1. (2003).

the spatiality and temporality of individual life is broken. The technologies of disability and desire suggest that the superiority of the strictly human will be rapidly overtaken by forms of life comprised by the multiple intertwinings of the human, animal and machine, where none of the elements is stable or predictable. In the era of postmodernity, theories of the body are unlikely to settle. As I understand it, disability studies and cultural studies are instinctive supplements to one another that will flourish to the extent that they are co-constituted, co-operative and contestational at once, pushing forward to develop new theorisations of embodiment that will enable us all to go on living.

REFERENCES

Biro, M. "The New Man as Cyborg: Figures of Technology in Weimar Visual Culture." *New German Critique* 62 (1994). 71-110. Print.

Braidotti, Rosi. *The Posthuman.* Cambridge: Polity Press, 2013. Print.

Deleuze, Gilles and Félix Guattari. *Anti-Oedipus: Capitalism and Schizophrenia.* Trans. R. Hurley. London: Athlone Press, 1984. Print.

—. *A Thousand Plateaus: Capitalism and Schizophrenia.* Trans B. Massumi. Minneapolis: Minnesota University Press, 1987. Print.

Derrida, Jacques. *Speech and Phenomenon.* Trans. D. Allison. Evanston, Illinois: Northwestern University Press, 1973. Print.

—. *Of Grammatology.* Trans. Gayatri Spivak. Baltimore: Johns Hopkins University Press, 1974. Print.

—. *The Truth in Painting.* Trans. Geoff Bennington and Ian McLeod. Chicago: University of Chicago Press, 1987. Print.

—. *Points...Interviews, 1974-1994.* Ed. Elisabeth Weber. Stanford: Stanford University Press, 1995. Print.

Gibson, Barbara. "Disability, Connectivity and Transgressing the Autonomous Body." *Journal of Medical Humanities* 27 (2006). 187-196. Print.

Gibson, Barbara, Franco Carnevale and Gillian King. "'This is my way:' Reimagining Disability, In/dependence and Interconnectedness of Persons and Assistive Technologies." *Disability & Rehabilitation* 34 (2012). 1894-1899. Print.

Grosz, Elizabeth. *Time Travels: Feminism, Nature, Power.* Chapel Hill: Duke University Press, 2005. Print.

Guattari, Félix. *Soft Subversions.* Ed. S. Lotringer. New York: Semiotext(e), 1996. Print.

Haraway, Donna. "A Cyborg Manifesto: Science, Technology, and Socialist-Feminism in the Late Twentieth Century." *Simians, Cyborgs, and Women: The Reinvention of Nature.* London: Free Association Books, 1991. Print.

—. *The Companion Species Manifesto: Dogs, People and Significant Otherness.* Chicago: University of Chicago Press, 2007. Print.

Kamuf, Peggy. *A Derrida Reader: Between the Blinds.* Hemel Hempstead: Harvester Wheatsheaf, 1991. Print.

McRuer, Robert. "As Good As It Gets: Queer Theory and Critical Disability." *GLQ: A Journal of Lesbian and Gay Studies* 9.1 (2003). 79-105. Print.

McRuer, Robert and Abby Wilkerson. "Introduction: Cripping the (Queer) Nation." *GLQ: A Journal of Lesbian and Gay Studies* 9.1 (2003). 1-23. Print.

Mitchell, David T. and Sharon L. Snyder. *Narrative Prosthesis: Disability and the Dependencies of Discourse.* Ann Arbor: University of Michigan Press, 2000. Print.

Neumann, Boaz. "Being Prosthetic in the First World War and Weimar Germany." *Body & Society* 16.3 (2010). 93-126. Print.

Ott, Katherine, David Serlin and Stephen Mihn, eds. *Artificial Parts, Practical Lives: Modern Histories of Prosthetics.* New York: New York University Press, 2002. Print.

Poole, Jennifer, Margrit Shildrick, Patricia McKeever, Susan Abbey and Heather Ross. "'You Might Not Feel Like Yourself:' On Heart Transplants, Identity and Ethics." *Critical Interventions in the Ethics of Healthcare.* Eds. Stuart J. Murray and Dave Holmes. Farnham: Ashgate, 2009. Print.

Rossini, Manuela. "To the Dogs: Companion Speciesism and the New Feminist Materialism." *Kritikos* 3. (2006). <http://intertheory.org/rossini>. Web. 21 Oct 2013. Print.

Sedgwick, Eve Kosofsky. *Tendencies.* London: Routledge, 1994. Print.

Serlin, David. "Engineering Masculinity." *Artificial Parts, Practical Lives: Modern Histories of Prosthetics.* Eds. Katherine Ott et al. New York: New York University Press. 2002. Print.

—. "Crippling Masculinity: Queerness and Disability in U.S. Military Culture, 1800–1945." *GLQ: A Journal of Lesbian and Gay Studies* 9.1 (2003). 149-179. Print.

Shildrick, Margrit. *Dangerous Discourses of Disability, Subjectivity and Sexuality.* London: Palgrave Macmillan, 2009. Print.

—. "Imagining the Heart: Incorporations, Intrusions and Identity." *Somatechnics.* 2.2 (2012). 233-49. Print.

—. "Re-imagining Embodiment: Prostheses, Supplements and Boundaries." *Somatechnics* 3.2 (2013). 270–286. Print.

Shildrick, Margrit, Patricia McKeever, Susan Abbey, Jennifer Poole and Heather Ross. "Troubling Dimensions of Heart Transplantation." *Medical Humanities (BMJ Supplement)* 35.1 (2009). 35-38. Print.

Smith, Marquand and Morra, Joanne. *The Prosthetic Impulse: From a Posthuman to a Biocultural Future.* Cambridge: MIT Press, 2006. Print.

Sobchack, Vivienne. "Living a 'Phantom Limb:' on the Phenomenology of Bodily Integrity." *Body & Society* 16.3 (2010). 51-69. Print.

Warner, Michael, ed. *Fear of a Queer Planet*. Minneapolis: University of Minnesota Press, 1993. Print.

Wills, David. *Prosthesis*. Stanford, CA: Stanford University Press, 1995. Print.

Responses to Margrit Shildrick

Jan Söffner
EMBODYING TECHNOLOGIES OF DISABILITY

Crossing boundaries between disciplines – in this case the boundaries between cultural studies and disability studies – can produce new encounters, connections, assemblages of concepts, and notions. In Margrit Shildrick's highly innovative account, these 'theoretical' assemblages become a criterion to reflect further assemblages: machinic embodiments that are involved in technologies of disability. Shildrick observes these assemblages in every form of human bodily existence, but considers them to be especially visible and common in the prosthetic and cyborgian embodiment of disabled bodies. In describing this embodiment, she draws on postmodern concepts of queering and desire. I appreciate her account, and wish to highlight a particular merit of her approach: its ability to overcome the subject-object dichotomy (i.e., the presumption that an autonomous subject uses a given technology in an instrumental way), and in turn to overcome any extension of this dichotomy into concepts of prosthetic *replacement* (i.e., the presumption that a prosthesis 'replaces' a missing or deficient organic body part and thereby restores a perceived inherent 'integrity' of a body). Crucial to this overcoming is a Deleuzian notion of a proliferous desire: a desire that is not grounded in a lack of something but played out in the productive use of linkages and relations between the animate and the inanimate, between open and extended bodies; a desire that does not take place in forms of 'being,' but in forms of 'becoming.'

Thinking of bodies that live in constant prosthetic conjunctions in these terms is very convincing – especially when a dis-unified body is opposed to the norms of the integrity of a clearly delimited bodily self. It is certainly true that people with disabilities are more used to the inherent challenges of such a self, continually crossing the implications of a subjective authenticity grounded in an ideology of a distinctly delimited body. So the problem of my response is that it risks becoming (or remaining) a boring summary. To avoid this, I will raise some questions that stem from an *enactivist* approach, starting with the embedded and skillful enactions of an extended body.

Approaches such as Shildrick's start with what bodies (can) 'do' rather than with what they 'are;' an enactivist account is similarly opposed to the normative imaginary of a monadic body closed upon itself (see Varela, Thompson and Rosch). It focuses on what Shildrick addresses as "transcorporeality," a notion very similar to enactivist notions of "isopraxis" (see Despret), "shared embodied interaction" (see Gallagher and Zahavi 191-218) or "participatory sense-making" (see Fuchs and De Jaegher). The prosthetic and cyborgian existence of our bodies is reflected very well in this line of theory (see Clark), as is the "plasticity of the body" (see Gallagher).

What are the major differences that allow for a renewed discussion of Shildrick's account? First, enactivist theory offers a much broader discussion about skill (see Dreyfus; Ingold): The plasticity of the body is conceived in terms of learning and training rather than in composing and assembling only. This leads to a different interest concerning prostheses. To give an example: For nearly fifty years, researchers have been developing visual-to-tongue prostheses for blind people, where a kind of a haptic screen that can be placed on the tongue of a blind person displays the 'image' of what the camera records, or visual-to-auditory prostheses where the optic signal is transformed into an acoustic one. Research on the plasticity of the brain has shown that, after some training, some individuals are able to do something that – at least in neurological terms – very much resembles 'seeing:' haptic perception was wired to the visual centers of the brain. Of course such a perception is not a replacement of vision; it has a completely different phenomenology; in particular, it has a different phenomenology of space (see O'Regan et al., especially pp. 60-63). Nonetheless, it offers a potential of perceptive experience completely unknown to seeing people. This finding is completely in line with Shildrick's assertion that the embodiment of prostheses cannot and should not be subsumed under a teleological quest for the restoration of some hypothesized integrity. Rather, bodily functions are technically opened by prostheses in ways allowing for new forms of experiencing. But I hesitate to describe this effect as 'assemblage,' preferring Alva Noë's discussion of a perceptual *skill*. Plasticity cannot be reached simply by assembling a machinic body and an equally machinic technology. It requires training and habituation beyond the initial coupling, which results in the development of a precise 'feel' and does not only concern the 'intensity' of sensation. This is not to say that I would like to discard the notions of 'assemblage,' 'coupling,' 'desire' and 'intensity.' But I think that these terms are one-sided and need a different – enactivist and phenomenological – background to avoid becoming all too theoretical and abstract formulas.

Secondly, enactivism has chosen a different route for overcoming René Descartes than Gilles Deleuze. Put bluntly, Descartes conceived of the body as a machine – to set it apart from the non-machinic mind. In trying to overcome this dualism, postmodern embodiment – and Deleuze is no exception here –

describes the mind as an ideological construction and focuses on machinic constellations as an alternative for a transgressive human existence. Deleuze and Félix Guattari likewise challenge the monadic functional organization of an organic body by the notion of an open body without organs. However, their fundamental critique of Descartes took place before the digital revolution, in which Cartesian dualism was proven wrong in a very unexpected manner: It turned out that machines like computers are very much able to emulate the functioning of what Cartesianism has conceived of as a *disembodied mind*. They look incredibly clumsy, however, when they try to emulate the *body and the embodied mind* (see Dreyfus or Pfeiffer and Bongard). Computers easily beat the best human chess players but watching the world championship of robot-soccer is a rather sobering experience for any soccer enthusiast. This is not even the best example – it is even more productive to think about the still-hypothetical task of giving (embodied) emotions to machines and making them have 'a good feel' for a certain situation. When thinking about the fact that Descartes had thought of similar emotional issues as bodily and machinic, and moreover considering that Deleuze's and Guattari's account of senso-emotional 'intensities' echoes this very premise, the problem of a theory of machinic embodiment becomes even clearer. Similar findings have opened a different way of challenging Descartes: While the disembodied and 'informational' *mind* can be described as machinic, enactive embodiment cannot. As such, if one is to describe embodiment, I find it very promising to follow Hubert Dreyfus in focusing on what (computational) machines *cannot* do. This, too, makes me doubt whether a machinic body is really a good starting point for describing the phenomenology of embodiment.

Thirdly and finally, there is a grounding of enactivist theories in a phenomenological tradition (mostly in relation to Edmund Husserl, Martin Heidegger and Maurice Merleau-Ponty). Deleuze's own relationship with phenomenology was complex: He sometimes appears to be as indebted to it as he opposed it (for a close examination of this relationship, see Hughes). Today, observing something of a renaissance of phenomenology (which I personally very much applaud), there are similar challenges and complexities in the integration of postmodern and phenomenological theories. The problems of such a re-integration become most obvious where embodiment is concerned; and prosthetic bodies are perhaps even paradigmatic for this discussion. Phenomenological theory here offers a broad variety of precise notions, such as the diverse forms of 'directedness' – be they 'intentional' (i.e. provided with 'aboutness') or provided with an intrinsic 'contentless' orientation of motion. One could think about the Husserlian terms of 'protention' and 'retention' as temporal forms of directedness (see Husserl 20-27) – as opposed to the expectation of 'something' (e.g., a dancer's intentional directedness of movement merges with the ongoing rhythm rather than expecting a certain discrete sound to come along). Alternately, one could consider the Heideggerian distinction between 'vorhanden' (present at hand) and 'zuhanden' (ready at hand) (see Heidegger 66-76): A hammer that is only looked at or observed is a 'present at hand' object with properties; once it is used, it becomes part of a 'ready at hand' embodied activity and ceases to be an object. Finally, one could reference James Jerome Gibson's notion of 'affordances,' i.e. the fact of perceiving the environment not in terms of observation but in terms of what activities they afford – e.g. perceiving a chair not just as brown and antique, but as sit-on-able or climb-on-able. *All these issues* can become an integral part of 'becoming,' of bodily transformations, of bodily connections; and in these cases, a term like 'desire' can be productive. But it cannot be sufficient. If one takes seriously Husserl's *Zu den Sachen selbst!* (*To the things themselves!*), it is necessary to be much more precise.

So what critiques and alternative proposals arise from an enactivist account on technologies of disability? First, I think, it leads to more scrutiny concerning the question of *how* technologies of disability are embodied, how machines become an integral part of lived experience and the extended body. Here, skills play a crucial role. Indeed, I suspect that training and habituation count very much for a transparent experience of prostheses. A person does not simply *assemble* organic leg-movements and an inorganic bouncing-technology when learning to walk using Flex-Foot Cheetahs. There is merging and molding in a process not at all adequately described by the term 'assemblage.' I believe that Deleuze and Guattari's 'fluidity of becoming' is much more about how we conceive of ourselves, how we (re)present and (de)construct our identities, than it is about these concrete bodily tasks. As far as I understand Deleuze and Guattari, in their eyes, habituation and training of skills should even tend towards stratification and codification; in short, in a Deleuzian theory, they lead to territorialization standing in contrast with the *fluidity* of becoming, to which Shildrick refers. But what can this fluidity be, after all, if it does not care about these crucial issues? Can it really reflect the embodied existence properly? And do trained and habituated forms of bodily behavior (i.e., what Pierre Bourdieu called the 'habitus') not constitute an important aspect of identities as well?

My second doubt about the concept of assemblages regards the Cartesian premises of machinic embodiment. Indeed, when I think about where human-machine-interfaces really work in terms of connectivity and assembling (i.e., not in terms of skillful integration), those machines that emulate the Cartesian mind occur to me first. For example, I see a huge power of connectedness and indeterminate productive force of invention in everyday human-computer interaction. That is, I see well-functioning assemblages where the coupling takes place between software and a human mind trained by this software to become as Cartesian as possible – i.e., where a 'cognitio clara et disctincta' and thus the reading and production of discrete signals is necessary for putting computational functions to work. I also see how well this technology works when it comes to *replacing* skills and *inventing* new identities in such a way that no spontaneous and involuntary forms of bodily communication occur: It is, indeed, much easier to reinvent oneself on a virtual social network than it is to make one's body acquire the skills of an even slightly different embodied existence. Most crucially, it is much easier to execute this reinvention in terms of combining, connecting and assembling. Similar technologies can be a blessing for people (disabled or not) for whom a face-to-face interaction poses difficulties or challenges; but they do not really help the embodied existence – to the contrary, they contribute to making the body superfluous. Smartphone apps push this logic even further and replace skills (thereby omitting long and slow forms of training): Whoever can use a smartphone correctly no longer needs to cultivate – to train – an internal sense of orientation or a good feel for changing weather. This replacement of skills by technology does not lead to a more embodied and sensually intense experiencing – rather, the opposite occurs. This leads me to the suspicion that machinic assemblage is indeed a very valid description for some prosthetic experiences, but in these cases it has a tendency towards phenomena of disembodiment as well.

This leads to my third uncertainty, regarding desiring machines. Indeed, I hesitate to describe technologies of disability in terms of Deleuzian desire, because, for me, the term registers too vaguely (as adequate as I find it for describing the internet) to describe prosthetic bodies. This is not to say that Shildrick is wrong about the openness of these bodies; rather, I think this openness is too complex to be approached through Deleuzian terms. To give an example, the so-called Rubber-Hand illusion (see Botvinick and Cohen) is broadly discussed in the phenomenology of embodiment. This illusion completely queers the so-called 'sense of ownership' for one's limbs and has also been used for an enactivist distinction between sense of ownership and sense of agency concerning one's limbs. A person is put into a sitting position at a table so that they cannot see their 'own' hand, but instead sees a rubber hand placed in a correspondingly appropriate spot on the table. The real hand and the rubber hand are then stimulated in identical ways; at a certain point, the person will comprehend and experience the rubber hand as their own. This experiment can even be radically extended: The synchronous stimulation of a person's body and of a dummy the person sees can even lead to the sense of ownership of a whole body, to out-of-body experiences and even to body-swap experiences (see Petkova and Ehrsson).

Similar experiences may be much more unsettling for non-prostheticised bodies than they are for people used to a prosthesis as part of everyday life. In addition, these findings defy the notion of a normative and integrated body-experience in a way that can help describe the queering of bodies enacted by the use of prostheses. But again: What counts is the logic of habituation, of getting a feel for a certain activity, of developing a skill for feeling what cannot be felt without making it an integral part of the phenomenology of one's embodied existence – and it would be difficult to call all this 'desire.' What is needed are less generic terms; and I think that the terms offered by phenomenology are appropriate, at least partially. Protentions and retentions, for example, are crucial for timing while skillfully maneuvering a wheelchair; prosthetic limbs help with everyday phenomena of 'Zuhandenheit;' voice prostheses 'afford' speaking in a special manner (that can require preliminary logopaedic training). These technologies do not just queer the integrity of a normative body (as, indeed, any technology does in a way); they do so in a very complex way, creating autonomous niches, action loops, skills, sensualities, feels, etc. of embodied interaction with technology and environment. My suspicion here is that terms like 'connectivity' and 'assemblage' – as helpful as they are – can also lead to an all-too-abstract approach omitting the complex phenomenologies involved in the skillful practices that constitute the functionality, aesthetics, and phenomenology involved in technologies of disability.

I conclude with one more thought focusing on the problems of the notion of assemblage when applied to the prostheses of human bodies. The brain, too, is a part of the body, and enhancements for the neurologically impaired seem to follow a similar logic of assemblage; but they raise different issues than those already addressed. Take the currently developed implants for effective decision-making as an example. Sam Deadwyler (see Hampson et al.) has studied the brain functions active in decision-making, and the way these functions may be disabled for people affected by Alzheimer's disease. A result of this research is an implant short-circuiting neural networks, which can both restore certain lost abilities in brains with impaired function and enhance the critical decision-making process in neurotypical brains. To be sure, this example of becoming-machine contrasts with the Deleuzian idea of becoming-minoritarian. Nevertheless, it is a clear fact that similar prostheses are still opposed to the ideology of a metaphysical self. In addition, these prostheses entail decisive post-human transformations, creating hybrids and machinic assemblages. Again, this is of course not what Deleuze had in mind when pondering these issues. His theories were written at a time when this sort of technology was inconceivable. But now, as it is being realized, I think, technologies of disability raise an important issue that risks becoming a blind spot in cultural studies.

This is not to question the insights Margrit Shildrick offers. The path she opens – in my eyes – leads in a good, perhaps the best, possible direction. As stated, I very much agree with most of her positions: Technologies of disability can, indeed, be a formidable catalyst for overcoming normative ideologies of a healthy and unified body and entail an excellent deconstruction and/or queering of bodies. My aim is to complement these arguments, rather than to contrast them; and here, my focus was dedicated to the drawbacks in reiterating certain notions proposed by Deleuze and Guattari. Much time has passed since Deleuze and Guattari proposed their theories about desire and assemblage; I think it might be time to let go of some of their notions, in order to fully explore those lessons they still *can* teach us. This is why I advocate for further discipline crossings that involve an enactivist phenomenology.

References

Botvinick, Matthew and Jonathan Cohen. "Rubber Hands 'Feel' Touch that Eyes See." *Nature* 391.6669 (1998). 756. Print.

Clark, Andy. *Natural Born Cyborgs: Minds, Technologies, and the Future of Human Intelligence.* New York and Oxford: Oxford University Press, 2003. Print.

Despret, Vinciane. "The Body We Care for: Figures of Anthropo-Zoo-Genesis." *Body & Society* 10.2–3 (2004). 111–134. Print.

Dreyfus, Hubert. *Being-in-the-World.* Cambridge, MA: MIT Press, 1991. Print.

—. *What Computers Still Can't Do.* Cambridge, MA: MIT Press, 1993.

Fuchs, Thomas and Hanneke De Jaegher. "Enactive Intersubjectivity: Participatory Sense-Making and Mutual Incorporation." *Phenomenology and the Cognitive Sciences* 8 (2009). 465–486. Print.

Gallagher, Shaun. *How the Body Shapes the Mind.* New York and Oxford: Oxford University Press, 2005. Print.

Gallagher, Shaun and Dan Zahavi. *The Phenomenological Mind.* New York: Routledge, 2008. Print.

Gibson, James Jerome. "The Theory of Affordances." *Perceiving, Acting, and Knowing – Toward an Ecological Psychology.* Eds. Robert Shaw and John Bransford. Hillsdale: Erlbaum, 1977. Print.

Hampson, Robert E., et al. "Facilitation and Restoration of Cognitive Function in Primate Prefrontal Cortex by a Neuroprosthesis that Utilizes Minicolumn-Specific Neural Firing." *Journal of Neural Engineering* 9.5 (2012). Web. 23 Oct. 2013. <http://iopscience.iop.org/1741-2552/9/5/056012/pdf/1741-2552_9_5_056012.pdf>.

Heidegger, Martin. *Sein und Zeit.* Niemeyer: Tübingen, 1993. Print.

Hughes, Joe. *Deleuze and the Genesis of Representation.* New York: Continuum, 2008. Print.

Husserl, Edmund. *Gesammelte Werke: Die Bernauer Manuskripte über das Zeitbewusstsein (1917-18).* Eds. Rudolf Bernet and Dieter Lohmar. Dortrecht: Kluver, 2001. Print.

Ingold, Tim. *The Perception of the Environment: Essays on Livelihood, Dwelling and Skill.* Abingdon: Routledge, 2011. Print.

Menary, Richard. *Radical Enactivism: Intentionality, Phenomenology, and Narrative (Focus on the Philosophy of Daniel D. Hutto).* Amsterdam and Philadelphia: John Benjamins, 2006. Print.

Petkova, H Valeria I. and Henrik Ehrsson. "If I Were You: Perceptual Illusion of Body Swapping." PLoS One 3.12 (2008). Web. 23 Oct. 2013. <http://www.plosone.org/article/info%3Adoi%2F10.1371%2Fjournal.pone.0003832>.

Pfeifer, Rolf and Josh Bongard. *How the Body Shapes the Way We Think: A New View of Intelligence*. Cambridge, MA: MIT Press, 2007. Print.

O'Regan, J. Kevin, Eric Myin and Alva Noë. "Skill, Corporality and Alerting Capacity in an Account of Sensory Consciousness." *Progress in Brain Research* 150 (2005). 55-68. Print.

Thompson, Evan. *Mind in Life: Biology, Phenomenology and the Sciences of Mind*. Cambridge, MA: Harvard University Press, 2007. Print.

Varela, Francisco J., Evan Thompson and Eleanor Rosch. *The Embodied Mind: Cognitive Science and Human Experience*. Cambridge, MA: MIT Press, 1991. Print.

Moritz Ingwersen

CYBERN*ETHICS:* THINKING BODIES AND BOUNDARIES THROUGH SCIENCE

This response to Margrit Shildrick aims to link critical disability studies to a paradigm shift in the natural sciences in the attempt to reveal an analogy regarding the ways in which both disciplines come to problematize the notion of boundaries and closure. Where Shildrick speaks of bodies, the physicist may speak of systems. Key insights in contemporary physics – as well as chemistry and biology – arise from the recognition that closed, self-contained systems are an idealization. While classical Newtonian physics rests on the assumption that physical entities can be observed in isolation from the energetic flow of their environment, 20th century science, from quantum mechanics to non-equilibrium thermodynamics and epigenetics, reveals a fundamental inseparability of system and environment.[6] Following the biologist and founder of general systems theory Ludwig von Bertalanffy, this shift corresponds to the increasing tendency to view living organisms as thermodynamically open systems. As he explains: "An open system is defined as a system in exchange of matter with its environment, presenting import and export, building-up and breaking-down of its material components. Up to comparatively recent times physical chemistry, in kinetics and thermodynamics, was restricted to closed systems; the theory of open systems is relatively new and leaves many problems unsolved" (141). Prodded by scientists trained in the wake of systems theory and quantum physics, walls, skins, edges, and membranes have become permeable and fuzzy, and some of the most interesting and complex phenomena are

---

6 | For an insightful problematization of the distinction between system and environment within the discourse of quantum mechanics, see Karen Barad's *Meeting the Universe Halfway: Quantum Physics and the Entanglement of Matter and Meaning* (153-161). One lesson she draws from the writings of quantum physics pioneer Niels Bohr is the fundamentality of "differential material embodiment (and not merely of humans), not in the sense of the conscious subjective experience of the individual human subject but in terms of different material configurations of ontological bodies and boundaries" (155). As an immediate follow-up to a reference of analogous concerns in postcolonial, feminist, queer, and disability studies she quotes physics Nobel laureate Richard Feynman on the visual construction of boundaries: "What is the outline? The outline is only the edge difference between light and dark or one color and another. It is not something definite. It is not, believe it or not, that every object has a line around it! There is no such line. It is only in our own psychological makeup that there is a line" (Feynman cited in Barad 156).

described with predominant attention to the precarious conditions at thresholds and boundaries.[7] As Manuel DeLanda elaborates:

"The last thirty years have witnessed a [...] paradigm shift in scientific research. In particular, a centuries-old devotion to 'conservative systems' (physical systems that, for all purposes, are isolated from their surroundings) is giving way to the realization that most systems in nature are subject to flows of matter and energy that continuously move through them. This apparently simple paradigm shift is, in turn, allowing us to discern phenomena that, a few decades ago, were, if they were noticed at all, dismissed as anomalies." (129)

Accompanying this paradigm shift in modern science is a change in focus from the system's interior towards its edges, from its essence to its conditions of transition and transformation: "Ask not what a body *is* but what a body can *do*," writes Shildrick paraphrasing Gilles Deleuze and Félix Guattari ("Border Crossings" 144). In *A Thousand Plateaus* they translate this interrogation of bodies in flux into a problematization of affect as the fundamental parameter of transcorporeal attachment.[8] Arguably, Shildrick's reading of Deleuze and Guattari encourages the suspicion that the dominant contemporary notions of subjectivity are still too heavily invested in the problematic heritage of a Newtonian worldview. In this vein, the tendency to view disability not only as an essential characteristic independent of its social and physical environment, but moreover as an intrinsic deficiency in need of rehabilitation, harkens back to a more than 300-year-old privileging of ideal bodies, closed systems, and external observers. Yet, cognate to a scientific mindset in which systems in a non-static equilibrium were dismissed as anomalies (see DeLanda), "[t]he modernist myth of the norm of 'bodily perfection,'" as Rosi Braidotti and Griet Groets note, is "little more than a hostile imposition upon necessarily fluctuating organisms" (165). This is, of course, not to say that Newtonian physics and liberal humanism must be done away with altogether, but rather that some of their tacit

---

7 | In particular, consider the 'observer effect' in the Copenhagen Interpretation of quantum mechanics, Ilya Prigogine's Nobel Prize in chemistry (1977) for his research in non-equilibrium thermodynamics and the introduction of "dissipative structures" in his seminal book *Order Out Of Chaos* (1984), and the nomination of Adrian Bird, Howard Cedar and Aharon Razin for the Nobel Prize in medicine (2013) for their research in epigenetics on environmental effects on DNA methylation.

8 | See Deleuze and Guattari in *A Thousand Plateaus*: "We know nothing about a body until we know what it can do, in other words what its affects are, how they can or cannot enter into composition with other affects, with the affects of another body, either to destroy that body or to be destroyed by it, either to exchange actions and passions with it or join with it in composing a more powerful body" (284).

assumptions need to be reconsidered and their claim to universality curtailed. In a way then, what quantum mechanics and complexity theory are to physics, recent interventions on behalf of 'the posthuman' are to modern subjectivity. Anchored in a profound incredulity towards the "ontological hygiene of the humanist subject" (Graham 12), articulations of posthumanist subjectivity – among which Shildrick's work should be included – are moreover frequently quite explicit in their indebtedness to the sciences, in particular to the field of cybernetics (see, for instance, the work of Katherine Hayles).

Shildrick's consideration of prosthetic corporeality rests on the premise that bodies are always already diversified, that their boundaries are permeable, and that they cannot be separated from the material and energetic flows that suffuse their environments. A precedent for this line of thinking can be found in first-generation cybernetics spearheaded by Norbert Wiener, a discourse whose most "disturbing and potentially revolutionary" implication might have been "the idea that the boundaries of the human subject are constructed rather than given," as Katherine Hayles puts it in her widely received study *How We Became Posthuman* (84). By shifting the focus from a system's (organic or inorganic) internal mechanics to its modes of communication and exchange with other systems, cyberneticists describe the world not in the search for essences but instead point at the productivity of relations and feedback channels. Their most powerful tool, as Hayles reminds us (see 91 and 93), is analogy and their inherent mode of inquiry is the problematization of a boundary, a border crossing.

Echoing the subtitle of Wiener's foundational book *Cybernetics*, Shildrick's account of prosthetic embodiment explores the "fusions of animal and machine" ("Border Crossings" 139) with an emphasis on intercommunication and what the new-materialist political theorist Jane Bennett might call the "material vibrancy" at the threshold between organic and inorganic surfaces (Bennett xiii). The standard conception of prostheses, Shildrick notes, is that of a "concordant reparation – the making 'whole' of the disabled person" ("Border Crossings" 142). If, however, the closure associated with the idealized whole body is itself recognized as fictitious and all corporeality, as Shildrick notes elsewhere, "is inherently leaky, uncontained, and uncontainable" ("Bioethics" 7), her inversion that "we are all always already prosthetic" characterizes selfhood as a state in flux ("Border Crossings" 140).

Categorical distinctions between disability and non-disability are often drawn in terms of the degree of a person's independence and autonomy, in other words they are measured in degrees of closure. Drawing insights from Barbara Gibson's therapeutic practice with wheelchair and gastric feeding tube users, Shildrick offers, in turn, the possibility to conceptualize corporeality in terms of degrees of connectivity and linkage and she seems to suggest the obsolescence of the essentialized separation between physical autonomy and the need for assistance. This move allows us to reformulate the underlying chorus of what is usually known as the 'social model of disability' as follows: Let us not ask about people's essentialized lack of autonomy and self-sufficiency, but let us instead uncover the ways in which their channels of connection with their environment are socially limited or obstructed. By thus making disability a matter of communication between subject and surroundings we can begin to question the channel: How are stairs more jammed than ramps? To what types of perturbations are wheelchairs more susceptible than shoe soles? Can we envision a mode of dealing with disruptions that is not rehabilitative and seeking to restore unambiguity, but instead, one that is creative, embracing the noise that inevitably occupies the channel?

Consider the 'telephone game' popular among children, where the distortion of the message becomes a source of delight and players revel in its unforeseen transformations. It is along these lines that I understand Shildrick's Deleuzian reading of prosthetic embodiment when she speaks in favor of moving from "the givenness of being to the fluidity of becoming" ("Border Crossings" 145). The demarcation of prosthetic, deaf or cognitively divergent embodiment against the imaginary unity considered nondisabled can consequently be reviewed as a normalizing reduction of the multiplicities of potential interactions between what seems to lie inside and what seems to lie outside of the skin. While Shildrick limits her analysis to "crossings between human, animal and machine" (ibid.), let me draw out the environmental extension of embodiment implicit in her argument by considering a performance by autism rights activist Amanda Baggs.

Baggs gained the attention of major media outlets such as Wired Magazine and CNN for an 8-minute video clip titled "In My Language" that she released on Youtube in 2007. In the first part of the clip we see her rocking back and forth, caressing the knob of a drawer, rubbing her fingers on a computer keyboard, burying her face in the pages of a book, and batting a swinging necklace with her hand. Viewers will likely recall behavior patterns that have come to be associated with the autism spectrum, and some might find themselves sympathizing with the CNN journalist who visited Baggs for an interview in 2007 and who recounts "having a hard time discerning whether she even knows I am there" (Gajilan n.pag.). Accompanied by a continuous two-tone humming, Baggs' performance has the effect on the neurotypical viewer of not only estrangement, but also the potentially reassuring retreat into familiar categories of proper and improper subjectivity. This person, one is inclined to reassert, is disabled; her movements appear random or compulsory, and from this seeming vacuity the liberal humanist might end up extrapolating the absence of a rational self. All the more challenging it is to the viewer when, in the second part of the video, instead of a human voice we hear an artificial voice synthesizer translate Baggs' typing into speech. Against the backdrop of Baggs' erratic movements, the coupling of a nonhuman voice and a very articulate message will provoke a rupture in some neurotypical viewers' expectations.

Initial reactions will likely include the suspicion that the sentences introduced in subtitles as 'A Translation' do not stem from the same self that previously seemed to elicit the labels 'atrophic' or 'disabled.'[9] If this disbelief can be dispelled, viewers are invited to disroot their customary (potentially ableist) perspective and open their conceptual frameworks to a powerful alternative vision of selfhood. Her "native language," Baggs explains, "is not about designing words or even visual symbols for people to interpret. It is about being in constant conversation with every aspect of [her] environment reacting physically to all parts of [her] surroundings" (Baggs). Rather than circumscribing a Cartesian interiority, Baggs' language is expressive of a subjectivity that subsists in relationality. In an even more radical way than the human-machine assemblages considered by Shildrick, Baggs demonstrates what Shildrick calls the opening and "immersion of the singular human 'I' in its environmental context of multiple complex relations" (Shildrick, "Border Crossings" 142). When Baggs flaps her hands in resonance with an undulating flag outside her window, a suffusion of self and environment occurs that recalls a fever sensation related by Wiener in his autobiography and framed by Hayles as an allegorical founding moment of cybernetics. He writes: "It was impossible for me to distinguish among my pain and difficulty in breathing, the flapping of the window curtain, and certain as yet unresolved parts of the potential problem on which I was working" (Wiener cited in Hayles 92). Perceptively recognized by Hayles as a "boundary problem" (Hayles 93), Wiener's experience, which may or may not have lead to a mathematical epiphany, may serve as a reminder of the link between transcorporeality and cybernetics, and highlight the historical lineage of a paradigm shift from closed to open systems and embodied subjects. Unlike the purely cognitive self envisioned by

---

9 | In fact, Baggs' video provoked scorn and accusations of fraud from numerous bloggers associated with the autism community doubting the veracity of her diagnosis. A prolific blogger herself, Baggs has since responded posting copies of her medical case history on her blog *Ballastexistenz* and persists as a very outspoken and articulate commentator on issues relating to the lives of people with disabilities. These controversies regarding the legitimacy of her presence in a political debate over minority identity and 'proper' representation testify to a humanist bias of activists who wish to police and regulate what counts as authentic and containable expression of selfhood. Furthermore, Baggs' performance seems to evoke a Cartesian unease about the coupling of a purportedly dysfunctional body with profound intellectual reflection. Her use of a speech synthesizer heightens the challenge to notions of selfhood anchored in the Western tradition which, as Jacques Derrida has shown in *Of Grammatology*, suggests a mapping of voice and presence.

Descartes as a "thing that doubts, understands, affirms, denies, wants, refuses, and [...] imagines" (Descartes 24), Baggs illustrates an affective interaction with her environment that celebrates an opening of corporeal interfaces to noise and creative interferences. Just as the linkage to a technological appendage, in Shildrick's words, opens up "transformative possibilities of becoming other along multiple lines of flight" for Gibson's clients (Shildrick, "Border Crossings" 145), Baggs' bodily conversation with the objects surrounding her effectively deterritorializes habitual patterns of interaction. The computer keyboard, the door handle, the flag, or the book are not subordinated to the appropriate socialized imperatives, but rather are defamiliarized as vibrant surfaces for immediate sensorial contact. Employing her senses to explore the back of her hand, a spinning top, a towel, a pen, and the camera lens (in this order), Baggs insists: "I smell things. I listen to things. I feel things. I taste things. I look at things. It is not enough to look and listen and taste and smell and feel, I have to do those to the right things [...] or else people doubt that I am a thinking being" (Baggs). Cognate with Shildrick, Baggs is criticizing an idea of personhood anchored in the humanist tradition which curtails, reduces, and contains the multiplicities of human embodiment:

"Ironically the way that I move when responding to everything around me is described as 'being in a world of my own' whereas if I interact with a much more limited set of responses and only react to a much more limited part of my surroundings people claim that I am 'opening up to true interaction with the world'" (ibid.).

Baggs is, in fact, diagnosing her diagnosers with a severe case of Newtonianism where only a closed system is a good system and noise needs to be shut out. Her criticism of the reductionist consensus about consciousness and responsivity inadvertently echoes affect theorist and Deleuze translator Brian Massumi who, illustrating the material excess that characterizes the preconscious formation of affect, comes to the conclusion that "[w]ill and consciousness are *subtractive*. They are *limitative, derived functions* that reduce a complexity too rich to be functionally expressed" (29). Neither Baggs' nor Shildrick's account presents the motor behind transgressive corporeality as a unilateral consciousness or will, but rather as the reciprocal exchange of material forces and affects. In the work of Deleuze and Guattari, which provides the conceptual infrastructure to Shildrick's argument, a theorization of affect directly derives from a reading of Spinoza's *Ethics*; affect thus becomes the key to ethics.[10]

---

10 | See Deleuze's *Spinoza: Practical Philosophy* (1988) and "On Spinoza."

Indeed, what binds recent intersections between Deleuzian scholarship and critical disability studies[11] is the demand for a "radical reconfiguration of bioethical thought" (Shildrick, "Bioethics" 4) which takes into account the affective relays between bodies and their organic as well as inorganic supplements. Contained in this line of thinking is a radical disavowal of the divisions between self|other, subject|environment, or whole|fragmented that have become so ubiquitous in demarcations of disability. "So what then," asks Braidotti, whose work in many ways resonates with Shildrick's project, "What if the subject is 'trans' or in transit, that is to say no longer one, whole, unified and in control, but rather fluid in process and hybrid? What are the ethical and political implications of a non-unitary vision of the human subject?" (Braidotti, *Transpositions* 9). These questions must be understood in direct response to a Cartesian ideology whose legacy, in philosophy as much as in the natural sciences, as science philosopher Michel Serres notes, "excludes the compound, the chimera that consists of disjoint parts, pieced together without rhyme or reason, in which adjacent elements seem to exist in bad neighborship and things connect that do not quite fit together [...] equally in view of their edges" (Serres 53; translation by author).

Mirroring Shildrick's benign integration of nonhuman components such as the wheelchair, the ventilator, the gastronomy tube or the voice synthesizer, Jane Bennett also aims at a more inclusive conception of subjectivity by drawing attention to our affective relationship with objects. She likewise speaks of an "ethical task [...] to cultivate the ability to discern nonhuman vitality, to become perpetually open to it" (Bennett 14), which, she hopes, will "inspire a greater sense of the extent to which all bodies are kin in the sense of inextricably enmeshed in a dense network of relations" (13).[12] Advocating the levelling of hierarchies and the emphasis on exchange between the (human) subject and its (non/human) environment, Shildrick, like Braidotti and Bennett, not only revokes the Enlightenment anthropocentrism that helped shape a humanist regime of normalcy, but she moreover imbricates the study of trans-subjective conduct – ethics – with the study of feedback relations – cybernetics. To capture this link I would like to propose a neologism that is commonly

---

11 | See, for instance, the work of Braidotti, in particular, *The Posthuman* (2013) and *Transpositions: On Nomadic Ethics* (2006), Patricia MacCormack's *Posthuman Ethics* (2012), or Dan Goodley, Rebecca Lawthom, and Katherine Runswick Cole's "Posthuman Disability Studies" (2014).

12 | It is not difficult to detect Bennett's indebtedness to the work of Bruno Latour who in *We Have Never Been Modern* (1991) uncovers the neglected investment of Western Modernity in hybridization and networks of human and nonhuman actors.

credited to Heinz von Förster: cyber*nethics*.[13] As the chronicler of the Macy conferences (the ground zero of cybernetics, held between 1946-1953), Förster was one of the earliest commentators on Wiener's treatise on self-regulating machines. On this basis he spent his life outlining the stakes of what he called a 'second-order cybernetics' which, in extension of Wiener's work on self-control mechanisms (considered first-order cybernetics) and in support of Bertalanffy's biological systems theory, marries informational closure with thermodynamic openness as a viable model to describe interactions between self-reflexive human observers and their environment (see "Cybernetics of Cybernetics"). From the recognition that the human system is itself engaged in a perpetual reorganization of its faculties as it is caught up in a continuous feedback loop with its environment, Förster distils an ethical imperative: "Act always so as to increase the number of choices" ("Ethics" 227). Freedom and autonomy for Förster result only when potential channels of interaction are multiplied and not regulated and normalized; when, confronted with new input, unpredictability, inventiveness and undecidability are encouraged; and when human agents recognize their energetic openness instead of idealizing closure. In other words, his code of conduct follows an imperative to connect. Although it functions as little more than a recurring rhetorical punchline in his writings, Förster's 'cyber*nethics*' might serve as an anchor for the transformation of bioethical thought envisioned by Shildrick. Both frameworks, while entering the field from different disciplinary angles, ultimately aim at the appreciation of transgressive corporeality not as a marker of pathology, but as a mode of being that can be instructive in reconsidering the customary perception of the relationship between embodied agents and the world.

References

Baggs, Amanda. "In My Language" (Video). 2007. Web. 18 Nov 2013. <http://www.youtube.com/watch?v=JnylM1hI2jc>.

Barad, Karen. *Meeting the Universe Halfway: Quantum Physics and the Entanglement of Matter and Meaning*. Durham and London: Duke University Press, 2007. Print.

Bennet, Jane. *Vibrant Matter: A Political Ecology of Things*. Durham and London: Duke University Press, 2010. Print.

Bertalanffy, Ludwig von. *General Systems Theory: Foundations, Developments, Applications*. Revised Edition. New York: George Braziller, 1973. Print.

Braidotti, Rosi. *The Posthuman*. Cambridge: Polity Press, 2013. Print.

—. *Transpositions: On Nomadic Ethics*. Cambridge: Polity Press, 2006. Print.

---

13 | See especially Förster's *KybernEthik* (1993) and "Ethics and Second-Order Cybernetics" (2003).

Braidotti, Rosi and Griet Groets. "Nomadology and Subjectivity: Deleuze, Guattari and Critical Disability Studies." *Disability and Social Theory: New Developments and Directions*. Eds. Dan Goodley, Bill Hughes, and Lennard Davis. New York: Palgrave Macmillan, 2012. 161-178. Print.

DeLanda, Manuel. "Nonorganic Life." *Incorporations*. Eds. Jonathan Crary and Sandford Kwinter. Cambridge: Zone Books, 1992. 129-167. Print.

Deleuze, Gilles and Félix Guattari. *A Thousand Plateaus: Capitalism and Schizophrenia*. Trans. Brian Massumi. London and New York: Continuum, 2004. Print.

Deleuze, Gilles. *Spinoza: Practical Philosophy*. San Francisco: City Light Books, 1988. Print.

—. «On Spinoza.» *Lectures by Gilles Deleuze*. Trans. Unknown. Web. 15 April 2014. <http://deleuzelectures.blogspot.de/2007/02/on-spinoza.html>.

Derrida, Jacques. *Of Grammatology*. Trans. Gayatri Spivak. Baltimore and London: The John Hopkins University Press, 1997. Print.

Descartes, René. *Meditations on First Philosophy*. Ed. John Cottingham. Cambridge: Cambridge University Press, 1996. Print.

Förster, Heinz von. *KybernEthik*. Berlin: Merve Verlag, 1993. Print.

—. "Ethics and Second-Order Cybernetics." *Understanding Understanding: Essays on Cybernetics and Cognition*. New York: Springer, 2003. 287-304. Print.

—. "Cybernetics of Cybernetics." *Understanding Understanding: Essays on Cybernetics and Cognition*. New York: Springer, 2003. 283-286. Print.

Gajilan, A. Chris. "Living with Autism in a World made for Others." CNN. 2007. Web. 18 Nov 2013. <http://www.cnn.com/2007/HEALTH/02/21/autism.amanda/>.

Goodley, Dan, Rebecca Lawthom and Katherine Runswick Cole. "Posthuman Disability Studies." *Subjectivity* 7.4 (2014): 342-361. Print.

Graham, Elaine L. *Representations of the Post/Human: Monsters, Aliens and Others in Popular Culture*. Manchester: Manchester University Press, 2002. Print.

Hayles, Katherine N. *How We Became Posthuman: Virtual Bodies in Cybernetics, Literature, and Informatics*. Chicago and London: The University of Chicago Press, 1999. Print.

Latour, Bruno. *We Have Never Been Modern*. Trans. Catherine Porter. Cambridge: Harvard University Press, 1993. Print.

MacCormack, Patricia. *Posthuman Ethics*. Farnham and Burlington: Ashgate, 2012. Print.

Massumi, Brian. *Parables for the Virtual: Movement, Affect, Sensation*. Durham and London: Duke University Press, 2002. Print.

Prigogine, Ilya and Isabelle Stengers. *Order out of Chaos: Man's New Dialogue with Nature*. New York: Bantam Books, 1984. Print.

Serres, Michel. *Die Nordwest-Passage.* Trans. Michael Bischoff. Berlin: Merve Verlag, 1994. Print.

Shildrick, Margrit. "Border Crossings: The Technologies of Disability and Desire." This volume. 137-151. Print.

—. "Beyond the Body of Bioethics: Challenging the Conventions." *Ethics of the Body: Postconventional Challenges.* Eds. Margrit Shildrick and Roxanne Mykitiuk. Cambridge: MIT Press, 2005. 1-26. Print.

Wiener, Norbert. *Cybernetics: Or Control and Communication in the Animal and the Machine.* Cambridge: MIT Press, 1985 (1948). Print.

Superhumans-Parahumans

Disability and Hightech in Competitive Sports[1]

Karin Harrasser

The visual language of the Paralympic Games 2012 provides a good point of departure to examine how public perception of disability in sports and, perhaps of impairment in general, has changed in recent years. The Paralympics in London were the biggest games of their kind with the greatest media coverage up until that point and 4,237 competing athletes from 146 nations. Already during the preliminaries of this event, spectacular pictures were brought to the public's attention through campaigns such as "Meet the Superhumans," which was the widest-ranging campaign ever launched by Channel 4, a private TV company based in Britain.

Image: Campaign Poster "Meet the Superhumans," Channel 4, 2012 [2]

---

1 | This article is based on a translation from German into English by Eleana Vaja.

2 | Source: http://leidmedien.de/sprache-kultur-und-politik/sport-analyse/paralympics-london-sotschi/. Accessed September 22, 2016.

The poster series and television commercial advertises the Paralympics and, naturally, Channel 4's coverage of it. The short film is driven by the song "Harder Than You Think" by *Public Enemy*. It focuses on the training activities of eight athletes from the United Kingdom and presents a narrative of how impairment can be overcome through self-discipline. The visual language of the spot connects dramas of accidents and war injury with elements taken from action movie and video clip aesthetics. For congenitally disabled athletes, who have no dramatic incident to narrate, images of sonograms and shocked mothers are inserted. The final scene depicts the group of athletes as a league of superheroes. All of them look straight into the camera, displaying a body language of defiance.

Although these elements are well known, the staging of disability in this specific combination is relatively new. Its impact on disability sports and disability politics is difficult to estimate. On the one hand, the spot highlights the professionalization of disabled athletes. Echoing Oscar Pistorius' demand to participate in the 2008 Summer Olympic Games, these athletes demonstrate strength and will power. This is what is written in their faces. The term "superhumans," as used in the campaign, however, is ambivalent. One trajectory of the visual argument is that impairment, the biological 'deficiency,' *enables* these bodies to be enhanced by the latest developments in technology, thus transforming them into "humans 2.0," a term used to advertise a conference on prosthetics and robotics at the MIT Media Lab in 2010. Hugh Herr, one of the organizers, uses it in a quite straightforward manner to connect with posthumanist discourses.[3]

Secondly and probably more importantly, the video clip promotes motifs of will, self-conquest, and self-mastery. Peter Sloterdijk's considerations on "crip-anthropology" echo through these images (see Sloterdijk 40-60). By examining cases from the Weimar Republic, Sloterdijk reconstructs a self-concept of disabled persons that he calls "existentialism of defiance." The 'heroes' of his narrative not only integrate adversities of life as part of the game, they also consider these as sources of self-enhancement. A historically striking example Sloterdijk provides is Hans Würtz's 1932 book *Zerbrecht die Krücken: Krüppelprobleme der Menschheit* [*Smash the Crutches: Cripple Problems of Humankind*]. Würtz was a pioneer in pedagogy for disabled people in his time. This book encompasses an extensive register of over 472 "known invalids and deformed people," a collection of the depiction of "cripples" in art (2,502 examples), an annotated bibliography on *belle-lettres* and "cripples" (Würtz 779), as well as information on "cripples" in myths, fairy tales, and proverbs. Würtz's downfall resulted from mentioning Joseph Goebbels club foot (88). In spite of his being put into the rather upscale category of "revolutionary politicians,"

---

3 | See the website of the *h2.0* conference (http://h20.media.mit.edu/).

Goebbels did not appreciate this impairment-based classification at all and thus could not be convinced of the Würtzian concept. The book was banned, and Würtz left Germany.

Würtz's concept, despite its awkward terminology, positions itself against an ideology of exclusion of differently abled people. In fact, it views and depicts "cripples" as initiators of cultural evolution. The slogan "Meet the Superhumans: Forget Everything You Thought You Knew About Humans" in certain ways echoes Würtz's concept, which addressed and was aimed at motivating disabled veterans. "The will is the one true prosthesis" Würtz claimed in one of his pamphlets for veterans. Of course, from a contemporary perspective this guiding idea is highly questionable. Yet, it resonates well with the new spot. What is striking, in any case, is how the same combination of two narratives occurs in both accounts: impaired bodies as sources of technological enhancement and the metaphysics of will, and overcoming of adversities. How could a concept of self-discipline resulting from the devastations of war and a general crisis of European subjectivity nowadays be reanimated and recombined with technophilic futurism?

THE X-MEN'S POLITICS OF PHYSICAL DIFFERENCE

The visualization of the Paralympic athletes as a league of superheroes triggers images of another famous group of "disabled" superheroes: The X-Men (who of course include quite a number of X-Women).[4] The X-Men comic books were created by Stan Lee and Jack Kirby in 1963. Since 2000, five popular movies about the league and another two with the character of Wolverine at the center of the narration have been published. These movies deal in a multi-faceted way with issues of otherness, biopolitics, normalism, and with phantasies of superiority: The protagonists are mutants whose X-Gene makes them social outsiders. They possess wings, wolves' claws, or lions' manes, they can release storms, and have telepathic or magnetic abilities. As the mutation of one of the protagonists manifests while he is imprisoned in a Nazi concentration camp, it is evident that we should understand these movies as a critical commentary on the treatment, or in the worst case, on the extermination of minorities. The movies address two generic ways of handling minority status (see X-Men: First Class). One group, led by the character Magneto, regards itself as an evolutionarily superior "species" and relies on identity politics, the idea that (biological) otherness means physical superiority, and recodes past experiences of suppression as moral superiority. Charles Xavier, a Holocaust survivor, is the leader of the second group, whose strategy aims at assimilation or normalization:

---

4 | Regarding otherness and disability in the X-Men movies, see Harrasser and Lutter.

Young mutants, mainly adolescents, are taught to apply their talents for the benefit of society at the 'Xavier's School for Gifted Youngsters.' Simultaneously, they are trained to protect themselves against Magneto's people by channeling their powers as efficiently as possible towards the enemy. Society is ambivalent with regard to the mutants: Politics oscillate between political inclusion (the attempt to make use of the X-Men's power) and physical violence, between fear of otherness and fascination with 'the other.'

The plot of the third X-Men movie (*X-Men: The Last Stand*) revolves around a drug that reverses the mutation. It has been developed by the father of the mutant Angel and as part of the plot the biopolitical strategies of the drug's application are discussed and juxtaposed. Both the compulsory administering of the drug and a policed intake on a voluntary basis are considered issues of political controversy. The movie does not give a simple answer to this question. Angel decides not to take the drug and to keep his wings, while Rogue, a fellow mutant who is unable to touch other beings without killing them, in the end decides to take it.

A large variety of strategies to deal with physical difference is presented in the X-Men series, all of them problematizing individual happiness, identity conflicts within the group of mutants, the historicity of experienced violence, and finally scientific expertise as a foundation for decision-making. The movie poses questions that are discussed in postcolonial, gender, and disability studies today, and which become essential with regard to the example of the "Superhumans" in the Paralympics trailer: What role does bodily otherness play with regard to participation in political and social institutions? Is 'identity' an adequate foundation for political agency? How are otherness and difference to be understood in the context of normative and normalizing regulations?[5] Which models of agency are feasible and imaginable beyond a Kantian conception of the subject as autonomous and 'abled?' And, how does the notion of otherness change in the context of the growing possibilities presented by medical-technical procedures?

This issue is literally embodied by the character of Wolverine. His mutation is characterized by his ability to heal extremely quickly, an ability that makes him an attractive object of investigation for military research. Due to his self-healing powers – the claws can cut through flesh and skin but both heal immediately – he is experimentally and involuntarily equipped with lethal claws to be released in a fight. In order to escape from military research and instrumentalization, Wolverine withdraws from human contact as far as possible. However, he cannot flee from his past which, as it is implanted in his body, haunts him. As a result of his irascibility (presumably a relic of the forced surgery) he is not in full control of his fighting-claws. Both physical (and social)

---

5 | On the shift from normative/disciplinary to normalizing regulations, see Krause.

disability and physical superiority are placed in a fragile relation as a result of their technical incorporation.

FICTIONS OF EQUALITY AND THE MEANING OF TECHNOLOGY IN SPORTS

With these fictional and semi-fictional, rather spectacular images in mind we can reassess the Würtzian paradigm of self-mastery under technological conditions. How are ethics of self-mastery and technical enhancement related? The issue was discussed broadly with respect to South African runner Oscar Pistorius: Are disabled people who use state-of-the-art technologies still 'disabled' or are they 'superabled?' In the language of sport officials: Are prostheses to be seen as 'neutral' or rather as 'performance-enhancing?' In the language of the media: Is Pistorius a *wunderkind* or are his prostheses the actual wonder? When it comes to technology in sports, we are usually trapped in a pattern of arguments that considers technology (be it drugs, clothes, equipment, or prosthetic devices) to be 'barely acceptable' or 'no longer acceptable.' Can the swimsuit which imitates a shark's skin still be regarded as neutral or is it already performance-enhancing? How much engineering is allowed when it comes to running shoes? Which chemical substances maintain and provide the health of an athlete, and which should be considered doping?

The idea of the neutrality of technology becomes even more questionable when one thinks of sports such as skiing and Formula 1 racing. In fact, despite a certain mystification which sees the pilot as the key agent, motor sports has always been an arena where the engineers, the car, the speedway, and the weather conditions are the focus of interest. The equipment is shown, so to say, to be the *milieu* of the pilot, an environment which enables him to perform. One could therefore consider coaches and training facilities in other sports as such milieus. They demonstrate the 'technical' character of every other kind of training. The athlete is always an assemblage consisting of various ingredients: the body s/he is working on, the training team, the facilities, sports regulations. I therefore wish to bring the discussion surrounding Oscar Pistorius' Flex-Foot Cheetahs to a different realm by questioning the implicit presuppositions about body, performance, and technicality in competitive sports in relation to this prominent case. The Pistorius case illustrates how deeply the competitive body is an artifact, something fabricated, intertwined in social and technical networks, a 'construction' full of preconditions. This of course marks a contrast to the defining myth of sports based on the principal equality of bodies that are perfected by individual performance. The body in sports is a construction in a literal sense: culturally, materially, socially, and even biologically.

If we study Pistorius' childhood, we learn that his parents decided to surgically remove his dysplastic legs when he was very young. The motif behind this decision (and every following decision) was to enable Pistorius to grow up 'normally:' If a child learns to walk with prosthetic legs from early on, it will 'walk normally' compared to a child that, due to an impairment, cannot walk at all and instead learns how to use a wheelchair. Judging from Pistorius' statements, the family cultivated an ethics of competition. In his autobiography Pistorius recounts scenes in which he and his siblings arranged races the winner of which earned the bigger plate of food or more pocket money. Individual motivation and self-conquest are thus integral parts of Pistorius' value system. He relates to his body from within a set of values strongly attached to a protestant ethics of achievement. This is the topic of his tattoo, an inscription of 1 Corinthians 9:26-27: "Therefore I do not run like someone running aimlessly; I do not fight like a boxer beating the air. No, I strike a blow to my body and make it my slave so that after I have preached to others, I myself will not be disqualified for the prize." The pride he takes in self-discipline and in suffering in the line of duty are framed by the doctrine of salvation. One's own accomplishment is essential for this ethos. But how do the performance-enhancing character of the prostheses and the ethos of self-conquest and fairness go together? Through the discussion of Pistorius' case rings the suspicion that he behaves unfairly, that he extracts advantages from his disability. Taking his ethos seriously, and not simply as a clever way of self-marketing, it is necessary to take a closer look at the threshold between 'permitted self-technologies,' which are those that legitimately form the athlete's body and are grounded in this very ethics, and those that are only partly permitted and often seen as 'external technologies.' With increasing technological possibilities, the line between these domains becomes more and more blurry. It is not the dilemma of deciding between a natural versus a technified body that troubles the debate, but the fact that every body in sports is technical in some sense.

The scientific studies on the Pistorius case dealt exclusively with the question of the possible 'advantages' of running with the blades. As the Cheetahs are not patterned on the human leg but, as the name implies, on the legs of cheetahs, the question arose whether the cheetah-like motion is a) comparable to the human way of running, b) tantamount or c) even superior to it. Scientists tried to solve the case through measurements made in high-tech laboratories, which added even more technology to the assemblage. The first study by the International Association of Athletics Federation (IAAF) on the case, commissioned by Gert-Peter Brüggemann, stated that the prostheses' suspension benefits the athlete's performance (see Brüggemann et al.). The study in favor of Pistorius' plea argued that although the Cheetahs lead to a different running style, it might not automatically be a better one. The core of the latter argument is based on the acceleration force of the bouncy prostheses: At the beginning of a race they are rather slow. They evolve their marvelous acceleration skills only in the course of the race. Brüggemann's first study only focused on this last sequence and did not take into account the acceleration time needed to achieve speed.

In 2008, the Court for Arbitration in Sport (CAS) in Lausanne allowed Pistorius to participate in the Olympic Games in Beijing, based on the argument of the second study. However, the verdict included the addendum that despite the fact that the performance-enhancing features of the prosthetic legs could not be verified, this issue was still regarded as unresolved. A strange result: No violation of the regulations could be attested to, but the fundamental question is still under discussion. Similar verdicts had already been announced. In 2009 Usain Bolt, for example, set the world record in sprint, wearing shoes uniquely designed for him. Again, no violation of the regulations could be attested to, but the fact that only top-ranking athletes have access to such high-tech products initiated many discussions about fairness in competitive sports. To further complicate this discussion, on the occasion of the Paralympics in 2012, Oscar Pistorius suffered a defeat in the 200-meter race. He was relegated to second place by the Brasilian sprinter Alan Oliviera, whose blades were higher than Pistorius'. Pistorius commented on Oliviera's victory in the following way: "It was not unfair, he stuck to the rules, but the fact is he has never been that fast before, not even close to it" (cited in "Pistorius verliert gegen Wunderstelzen;" translation by Eleana Vaja). Again, the same dilemma: Oliviera's prostheses are not unfair, but neither are they fair. What, then, are they? It seems that using sports terminology we are not able to address what is at stake here. Let me try some detours.

POSTHUMANIST SPECULATIONS

Some studies from sports science approach these multilayered problems by correlating legal (regulations), ethical (fairness, economic accessibility to technology), and physiological questions. They formulate questions traditionally dealt with in cultural studies and media studies: the entangledness of biology and technology, and the cultural codification of corporality. Brendan Burkett, Mike McNamee, and Wolfgang Poothast raise the question of the modalities of human running, and how 'disability' is to be understood in terms of competitive sports (see "Shifting Boundaries"). Interestingly, biomechanical research approximates the question of the status of 'the human' and of the cultural construction of the body. If the debate on the enhancing abilities of the blades is tackled, the demarcation between humans and machines on the one side, and humans and animals on the other side is simultaneously called into question – a prevailing issue in cultural theory situated within the scenario of the human as *Mängelwesen*, as 'deficient by nature' (an idea conceived already by Johann Gottfried Herder that was prominently advocated by Arnold Gehlen in the twentieth century). In this sense, Pistorius would be the master of successful 'technological' adaptation. He would be paradigmatic for all humans and their ongoing struggle for survival against specialized and brutal nature by technological means.

On the one hand, the Nietzschean *Übermensch* who overcomes the softly cultivated form of the 'humanist human' is knocking on our door. On the other hand – and this might be the really disturbing part of that discourse – some contributions in disability studies (Swartz and Watermeyer) call to attention to how such a perspective on people with disabilities puts them into a categorical system that might be devaluating, as it operates through categories such as 'not-human-anymore' or 'not-human yet,' with the 'human' as the unquestioned center. I want to understand categorization in its original Greek sense: an accusation that entails social consequences. Images as a way of representing disability are a means of drawing the line to the 'non-human,' for instance through the decomposition of the human figure or, as in the case of Pistorius, by showing him as predator-like and ready to 'hunt.' With this discussion we enter the dangerous terrain of the monstrous that is guarded by the 'non-thinking animal' on the one side of the border, and the *Übermensch*, the robots and cyborgs, on the other. Along with Pistorius' blades, which are technically quite simple, well-built mechanical cat-stilts, we risk either under- or overestimating what is commonly understood as 'human.' This territory requires careful and deliberate intellectual exploration, and an encapsulation of all presuppositions about animals, humans, and machines.

In their article "Cyborg Anxiety," Leslie Swartz and Brian Watermeyer place Pistorius' case within a posthumanist discourse, which argues that the territory of the "exclusively human" is shrinking. Posthumanist theory deals with the emancipatory revaluation of various modes of existences and forms of life that do not conform to the normative ideal of an autonomous, self-transparent, reflexive, and conscious thinking subject, namely the 'humanist human.' It takes the side of modes of existences and agents which, when measured against these norms, easily appear to be 'deficient' and have therefore been excluded from political and societal participation. This is a political promise of inclusion, but it should be handled with care as it bears the danger of a loss of rights: As long as positive and negative rights are tied to humanness and personhood, it is extraordinarily dangerous to not be able to claim this status for oneself.

The strategy of Pistorius and Herr is to reach out for a posthuman that is 'superhuman.' This strategy, so to say, includes the cultivation of one *ability* that is considered to be specific to the human in many philosophical discourses: to overcome the given and to leave all obstacles behind. The price they pay for this leap into a techno-evolutionist future is high, both individually and socially. The superhuman individual has to achieve complete self-mastery, abolish every weakness, and embrace competition as the driving force of the social. Socially and culturally the price is equally high: Whoever establishes the superman as an ideal affirms the concept of the human as a *Mängelwesen* (deficient by nature) and, more importantly in pragmatic terms, supports a neoliberal ideology of continuous self-improvement that pushes individuals to the limits of their biological and cognitive possibilities.

SPORTS REGULATION AND FAIRNESS

How do regulatory authorities in sport navigate through this minefield? They evidently know that Pistorius' case is only the tip of the iceberg. They struggle to maintain the threshold between genuine individual performance and technological, artificial performance. Also, quite often, fear of losing the 'purity' of sports is articulated. The whole idea of a purity of sports is based on the fiction of an equality of all bodies, the myth that every body can be virtuously perfected by training, but should not be spoiled by technology. Elio Locatelly, Members Service Department (MSD) director at IAAF, puts it like this: The Pistorius case "affects the purity of sport. The next step will be another device where people can fly with something on their back" (cited in Longman). Bluntly put, posthumanists would love to see flying athletes; for them, technology is a reliable means to propel us out of the humanistic swamp that holds back our transgressive abilities. The sports institutions, in opposition, hold on to the ideal of the natural, universal and therefore comparable body, while at the same time reworking it with the extensive use of technology. However, this ideal has already been damaged beyond repair through ongoing doping scandals and the like. Although they are the driving force behind them, sports institutions ignore the world-changing power of science and technology, the social character of exercise and training, and the historic-cultural genesis of physicality as a whole.

Some sports journalists address the problem at its core and come to a rather radical conclusion. In 2008, Eric Adelson wrote a long commentary for the sports magazine ESPN, whose tone alluded to the end of competitive sports:

"A swim cap is a prosthetic; it smooths the 'defective' surface of a swimmer's head, making it more hydrodynamic [...]. Some will complain that only the disabled have access to prosthetic limbs, while everyone can lace on space-age shoes [...]. Is any of this fair? [...] Advocates for the able-bodied will say that these athletes don't have fake parts; their advantages are natural, unlike those offered by prosthetics and performance-enhancing drugs [...]. What's the difference between an amputee with a prosthetic and a lineman who has lost and regained use of his limbs? Or a point guard with a pacemaker? If a right wing loses an eye, would we make him wear a patch on the ice even if a mechanical eye allowed him to see off of it?" (Adelson n. pag.)

Adelson's tone fits the well-informed coverage of a journalist who questions the very foundation myth of a natural body perfected by a talented individual. Nevertheless, the consequences of an increasingly blurred distinction between naturalness and artificiality are dangerous, especially since frivolous scenes of self-mutilation, as preconditions for super-performances, appear on the horizon. What is unquestionable, however, is that the future of sports lies in the hands of engineers:

"The International Association of Athletics Federations is supposed to decide if Pistorius is eligible for the Olympics this spring [2007]. The possibilities: If Pistorius is a black swan, a statistical freak who would have been a world-class sprinter on natural legs, too, then no problem – let him run. And, if being an amputee is what gave Pistorius something to prove and turned him into a world-class sprinter, then no problem – let him run. But if he is the vanguard of a legion of plastic track-and-field terminators whose upper speed is a function of materials science and software instead of determination and training? The International Olympics Commission better start hiring some engineers." (McHugh n. pag.)

'Statistical freak' or precursor of a future à la Terminator would be two sad alternatives indeed. Without doubt, even Pistorius has incorporated the myth of self-mastery, challenges such an understanding of mastery by way of technology. In his biography we find several situations that deal with the impact of his social milieu and the concrete doings of technical artifacts. We can see "parahuman" (see Sofoulis) agencies at work, all the agents that make – that literally fabricate – the assemblage we all too quickly call 'athlete.' Pistorius speaks at one point of the many hours of his childhood that were consumed by making adjustments to the prostheses. The prosthetic fitting is an extremely tedious matter, a process in which both the orthopedic specialist and the patient need to work together, measuring, fitting, testing, measuring again, fitting again, and testing again. The adjustment is important, as otherwise the stump is injured, which is very painful and, in a worst-case scenario, might obviate wearing the prosthetic leg for months. Pistorius describes how his brother was in charge of constantly observing and controlling the interfaces between the prostheses and the stumps to prevent injury.

When it comes to the *agency* of technology, the story of how Pistorius decided to become a runner is most interesting. Despite his being an ambitious sportsman, he used to be quite indifferent to running as a sports activity. "Becoming interested in running" is ascribed to the very materiality of prosthetic technology. The heavy prostheses of his childhood enabled him to wrestle, ride a bike, lift weights, play rugby, and water polo, but he was not able to run as fast as was necessary for competitive sports. It was only with the Cheetahs that he discovered his body as perfectly constituted for short-term performances such as sprinting. He had to quit all endurance sports in order to build up the necessary muscles for running. To put it in a nutshell: Many of Pistorius' descriptions highlight the important role of a human and non-human collective, to use Bruno Latour's terminology (see *Reassembling the Social*), to produce his 'individual' performance. From such a perspective, 'individual performance,' which constitutes the very regulation system of sports, appears as something of a fetish. It is probably no more than a relic of the 19th century idea which celebrated the individual's will and ability to master their own body. This view still structures athletes' ethics and the viewers' expectations today.

GROTESQUE SPECTACLES

Another interpretation of the increasing popularity of the Paralympics deals with the exotistic pleasure of 'grotesque' spectacles. The focus here lies on the body celebrating and exposing in a Dionysian manner its transgression of normalcy. In such a discourse, the interest is not in a body that is forced to adjust according to 'normal' distributions of attractiveness and popularity. Hans Ulrich Gumbrecht's commentary on the Paralympics 2012, which appeared in the daily newspaper *Frankfurter Allgemeine Zeitung* (FAZ), offers such a reading. He associates the classical ideal of Apollonian, graceful beauty with dull egalitarianism. Furthermore, he contrasts this dullness with a current, fundamental distrust in the adequacy of humanist ideals of equality. In his view, the drastic and grotesque body of disability sports hypostatizes this challenge for democratic politics. Similar to the aesthetics of the artistic avant-garde of the 20th century, the disabled body holds a particular erotic attraction and fascination that highlights an affinity to the horizon of the Dionysian.

"There is something potentially frightening about this new view because it distances itself from the friendliness of any progressive humanitarian. Then again, no one can tell me that the atmosphere in the sold out stadium at the London Paralympics closing ceremony was just another apotheosis of the ethics of tolerance and egalitarianism." (Gumbrecht, translation by Eleana Vaja)

Evidently the Paralympic bodies are fascinating. Moreover, they evolve into a sublime aesthetics that is more closely related to inaptitude and intangibility than to the Apollonian, athletic body. The closing ceremony of the Paralympics with its apocalyptic cyberpunk aesthetics evoked images of the "flesh fair" in Steven Spielberg's *A.I* (2001), where androids are forced to fight with each other for an audience salivating with pleasure at the sight. Yes, it is tempting to read this fascination as a revolt against the ethics of normalization or maybe also as an ethicization of the marked body as a political foundation. Furthermore, the Paralympics could be seen in the tradition of libertarian utopias of emancipation and exuberance, directed against the biopolitical institutions that softly regulate and navigate our desires into productiveness and reproduction. In this case, the Paralympics would be located in the tradition of the perverse or carnivalesque rituals that facilitate a temporary transgression of the acceptable and preferable.

Similar to normalization, transgression has its limits, which may paradoxically be caused by contradictory effects of what has been called "flexible normalism" (Link). Contrary to the disciplining model that restricts them, transgression expands one's possibilities. However, transgression as an ideal is also ambivalent, since it is already included in the system of cashing in on difference: Transgression has a symbolic value, it is capital. The power of the Paralympic athletes to fascinate is rooted perhaps in their verification of the myth of cognitive and affective capitalism. Everyone can transgress; you just need to work hard enough on yourself. *Hands Up for GOLD,* which celebrated its premier at the Berlin film festival in 2013, portrays three Paralympic athletes reiterating this particular message. Smaller movie productions such as the American *The Gimp Monkeys,* which deals with three disabled climbers and their ascent of El Capitan in Yosemite Valley, also stress the importance of self-discipline. Because it fascinates, the disabled body is an effective promoter for this message. This is the reason why Gumbrecht's statement requires modification. The fascination for the deformed, Dionysian body is not simply a revolt against a boring, Apollonian egalitarianism, but rather an expression of a last hope for equality in competitive sports: If *they* can make it despite their disability, then I (the 'normal' being) can certainly make it as well.

Is there a possibility to avoid the traps of normalization, exoticization, and posthumanization when it comes to disability and sports? I want to propose a *parahuman* perspective that allows for a re-interpretation of the Paralympics. The term Paralympics, although it is greatly problematic in terms of its history and my usage is consciously etymologically incorrect, fits, quite unexpectedly, quite well. The name can be traced back to 1948, when the physician Ludwig Guttman initiated the first competitions in sports for 'disabled people,' namely paraplegics. At that time they were called the Stoke Mandeville Games. Nowadays, "para" is also related to the location of the Paralympic Games, which is identical to that of the 'normal' Olympic Games. It would be a step forward to stress the prefix "para" in the sense of 'being next to each other' by synchronizing the competitions not only in place but also in time. Such a grouping would undermine the tendency to classify the Paralympics as second division sports and it would also bring to light the artificiality of all bodies in competitive sports. Finally, to consider the Paralympics as a parahuman event would stress the side-by-side principle of human and non-human agents, as outlined above. This could challenge the very foundation of our understanding of performance in sports. The Paralympics could work as a probing tool to question the presuppositions of those regulations which *produce* performances in the first place.

The fiction of equal bodies, the sense of equal 'primal conditions' that can be altered individually, connects to the idea of a 'free' and fair competition. It therefore links the body to the idea of freedom on a 'free' market: Every body and everybody is the same as long as they are marketing themselves. Both the market and the sports arena are not unfair and violent *because* they are full of preconditions and expectations. They are unfair and violent because they pretend not to be. The market and sports hide the inequality of their basic assumptions by way of fictions of equality and equivalence. In this respect, the obviously different bodies of the Paralympics could at least be a provocation. Let us not tame them all too quickly by inserting them into posthumanist narratives.

REFERENCES

A.I. Artificial Intelligence. Dir. Stephen Spielberg. Warner Bros. Pictures, 2001. Film.

Adelson, Eric. "Let'em Play." *ESPN* 14 April 2008. Web. 20 April 2015. <http:// sports.espn.go.com/espnmag/story?id=3357051>.

Angerer, Marie-Luise, Kathrin Peters and Zoe Sofoulis. *Medienkultur.* Wien, New York: Springer, 2002. 273-97. Print.

Brüggemann, Gert-Peter, et al. "Biomechanics of Double Transtibial Amputee Sprinting, Using Dedicated Sprinting Prostheses." *Sport Technologies* 1.4-5 (2008): 220-27. Print.

Burkett, Brendan, Mike McNamee and Wolfgang Poothast. "Shifting Boundaries in Sports Technology and Disability: Equal Rights or Unfair Advantage in the Case of Oscar Pistorius?" *Disability and Society* 26.5 (2011): 643-54. Print.

Gumbrecht, Hans Ulrich. "Dionysische Faszination der Paralympics." *Frankfurter Allgemeine Zeitung* 18 September 2012. Print.

Harrasser, Karin and Christina Lutter. "Spielräume. Zwei Szenen zur Differenz." *Dritte Räume. Homi K. Bhabas Kulturtheorie. Kritik. Anwendung. Reflexion.* Eds. Babka, Anna, Julia Malle and Matthias Schmidt. Wien: Turia + Kant, 2012. 237-48. Print.

H2.0: New Minds, New Bodies, New Identities. Conference Website. Hugh Herr and John Hockenberry. Web. 20 April 2015. <http://h20.media.mit.edu/>.

Krause, Marcus. "Von der normierenden Prüfung zur regulierenden Sicherheitstechnologie. Zum Konzept der Normalisierung in der Machtanalytik Foucaults." *Spektakel der Normalisierung.* Eds. Krause, Marcus and Christina Bartz. München: Fink, 2007. 53-75. Print.

Latour, Bruno. *Reassembling the Social: An Introduction to Actor-Network-Theory.* Oxford: Oxford University Press, 2005. Print.

Link, Jürgen. *Versuch über den Normalismus. Wie Normalität produziert wird.* Göttingen: Vandenhoeck & Ruprecht, 1998. Print.

Longman, Jeré. "An Amputee Sprinter: Is He Disabled or Too-Disabled?" *New York Times* 15 May 2007. Print.

McHugh, Josh. "Blade Runner." *Wired* 15 March 2007. Web. 20 April 2015. <http://archive.wired.com/wired/archive/15.03/blade.html>.

Pistorius, Oscar. *Blade Runner.* New York: Random House, 2009. Print.

"Pistorius verliert gegen Wunder-Stelzen." *Frankfurter Allgemeine Zeitung* 03 September 2012. Web. March 04 2013. <http://www.faz.net/themenarchiv/sport/paralympics-2012/paralympics-pistorius-verliert-gegen-wunder-stelzen-11877393.html>.

Sloterdijk, Peter. *You Must Change Your Life: On Anthropotechnics.* Trans. Hoban, Wieland. Cambridge; Malden: Polity, 2013. Print.

Sofoulis, Zoe. "Post-, Nicht- und Parahuman. Ein Beitrag zu einer Theorie soziotechnischer Personalität." *Future Bodies. Zur Visualisierung von Körpern in Science und Fiction.* Eds. Angerer, Marie-Luise, Kathrin Peters and Zoe Sofoulis. Medienkultur. Wien, New York: Springer, 2002. 273-97. Print.

Swartz, Leslie and Brian Watermeyer. "Cyborg Anxiety. Oscar Pistorius and the Boundaries of What It Means to Be Human." *Disability and Society* 23.2 (2008): 187-90. Print.

Würtz, Hans. *Zerbrecht die Krücken. Krüppel-Probleme der Menschheit. Schicksalsstiefkinder aller Zeiten und Völker in Wort und Bild [Smash the Crutches: Cripple Problems of Human Kind. Doomed Stepchildren of all Times and Peoples in Text and Image].* Leipzig: L. Voss, 1932. Print.

X-Men. Dir. Bryan Singer. Twentieth Century Fox, 2000. Film.

X-Men: The Last Stand. Dir. Brett Ratner. Twentieth Century Fox, 2006. Film.

X-Men: First Class. Dir. Matthew Vaughn. Twentieth Century Fox, 2011. Film

X-Men: Days of Future Past. Dir. Bryan Singer. Twentieth Century Fox, 2014. Film.

X2. Dir. Bryan Singer. Twentieth Century Fox, 2003. Film.

Responses to Karin Harrasser

Eleana Vaja
PROSTHETIC CONCRETIZATION IN A PARAHUMAN FRAMEWORK

In her essay "Superhumans-Parahumans. Disability and Hightech in Competitive Sports", Karin Harrasser attributes the public success of the 2012
Paralympics to the visual staging of the competing athletes as masters of
willingness, discipline, and self-conquest. These visual markers of individual
exceptionality rely on a concept of the human that at its core fortifies a pillar of
competitive sports: human comparability. Harrasser's overall aim is to demystify
this conceptualization and to highlight the constructed character of competitive
sports on the basis of an alterity of bodies. She begins her theorization of
disability in competitive sports with Peter Sloterdijk's existentialism of defiance, which is echoed in Hans Würtz's paradigm of disability and self-
mastery. These latter theories affirm the promoted ideal of exceptionality and
disability. By including the posthumanist reading of the Paralympics, she pays
tribute to the exhibition of these athletes as superhumans.

While impairments designate the pivotal parameter attesting to the Paralympics athletes' unique sense of determination, the relation between body and
technological enhancement amplifies the ideal promoted by superhumanism.
Impairments thus underscore the extraordinary strength needed to deal with
misfortune, thereby promoting an ableist view of impairments as obstacles. The
discourse on technological enhancement, which is simultaneously triggered in
this context of bodies and performance, deflects from this position and poses
impairments as platforms for biological engineering. These two leitmotifs
of disability allow Harrasser to address the coping mechanisms acquired by
many people with impairments confronted with an enforced normal ideal. She
generates three modes from this enforcement, framing her argument with
the X-Men movies as another group of staged disability: dealing with one's
minority status, one's self-concept, and the societal reaction to alterity. This
minority status can be dealt with either by assimilating to the alleged majority
or by exercising superiority over it. In terms of self-concept, one is torn between
either accepting or rejecting the biological difference that marks one's minority

status. The societal reaction oscillates between practices of inclusion and exclusion. Harrasser sees these antagonizing strategies of coping with physical difference best explicated by the X-Men character Wolverine. Wolverine's social and psychological predicaments, remains of his technological enhancement, frame Harrasser's addressing of the equality of bodies in competitive sports, focusing on technological neutrality.

By connecting the issue of technological enhancement with the Würtzian paradigm of self-mastery, Harrasser highlights the dispute between "permitted self-technologies" and "external technologies" *ad absurdum* by illustrating the artificiality of competitive sports as such (Harrasser 176); the milieu itself is technical. The technicality of each sport decisively influences the performance of the athlete. Her argument revolves around the technicality of physical contests that turns every participating athlete into a technical body. This derivation of the construction of competitive sports annihilates any difference between disabled and abled athletes, since the overall milieu is the one imposing the technicality on each body, constructing it "culturally, materially, socially, and even biologically" (175). She illustrates this thesis by referring to Oscar Pistorius's life as a professional athlete. From his birth onwards, every decision was based on forming and 'constructing' him into a perfect athlete. Thus, the issue of fairness in competitive sports cannot be solved from a technological standpoint. For Harrasser, discussing permitted technologies, as sport officials and the media continue to do, functions as a distraction from the main issue at stake, which is the illusion of bodies as equal and thus comparable.

Although the issue of fairness cannot be addressed from a technological standpoint, prostheses and performance enhancements trigger extreme positions in the posthumanist discourse that require attention. Biological enhancement through technology includes two positions, both of which tackle the *humanist* human. On the one hand, technical enhancement blurs the demarcation between animal and human by defining the human being as *Mängelwesen*. On the other hand, it endorses the fusion of humans with machine. Testing the normative kernel of the *humanist* human, as posthumanist voices endorse, is in Harrasser's view dangerous since it comes along with the rejection of legal rights. The chosen posthumanist ideal in the context of competitive sports is the superhuman. Athletes incorporating this implied perfectionism endeavor to exterminate all weaknesses. Like the staging of the Paralympics and the debate on the neutrality of sports technology, this superhumanism advocates self-mastery and instantaneously affirms the human as deficient by nature promoting, hence, an ethics of perfectionism.

This ethics resonates within the regulatory practices of competitive sports. They adhere to the ostensible fairness of physical contest, which affirms the equality of bodies. *Regulation* implies order; categorizing bodies in athletics sets forth a given standard of biological equality that would be disturbed by any enhancement other than the athlete's own determination. The alterity of bodies is again replaced by the illusion of their comparability which encourages, above all, self-mastery. By following this view, Harrasser criticizes the discourses that have evolved around the aesthetics of these bodies. The alluring eroticism of these bodies did not result from their somato-normative transgression, but rather from the advocacy of self-mastery.[6] The success of the visual staging of the Paralympic athletes is rooted in this perpetuation of self-mastery, which thrives on sustaining the comparability of bodies, the related notion of fairness in competitive sports, and the dismissal of this milieu's constructed character. Harrasser's proposed parahuman approach, however, places abled and disabled bodies next to each other, highlighting the constructed character of sports in general, and thus helps to initiate a demystification of the illusion of biological equality. *Para* first needs to be understood here in its etymological sense of *beside*. A contemporaneous staging of Paralympic and Olympic Games would dismantle the artificiality of all bodies in competitive sports, and contribute to a side-by-side principle of human and non-human agents.

My aim is to strengthen Harrasser's argument about competitive sports as constructed milieus by concentrating on the three modes of existence she introduces and intermeshes: human (individual), prosthesis (technical object), and environment (milieu). While she builds her argument from the perspective of the human in this milieu, I intend to revise the order by focusing on the prosthesis, the non-human agents in this configuration. The prosthesis' environment plays a decisive role in how it is perceived. In a milieu of mastery, discipline and willingness, the prosthesis becomes a device of pure utilization as well as a means of capitalistic interests. It is the prosthesis, its shape, form and technicality that, according to Harrasser, attract the interest of the media, philosophers, and sport officials. The questions that arise regarding the prosthesis in the juxtaposed milieus of superhumansim and parahumanism are: Why is the value of a prosthesis, its importance for the individual, bound to its serving to win? How is participation to be conceived in terms of the prosthesis and the individual? To answer these questions on the ground of technologies – since so far the *para* has addressed the human agents, and *super* has been discussed in terms of technical enhancement – I will develop Gilbert Simondon's notion of the genesis of the technical object and its associated milieu because

"[f]rom the opening lines, rather than a 'thinker of technics,' [he] appears as a thinker of the resolution of a crisis of humanity in its relation to the world of technics. The reasons for such a crisis seem to reside in the secular opposition between, on the one

---

6 | In her TED talk from 2014, Stella Young coins the term "inspirational porn" to designate the objectification of impairments as overcoming an obstacle.

hand, the world of culture as a world of *meaning*, and on the other, the world of technics considered exclusively from the angle of *utility*." (Combes 57-58)

For Simondon, our lack of understanding the technical objects surrounding us – even those which are part of our daily life, be it our cars or even our mobile phones – plays a decisive role in evoking an uncertainty towards them, which diminishes them into devices of utilization. They are thus separated from the world of culture. Regarding prostheses, the problems that derive from this utilization, this exclusion, becomes striking since these technical objects are connected to the humans who are using them. Understanding prostheses and how they develop would thereby help to harmonize the human and non-human agent relationship in this constellation. Understanding a technical object means, for Simondon, first and foremost to introduce its genesis. Through this perspective on the technical object as something that becomes, it enters both culture and ethics, which elevates the technical object from mere utility into a participating entity. This participation is based on the technical object's genesis in relation to the individual who is inventing or using it, as well as their common environment. Within a disability studies context, Simondon's philosophy of technology helps to theorize this relation between human and non-human agent, focusing however on the latter entity and on the consequences of an ideology of self-mastery, or rather anticipated perfection, with respect to the technical object, which is here the prosthetic leg. Therefore, this theorization introduces Simondon's notion of the coming into being of a technical object, its "concretization" (Simondon, *On the Mode* 11), and pays tribute to the constructed character of competitive sports.

The onset of this analysis first requires, nevertheless, a definition of the relation between technical objects that provide a "human reality" (*On the Mode* 1) and the individual. Technical objects and individuals, although both modes of existence for Simondon, are not equated with each other. Several features distinguish them from each other, such as the ability to rebel or to change one's aims, the difference between the learning processes of an individual in contrast to the adaptation of a technical object, as well as the human feature of questioning oneself and one's actions (*Note* 517). This relation is marked neither by any form of mastery of the one over the other nor by complete indifference toward the other, but rather by the principle of complementing each other. I consequently include a reference to Simondon's notion of "individuation" (*The Genesis* 298) in order to highlight this relation and also to apply these findings to the technical object at hand: the prosthetic leg. Finally, the resonance of the traits of the technical object's genesis within superhumanism and parahumanism are explicated.

'Concretization' describes the genesis of technical objects. The inherent potentiality of every technical object is to become more concrete rather than abstract. This means that the single constituents of a technical object undertake more tasks, interacting more smoothly with each other on several levels in order to decrease any occurring disturbances, which consequently reduce the need for maintenance, and ultimately increase the coherence of the object so that it can become "entirely unified"[7] (*On the Mode* 16). Neither unification nor coherence, however, should be equated with perfection. Perfection denotes an end-state of being incapable of further development, a static equilibrium or stability, an automatism, a closed system. To exemplify the process of 'concretization' according to our technical object of interest, the prosthetic leg, one needs to compare the first prosthetic leg made from wood with current versions. The latter anticipates the natural motion of walking by refining the material in terms of friction, weight, the relaxation of joints, the fitting to the body, the handling, weather resistance, and shape. These features already allude to the next two indispensible moments of the genesis of the technical object, its over-specialization[8] and its surrounding: "hypertelia" (*On the Mode* 51) and the "associated milieu" (ibid.).

According to Harrasser, one of the major debates around the prosthesis in a superhumanist idealism revolves around its technological enhancement. In dealing with the issues of technological neutrality in sports as well as the idea of fairness, it is helpful to consider the notion of technological over-specialization and its consequences for the technical object, as introduced by Simondon under the umbrella term of 'hypertelia.' Hypertelia is a phenomenon which occurs during the enhancement procedures of increasing a technical object's technicality and can, in some cases, strip the technical object of its autonomy, turning it into a "hypertelic-technical object" (*On the Mode* 52). A common example to illustrate one form of over-specialization is the Google Watch, where reading the time becomes a mere side effect of this technical object rather than its main function; it is not an enhancement that focuses on the 'schematic essence,' reading the time. Regarding Harrasser's discussion, the prosthesis' shape, its acceleration potentiality, material, or length initiated the analogy of athletes using prostheses with cyborgs, blurring the demarcation between human and machine. While Harrasser characterized these discussions as distractions from the main issue at stake, the constructed character of sports, a Simondonian philosophy of technology dismisses these readings even within

---

7 | Pascal Chabot also sets this feature of unification as the main aim of any technical object during its process of refinement; "[c]oncretization may be understood as the unification of certain fundamental concepts: synergy, superabundant functionality, coherence, internal resonance and formalization" (15).

8 | Although the English translation refers here to "specialization" (On the Mode 51), note that the original French version speaks of an spécialisation exagérée (MEOT 50) therefore I added the preposition "over."

a technological argument since the Cheetah preserves the 'schematic essence' of prostheses by supporting the individual in walking, standing, and running. The Cheetah marks a new phase in the becoming of prosthetic legs, engineered to strengthen the schematic essence by reducing maintenance and increasing the adaptation of the technical object to the individual and to the surroundings. This inclusive form of a technical object's genesis mirrors best what Simondon juxtaposes to hypertelia and coins "adaptation-concretization" (*On the Mode* 58).

Although Simondon does not include prostheses in his treatise, one can derive that prostheses fit his notion of "adaptation-concretization," which is the successful genesis of the technical object because it refines two milieus by connecting them during their geneses, and therefore enables them to form a synergetic compliance where the single elements of both milieus work in a multifunctional manner on both sides: in this case the individual and the prosthesis in daily life. Therefore, they strengthen each other's autonomy rather than depriving each other of it. Both the prosthetic leg and the individual are in individual processes of becoming, helping each other to become what is potentially inherent within themselves, and are not reduced to the pursuit of *self-mastery*. They do not form a closed system but participate with each other and with their surrounding, being sensitive to new information. They need to participate and react to their common 'associated milieu,' and this is where the constructed character of competitive sports enters and hinders both entities to become. Both agents, the non-human and the human, are deprived of their own genesis in favor of a given ideology: self-conquest and perfection. The individual in a parahuman framework perceives and lives from a new perspective and thus shifts into a subsequent phase of her/his becoming. Although the individual, as we have seen, is not equated with the technical object, the cases of individuals with prostheses require the genesis of the individual to be thought of in line with the technical object, since the technical essence of a prosthesis can only be constituted in relation to the individual. Additionally, "being as becoming" ("Genesis" 301) follows a similar principle in the technical object as it does in the individual, namely 'concretization' and 'individuation.' In the case of prostheses and individuals, these two modes of existence and genesis need to be thought of in accordance with each other in order to grasp the various notions and concepts applied to individuals using prostheses. Thomas LaMarre's comment on Simondon's theory stresses that "any inquiry into the relation between humans and machines [...] has to deal with a genealogy of the human alongside a genealogy of the technical object" (100). Relating this concept to prostheses and individuals highlights the difference between superhumanism and parahumanism from a prosthetic point of view which, in the case of 'adaptation-concretization' is always the individual and its own created 'associated milieu.' The associated milieu of any kind of prosthesis is daily life along with its variations, disturbances and challenges. New information appears naturally, be it the material, stability or fitting of the prostheses or the individual's decision to decide freely when to put on the prosthesis or to leave it:

"In the modern tendency toward the construction of technical individuals (machines) [or prostheses], Simondon sees the emergence of a new kind of relation in which technical objects become more and more like natural objects – in that they carry their associated milieu with them, generating it through their relations." (LaMarre 90)

Looking at the prosthesis' 'associated milieu' which is, on the one hand, identified by Harrasser as superhumanism in the form of competitive sports and, on the other hand, by parahumanism as individual bodies distinguished by and through their alterity, one can argue that the discussions around prostheses mirror the implied concepts of both settings. Superhumanism is marked by self-conquest, enhancement, self-mastery and competition, leaving no space for the prosthesis to be seen as a technical object in the process of 'adaptation-concretization' in relation to the individual, but rather as a mere tool to form the perfect athlete. This anticipated perfection, however, contradicts the genesis of the technical object as well as the genesis of the individual. It initiates in the first place the discussions of monstrosity, cyborgs, and the grotesque by defining the prostheses and the individuals as pure modes of function rather than of existence. Functionality runs smoothly when perfection as an end-state, an equilibrium, is achieved. Prostheses in everyday life, rather than heading towards perfection, highlight the moment of *para* as next to each other. This form of humanism captures the principles of both geneses; the technical object's and the individual's. Both participate with and influence each other, as well as react toward one another, forming an open milieu of their own. This reflects the prosthesis' and individual's moments of being. In their final instances, daily life, the *"rupture[s] in the process of becoming"* (Salter 123), mark the difference between superhumanism and parahumanism. While in superhumanism *ruptures* define failure and reveal the illusion of the comparability of humans, thus shattering the very foundation of self-conquest, they simultaneously form the essence of parahumanism. Oscar Pistorius's relation to his prostheses is from the beginning bound to success and to the elimination of *ruptures*, utilizing the prostheses to achieve this aim by mastering them. *Ruptures*, however, mark moments of despair, loss, acceptance, reorganization, and happiness. These obstacles add new characteristic features to the prostheses, and allow them to participate in the person's life as more than pure utility whose value is measured in terms of success. Parahumanism hints at another important aspect that highlights the prosthesis' upgrade from pure utilization and capitalization to culture. The prosthesis and the individual form a team in which both sides are connected with each other. The prosthesis participates in the life of the individual and gains a value that is not measured in numbers. Simondon introduces an ethics that emancipates the technical object from pure utilization and through this also liberates the individual and the prosthesis from any ideology of self-mastery and perfection.

References

Chabot, Pascal. *The Philosophy of Simondon. Between Technology and Individuation.* New York: Bloomsbury Academic, 2003. Print.

Combes, Muriel. *Gilbert Simondon and the Philosophy of the Transindividual.* Trans. Thomas LaMarre. Cambridge: MIT Press, 2013. Print.

Harrasser, Karin. "Superhumans – Parahumans. Disability and Hightech in Competitive Sports." This volume. 171-184. Print.

LaMarre, Thomas. "Afterword: Humans and Machines." *Gilbert Simondon and the Philosophy of the Transindividual.* By Muriel Combes. Cambridge: MIT Press, 2013. 79-108. Print.

Salter, Chris. "Just Noticeable Difference. Ontogenesis, Performativity and the Perceptual Gap." *Inflexions 5. Simondon: Milieu, Techniques, Aesthetics* March (2012): 119-129. Web. 6 Nov. 2014. <http://www.inflexions.org>.

Simondon, Gilbert. [MEOT] *Du Mode d'Existence des Objets Techniques.* Paris: Aubier, 1958. Print.

—. *On the Mode of Existence of Technical Objects.* Trans. Ninian Mellamphy. University of Western Ontario: 1980. Print.

—. "The Genesis of the Individual." Trans. Marc Cohen and Sanford Kwinter. *Zone 6. Incorporations.* Eds. Jonathan Crary and Sanford Kwinter. New York: MIT Press, 1992. 297-319. Print.

—. "Note Complémentaire sur les Conséquences de la Notion d'Individuation." *Individuation à la Lumière des Notions de Forme et d'Information.* Grenoble: Millon Krisis, 2005. 503-527. Print.

Young, Stella. "I Am Not Your Inspiration, Thank You." *TED.* 2014. Web. 20 Oct. 2015. <https://www.ted.com/talks/stella_young_i_m_not_your_ inspiration_thank_you_very_much>.

Olga Tarapata

PARALYMPIC, PARAHUMAN, PARANORMAL

In her article, Karin Harrasser elaborates on disability and technology in competitive sports, offering an alternative perspective on the 2012 Paralympic athletes whose medial representation, as she argues, leans towards the 'superhuman.' With the introduction of 'parahumanism,' Harrasser rivals the omnipresent 'posthumanism' that has been proposed as the emancipatory spearhead in the erosion of what, not only since the Enlightenment, it means to be 'human.' As one of the first to popularize 'the posthuman' in her 1999 book *How We Became Posthuman*, Katherine Hayles set the tone for future publications such as Cary Wolfe's *What is Posthumanism?* (2010), Patricia MacCormack's *Posthuman Ethics* (2012), and, most recently, Rosi Braidotti's *The Posthuman* (2013). In these works, the specter of disability is persistently evoked as the preeminent site for the negotiation of the cultural and political transformations of human embodiment in an age in which "[w]e cannot think realistically any longer of the human species" as Bruce Mazlish claims, "without a machine" (6). Although Harrasser agrees with the debunking of the "autonomous, self-transparent, reflexive and conscious thinking subject" as the myth ("Superhumans" 178) at the heart of posthumanism, Harrasser eventually comes to advocate an approach that eschews the progressive undertones of human obsolescence in this renegade discourse. Instead, by means of what she calls a 'parahuman perspective,' Harrasser proposes a re-interpretation of the Paralympics.

This response attempts to flesh out this notion of the 'parahuman' by complementing its vocabulary with philosopher and cognitive scientist Andy Clark's concept of 'wideware,' and finally by taking these observations into the realm of American science fiction literature. The fiction of cyberpunk icon William Gibson not only displays cyborgs, AIs, humans, non-humans and their milieu, but highlights their interplay, the ways in which collectives emerge, blend, and dissolve. Gibson's 1996 novel *Idoru*, in particular, embraces the mutually formative resonance between environment and protagonist, making the latter "the equivalent of a dowser" (25); a figure I consider most appropriate to ground Harrasser's conceptualizations.

The Paralympic Games 2012 constitute the anchorage for the numerous excursions[9] Harrasser undertakes in giving the conceptualization of disability a new spin. On her trajectory from disability to superability, from posthumanism to parahumanism, the 14th Summer Paralympic Games in London serve

---

9 | Harrasser moves swiftly from, for instance, the philosophy of Peter Sloterdijk and the writings of Hans Würz to the X-Men movies, from legal reports assessing Oscar Pistorius' athletic condition to Channel 4 advertisements and Formula One.

a threefold purpose. They function as a historic marker of a turning point in the "public perception of disability in sports and, perhaps of impairment in general" (Harrasser, "Superhumans" 171), as a focal point for the most divergent notions of the competitive disabled body and the technology involved, and finally, as an entry point for her introduction of parahumanism.

Paralympic

The strikingly visual conjunction of disability and high technology in the opening and closing ceremonies, as well as the individual contests, raises the question for Harrasser whether "disabled people who use state-of-the-art technologies [are] still 'disabled' or [whether] they [are] 'superabled'" (175). As Harrasser argues, the turning point in the perception of disability is reflected in the depictions of 'superability' not only invoked in the media coverage of and advertisement for the Games, but also underlying many scientific and legal reports and classification systems orbiting the participants. The sprint runner Oscar Pistorius serves as Harrasser's primary example for ambivalent ascriptions ranging from "disabled" to "too-abled" (Longman) and from "super-legs" ("5 Super Powers") to "No Legs" (*The Fastest Man*). Questioning the possible advantages that athletes draw from their disability leads to the evaluation of the technologies involved in their performance. Such questioning, however, proves deeply disruptive for competitive sports in general, since it also draws attention to the equipment involved in 'regular' sports, such as running shoes, swim caps, swim suits, and personal trainers. Despite the endangerment of the 'neutrality' or even the possible "end of competitive sports" this interrogation provokes (179), Harrasser illustrates how questions about the props and aids involved in sports reveal that "the competitive body is an artifact, something fabricated, intertwined in social and technical networks, a 'construction' full of preconditions" (175). Whereas Harrasser focuses primarily on the corporeal dimension of cultural, material, social, and biological agents, Andy Clark argues that "[o]ur cognitive profile is *essentially* the profile of an embodied and situated organism" (21). An advocate of the extended mind hypothesis, Clark contends that the skin no longer delimits the organism, which he conceives as a "deeply interanimated triad" (21) of brain, body, and environment. Human agency, he argues, "includes the humanly-generated 'whirlpools and vortices' of external, symbol-laden media: the explosion of wideware made available by the ubiquitous devices of language, speech, and text" (21). Clark's notions of wideware encompasses

"states, structures or processes that satisfy two conditions. First, the item in question must be in some intuitive sense environmental: it must not, at any rate, be realized within the biological brain or the central nervous system. Bodily aspects and motions, as well as truly external items such as notebooks and calculators, thus fit the bill. Second, the item (state, structure, process) must play a functional role as part of an extended cognitive process." (16)

Clark draws attention to the ways in which the environment is fundamental to an organism's functioning and subjectivity. Accordingly, the agency and abilities which one might believe to be inherent properties of the individual body only emerge in conjunction with the proper milieu, a notion that supplements Harrasser's break with the "defining myth of sports based on the principal equality of bodies that are perfected by individual performance" (Harrasser, "Superhumans" 175). From bathing suits that imitate shark skin to the trainer's instructions, the team-mates' cues or the spectators' cheers, all the innumerable props and aids that structure the athlete's performance contribute to the illusion of an autonomous, independent, and powerful individual. In this light and with a distinct Deleuzian undercurrent, Harrasser pointedly re-conceptualizes the athlete as "always an assemblage" (ibid.). In her discussion, Harrasser examines less a turning point from disability to superability, than the transition from posthumanism to parahumanism, implicitly acknowledging Clark's notion of the "organism-plus-wideware" (Clark 23). In this regard, both share the recognition of the specific milieu as an integral part of the organism itself. The distinction of disability and (super)ability is no longer an absolute, but rather a relational matter, a bodily formation that must be viewed in terms of its embeddedness in its material context. When "wheelchair users describe how the chair becomes 'part of them'" (Reeve 104), we can effectively understand the wheelchair to be what Harrasser identifies as a non-human agent, or what Clark characterizes as wideware. In the context of disability (or any other context), all sorts of assemblages are conceivable. Likewise against the backdrop of Gilles Deleuze and Félix Guattari's philosophy, Barbara Gibson, a professor of physical therapy and rehabilitation at the University of Toronto, conceives of her patients as interconnected in "human-machine assemblages [...]; human-animal assemblages [...] and/or human-human assemblages" ("Reimagining" 1895-6). Considering the infinite number of wideware agents involved, I strongly agree with Harrasser that the myth of the superhuman, as proclaimed by the Channel 4 video ad in its celebration of will power, self-mastery and self-conquest, is only half the story.

As a focal point, the Paralympic Games 2012 serve Harrasser's unfolding of the broad spectrum of implications regarding the competitive technologized disabled body, be they ethical, political or sociological. She reminds us that the acceptance and propagation of the myth of the superhuman "affirms the concept of the human as a *Mängelwesen* (deficient by nature) and [...] supports a neoliberal ideology of continuous self-improvement that pushes individuals to the limits of their biological and cognitive possibilities" ("Superhumans"

179). While her wide-ranging discussion reaches from Herder's *Mängelwesen* to Nietzsche's *Übermensch*, from official sports regulations to the protestant ethics of self-mastery, Harrasser manages to weave these strands into a lucid critique of the position of the human in the greater scheme of competitive sports.

While, for instance, Jürgen Link's sociological concept of flexible normalism, on the one hand, does not discard non-normative bodies per se and offers inclusion for commodifiable bodies, it is, on the other hand, the spawn of cognitive and affective capitalism, since it creates a 'new deviant' that is by and large responsible for its own exclusion. On this basis, the Games constitute a site of normalizing practices since athletes are presented as having to overcome their disabilities and master superabilies by broadly denying the wideware involved. Harrasser outlines this even more forcefully in her book *Körper 2.0* with reference to Aimee Mullins, whose claim for the acknowledgement of otherness is fundamentally competition-based. As Harrasser argues, Mullins embodies qualities valuable to capitalism, such as self-discipline, commitment, cleverness, wit and curiosity, all of which result in Mullins' self-proclaimed superability.[10]

Parahuman

From these ossifying categorizations, Harrasser concludes the need for a side-by-side-form of humanism, which I read as a need to bypass the static hierarchies implied by the prefixes of 'dis-' and 'super-' or the seemingly progressive linearity of 'post-.' Endorsing her colleagues' strong skepticism towards the posthuman, Harrasser takes up Zoe Sofoulis' idea of the 'parahuman' as a potent alternative framework for conceptualizing the (non-)human agents involved not only in the choreography of sports but of agency in general. While acknowledging certain aspects of Hayles' notion of the 'posthuman' in the 2002 volume *Future Bodies*, Sofoulis finally rejects the term altogether. Due to its tacit suggestion of human redundancy, insignificance and the consequential release from responsibility, Sofoulis argues that the 'posthuman' is neither an adequate nor a viable term to describe the state of the human and its subjectivity. Rather as an impetus

---

10 | Harrasser's original reads: "Die von Mullins propagierte Form der Anerkennung des Andersartigen ist nämlich nur in Form eines Wettbewerbs zu erreichen. Grundlage dieses Wettbewerbs sind einerseits teure, bei weitem nicht allen zugängliche Technologien und andererseits bestimmte persönlichen Eigenschaften, die im kognitiven oder affektiven Kapitalismus als wertschöpfend erachtet werden. An erster Stelle stehen Leistungsbereitschaft und körperliche Selbstdisziplin. Ebenfalls wichtig sind emotionale und kognitive Kompetenzen: Klugheit, Witz, Lernfähigkeit, Neugierde. Hand in Hand damit geht eine Idee von Schönheit, die den gegebenen Körper als empfangsfähiges und modellierbares Material behandelt und in den Fällen Mullins, Herr, Pistorius mit der Prothese als Technofetisch legiert ist" (*Körper 2.0* 21).

than as a full-fletched concept, Sofoulis proposes the 'parahuman' as a possible alternative to conceive of the agency and intelligence that exists – in a Latourian sense, symmetrically – outside and next to the human.

Carrying Sofoulis' notion from gender to disability studies allows Harrasser to consider all the partially sovereign agents involved in the Paralympic Games 2012. By adopting the idea of the "side-by-side principle of human and non-human agents," ("Superhumans" 183) Harrasser's argument exceeds mere discussions of disability as the resisting force threatening the normative body or the disordering force threatening the social body, as has been conceptualized under the medical and later the social model of disability. Rather, it allows her to draw attention away from the individual and its accomplishments and instead towards the form of association between humans, machines and infrastructures, which appear in their collectivity as virtuous. Not only is the athlete conceptualized as a collective of 'human and non-human agents' but in consideration of the athletic body, the term 'parahuman' foregrounds its spatio-temporal character side-by-side with other collectives. Here, Harrasser's conception of parahumanism, to my understanding, breaks with the Euclidean geometry underlying our Western thinking. While, the notion of 'side-by-side' existence connotes a Euclidean parallelism, the 'para' Harrasser endorses necessitates, by definition, the overlap, intersection and entanglement of trajectories. In other words, parahumans are in a continuous process of messy becomings with their wideware, constantly dissolving one collective and establishing another in a partly sovereign fashion. From such a parahumanistic perspective, ability is wideware-related and not tied to a statistical norm, as it is with the notions of dis- or superability. By means of the parahuman, Harrasser disposes of the normative ideal, as well as the norm as the static reference point for categorization. The abilities conceived under parahumanism are therefore, I would like to suggest, in effect paranormal.

Paranormal

Abounding with figures embodying both paranormal ability and a fundamental connectedness with the environment, the work of William Gibson provides an extensive repository of extraordinary corporeality. His invention of 'cyberspace' and the pervasive "[t]he body was meat" (6) morale found in his early work earned the author a reputation as a technophile supporter of virtual reality and disembodiment. However, I would argue that Gibson's fiction does much more than offer cyberpunk prophecies of dystopian futures. Rather, it meticulously negotiates the margins of the 'human,' the nature of its embodiment, the status of its flesh, its entanglement in technology, and its inseparability from the world.

Idoru (1996), set in 21st century Tokyo, revolves around the marriage of the characters Rez, a world-famous rock star, and Rei Toei – the idoru – a computer-generated virtual celebrity. Thus, at its core the novel addresses the relationship and unification of a human and a non-human actor. All characters intentionally or accidentally involved in this undertaking display forms of corporeal or mental damage, deformity, lack, suture, rehabilitation, or technological enhancement all of which challenge the white, autonomous, heterosexual, able-bodied, employed, Western male, which Rosemarie Garland-Thomson calls 'the normate' (8). As a data specialist, the protagonist Colin Laney is hired by Rez's team to initiate the marriage. In the course of the narrative, Laney is revealed to be an orphan with a "medically documented concentration-deficit" (25), whose mental deviance could not be cured or corrected during his childhood. Laney's condition, however, is presented as a binary flicker between disability and superability, in that his skill to "toggle [his concentration-deficit], under certain conditions, into a state of pathological hyperfocus" (25) turns him into "an extremely good researcher" (25). Because of his talent for scanning infinitely complex sets of data, Laney is characterized as

"an intuitive fisher of patterns of information: of the sort of signature a particular individual inadvertently created in the net as he or she went about the mundane yet endlessly multiplex business of life in a digital society. Laney's concentration-deficit, too slight to register on some scales, made him a natural channel-zapper, shifting from program to program, from database to database, from platform to platform, in a way that was, well, intuitive. [...] Laney was the equivalent of a dowser, a cybernetic water-witch. He couldn't explain how he did what he did. He just didn't know." (25)

While this depiction captures Harrasser's notion of a changed perception of disability, a parahuman perspective, in contrast to classificatory attempts, directs attention away from the states and essences of deficit and talent or dis- and super-abilities towards the 'associations between humans, machines, and infrastructures.' Such a focus reveals that it is only when suspended in the infinitely complex architectures of data that Laney's specific ability to identify so called 'nodal points' arises. During a job interview for the sensational television show Slitscan, employer Kathy Torrance asks for a demonstration of Laney's skills and instantly realizes its paranormal quality, stating,

"I could almost believe there might actually be something to that nodal point bullshit. Some of your moves made no logical sense whatever, but I've just watched you hone in, cold, on something it took three experienced researchers a month to excavate. You did it in just under half an hour." (38)

Similarly, Gibson writes, "Slitscan allowed him [Laney] to do the one thing he possessed a genuine *talent* for" (40; emphasis added). However, Laney's talent, strictly speaking, only arises in that 'proper context,' which consists of the deployment of computer facilities, the free access to "low-level, broad-spectrum input" (148), and the recognition of his paranormal abilities by his employer. As a consequence, Laney's ability cannot be regarded as an inherent skill enclosed in the individual but instead represents, in Harrasser's sense, a partially sovereign system in resonance with its environment. Since the milieu co-constitutes the netrunner as much as he co-constitutes the milieu, Laney illustrates precisely the fundamental entanglement between organism and wideware that marks Harrasser's parahuman|paranormal collectives.

When Gibson identifies Laney's ability to "locate key data in apparently random wastes of incidental information" (38) with that of dowsing, this analogy, in the context of Harrasser's materialist parahuman approach, proves even more appropriate. While the 'cybernetic water-witch' resonates with digital information, dowsing originally describes the act of locating subterranean substances such as water, oil, metals, or mineral deposits. The various instruments used by dowsers range from rods, sticks, and pendula to their material bodies, which usually demonstrate an attraction to the respective materials. Although explanations of dowsing vary widely and wildly, many center on the flow of corpuscles or atoms between the respective material and the body, between the environment and the dowser as, for instance, explained by William Pryce in his *Mineralogia Cornubiensis* from 1778:

"The corpuscles [...] that rise from the Minerals, entering the rod, determine it to bow down, in order to render it parallel to the vertical lines which the effluvia describe in their rise. In effect the Mineral particles seem to be emitted from the earth: now the Virgula, being of a light porous wood, gives an easy passage to these particles." (114)

The dowser, who must be of an appropriate "constitution of mind and body" (116), detects the flow of particles by means of a rod in order to enter into a material feedback loop with the environment and to form a temporary collective of human and non-human agents. Adopting Harrasser's parahuman lens and echoing Mazlish, we thus can no longer think realistically of the human without considering its fundamental entanglement with agents in networks. Reading the paralympic athlete as a parahuman being with paranormal qualities and thinking the sprint runner through the netrunner and back, this response embraces Harrasser's re-reading of the Paralympic Games and adapts this new approach to the non-humanist human in re-reading American literature.

References

Clark, Andy. "Where Brain, Body and World Collide." *Deadalus: Journal of the American Academy of Arts and Sciences* 127.2 (1998). 257-280. Print.

Garland-Thomson, Rosemarie. *Extraordinary Bodies: Figuring Physical Disability in American Literature and Culture.* New York: Columbia University Press, 1997. Print.

Gibson, Barbara, et al. "'This is my way': Reimagining Disability, In/dependence and Interconnectedness of Persons and Assistive Technologies." *Disability & Rehablilitation.* 34.22 (2012). 1894-1899. Print.

Gibson, William. *Idoru.* London: Penguin, 2011. Print.

Harrasser, Karin. "Superhumans – Parahumans. Disability and Hightech in Competitive Sports." This volume. 171-184. Print.

Harrasser, Karin. *Körper 2.0: Über die technische Erweiterbarkeit des Menschen.* Bielefeld: transcript, 2013. Print.

Hayles, Katherine N. *How We Became Posthuman: Virtual Bodies in Cybernetics, Literature, and Informatics.* Chicago and London: The University of Chicago Press, 1999. Print.

Longman, Jeré. "An Amputee Sprinter: Is He Disabled or Too-Abled?" *The New York Times.* 15 May 2007. Web. 12 August. 2015.

Mazlish, Bruce. *The Fourth Discontinuity: The Co-Evolution of Humans and Machines.* Yale: Yale University Press, 1993. Print.

Pryce, William. *Mineralogia Cornubiensis: A Treatise on Minerals, Mines, and Mining.* 1778. Web. 15 Jan. 2015. <http://www.mdz-nbn-resolving.de/urn/resolver.pl?urn=urn:nbn:de:bvb:12-bsb10214410-0>.

"5 Super Powers You Can Have Today." Weird News, 1 May 2009. Web. 22 Oct. 2015. <http://wtf.thebizzare.com/offbeat/science-and-technology/5-super-powers-you-can-have-today/>.

Reeve, Donna. "Cyborgs, Cripples and iCrip: Reflections on the Contribution of Haraway to Disability Studies." *Disability and Social Theory: New Developments and Directions.* Eds. Dan Goodley, Bill Hughes and Lennard Davis. London: Palgrave Macmillan, 2012. 91-111. Print.

Sofoulis, Zoe. "Post-, Nicht- und Parahuman." *Future Bodies: Zur Visualisierung von Körpern in Science und Fiction.* Eds. Marie-Luise Angerer. Wien: Springer, 2002. 273-300. Print.

The Fastest Man on No Legs. Dir. David Notman-Watt and James Routh. October Films, 2009. Documentary.

Disability Studies Reads the Romance

Sexuality, Prejudice, and the Happily-Ever-After in the Work of Mary Balogh[1]

Ria Cheyne

Cultural disability studies scholars have repeatedly criticised academics in the humanities for perpetuating a "critical avoidance" (Bolt 287) of disability and disability issues. Yet cultural disability studies scholars themselves have been reluctant to engage with certain types of cultural production, and romance novels are a prime example of this. As the most popular of the popular genres,[2] romance novels are an obvious site of investigation for a field concerned with the effects representations of disability have upon the world. Though recent articles by Kathleen Miller, Emily M. Baldys and Sandra Schwab indicate the productive potential of a dialogue between disability studies and popular romance studies,[3] the critical conversation about disability in romance novels has only just begun.[4] Focusing on selected novels by Mary Balogh, a bestselling author of historical romance, I argue that romances with disabled protagonists offer significant opportunities to challenge negative stereotypes around

---

1 | This essay is a revised version of "Disability Studies Reads the Romance," originally published in *Journal of Literary & Cultural Disability Studies* 7.1 (2013): 37-52. It is reprinted here with the kind permission of the editor of *JLCDS*.

2 | Statistics from Romance Writers of America indicate an estimated total sales value for romance of $1.08 billion in 2013 ("Romance Industry Statistics" n. pag.).

3 | Miller uses feminist and disability scholarship to analyse vampire romances by Tanya Huff and Charlaine Harris. Baldys analyses five novels with cognitively disabled protagonists, arguing that these novels "bring both compulsory heterosexuality and compulsory able-bodiedness to bear on disabled sexuality" (128). Schwab analyses visual impairment and the loss of sight in two historical romances by Teresa Medeiros.

4 | Bly states that criticism of popular romance as a whole is still "in its infancy" (n. pag.). For a detailed discussion of popular romance scholarship, see Selinger and Frantz.

disability. The frequent use of disabled characters in Balogh's novels, and the way in which those characters are presented, positions all disabled characters as potential romantic actants, and encourages readers to critically reflect upon how they conceptualise disability and the values they attach to it.

POPULAR ROMANCE

Though the romance novel has been variously defined,[5] in this piece I adopt the definition used by Romance Writers of America, under which every romance novel has two vital elements:

"A Central Love Story: The main plot centers around individuals falling in love and struggling to make the relationship work. A writer can include as many subplots as he/she wants as long as the love story is the main focus of the novel. An Emotionally-Satisfying and Optimistic Ending: In a romance, the lovers who risk and struggle for each other and their relationship are rewarded with emotional justice and unconditional love." ("About the Romance Genre" n. pag.)

Romance novels come in many different varieties,[6] but these two elements are essential. While there are numerous other conventions of the popular romance novel whose analysis rewards a disability-informed approach – for example, the fact that romance heroes and heroines typically have "not merely 'normal' bodies, but perfect bodies" (Schwab 287) – I focus on these two essential elements. As Pamela Regis notes, critics "attack the romance novel for its happy ending in marriage" (7). Frequently, the fact that all romances follow the same basic plot pattern has been the cause of critical dismissal – either as part of a rejection of the genre as formulaic or on ideological grounds. However, the focus on the developing relationship between the heroine and hero, and the requirement for a happily-ever-after ending ("HEA" in romance parlance) in which those characters are united, means that romance novels featuring disabled characters are of particular interest when examined from a disability studies perspective.

This can be seen in the work of Mary Balogh, a Welsh-born author of over 70 historical romance novels. Mindful of cautions against romance scholarship

---

5 | Regis traces a long historical lineage for the romance novel by defining it broadly as "a work of prose fiction that tells the story of the courtship and betrothal of one or more heroines" (19) and identifying eight essential narrative elements. In this piece I focus on contemporary popular romance novels rather than 'romance' in a broader sense.

6 | For explanation of subgenres and formats, see Romance Writers of America, "Romance Subgenres."

that makes sweeping generalisations based on a small number of texts,[7] I do not claim the selected novels by Balogh I analyse here are representative of *all* popular romance novels (or even all works by Balogh). Rather, this analysis of her work is intended to suggest some of the possibilities that might be opened up for cultural disability studies, and for popular romance studies, by bringing the two fields together. Within Balogh's prolific output, I focus on two sets of Regency-era[8] novels: the six books in the *Slightly* series (published 2003-04), and the *Simply* quartet (2005-2008). Disabled characters appear frequently in these books. *Simply Love* (2006) features a disabled hero, Sydnam Butler, who is an amputee with one eye and significant facial scarring. Secondary characters with impairments abound, such as Prudence Moore, who is cognitively disabled (*Slightly Scandalous*, 2003, and other novels) and one-eyed Sergeant Strickland in *Slightly Sinful* (2004). In addition to the main characters discussed below, there are constant glimpses of other disabled people in the society depicted in these novels, from the amputee soldiers nursed by the heroine in *Slightly Tempted* (2004), to the hero's mobility-impaired grandmother in *Slightly Wicked* (2003). Interconnections between the novels in each series, between the two series, and with other works by Balogh, allow the reader a longer-term picture of the characters' lives, including an indication of what happens after the HEA.

SEXUALITY AND COMMUNITY

Simply Love begins with the hero, Sydnam Butler, living in a state of relative isolation. Despite his aristocratic background, he has withdrawn from society to live a "quiet, semireclusive life" (*Simply Love* 20) as the steward of a country estate after torture by enemy soldiers in the Peninsular Wars left him with significant facial scarring and nerve damage, and caused him to lose an eye and an arm. Despite "fulfilling work and several good friends," he admits that he is "essentially lonely" (99). As a consequence of what Carol Thomas terms "*the psycho-emotional dimensions of disablism*" (46), Sydnam has, to a degree, segregated himself from wider society.[9] On hearing that the owner of the estate

---

7 | Selinger and Frantz note that even in contemporary romance scholarship, critics "perpetuate a second tic of early scholarship: the impulse to frame their discussion in terms of the genre as a whole" even where only a small number of texts are actually considered (n. pag.). See also Regis (5-7).

8 | The Regency is the period from 1811 to 1820, in which the future King George IV ruled the United Kingdom as Prince Regent. It is a popular setting for romance novels.

9 | Thomas defines the psycho-emotional aspects of disability as "social barriers which erect 'restrictions' within ourselves, and thus place limits on our psycho-emotional well-being: for example, feeling 'hurt' by the reactions and behaviours of those around

will be visiting for a month with a large party of family and friends, Sydnam plans to move out of the main house where he normally lives, into a cottage nearby, and "stay out of the way as much as he was able to" (*Simply Love* 21) – despite several of his old friends being among the party. The rest of the novel traces Sydnam's journey from a state of loneliness and isolation to being part of a fulfilling romantic relationship, a family unit, and a wider community.

Having avoided women since he was tortured, Sydnam is resigned to his status as a man who has "learned to live alone. [...] Without a woman for his bed or his heart" (36). He believes that women are repulsed by him – a belief that is given some justification when the heroine, Anne, encountering him unexpectedly, is so shocked by his appearance that she actually runs away. Despite this inauspicious start, the two develop a relationship, but part after their first sexual encounter is a failure. He believes her physical unresponsiveness is due to repulsion at his appearance, while she is struggling with the traumatic aftereffects of being raped a decade earlier. The pregnancy that results from their liaison, however, forces them to marry, but with each believing that they are, in some sense, unworthy of the other. As they support each other in recovering a sense of self-worth, the two develop a relationship that is both loving and sexually fulfilling.

In the context of a contemporary culture in which there is "a pervasive cultural de-eroticization of people with disabilities" (Mollow and McRuer 4), the emphasis placed on the development of a sexually satisfying relationship is significant. Anna Mollow and Robert McRuer note the "segregation" of "sex and disability [...] in dominant cultural representations" (2). Depicting disabled heroes and heroines in satisfying sexual relationships and as erotic agents, as Balogh does, challenges this segregation. The status of the romance genre as a mass-market popular form, and the importance of fulfilling sexual relationships as an element of the HEA means that romances featuring disabled heroes or heroines are uniquely positioned to challenge public perceptions of disabled people as asexual.[10] More broadly, the depiction of disabled characters

us, being made to feel worthless, of lesser value, unattractive, hopeless, stressed, or insecure" (47).

10 | The picture becomes less clear when another dominant stereotype, disabled people as sexually abnormal, is considered. Mollow and McRuer pose the questions: "But what if disability were sexy? And what if disabled people were understood to be both subjects and objects of a multiplicity of erotic desires and practices?" (1). While the romances I discuss here affirm the possibility of disability as sexy, they, like virtually all mainstream romance novels, offer their disabled characters access only to a narrow version of sexuality (heterosexual, monogamous, vanilla) rather than a "multiplicity of erotic desires and practices." See Kaplan and Baldys for further discussion of heteronormativity in romance novels.

achieving the HEA is significant in a society still dominated by tragedy-model perspectives and thus ambivalent about whether disabled people are worthy or desiring of love: Sara Hosey notes "the enduring stereotype that disabled women [...] are incapable of initiating or maintaining mutually fulfilling romantic relationships" (40), while Colin Barnes and Geof Mercer (citing Harlan Hahn) write that in television portrayals of disabled characters, "the 'good parts' of ordinary lives – love, romance and sex – are largely absent or not stressed" (94). In romance novels, these 'good parts' of life, and how the protagonists secure them, are the main business of the narrative. Romance novels with disabled heroes or heroines require the reader to enter into an imaginative engagement with a world where disabled people love and are loved – happily ever after.

Simply Love depicts Sydnam's incorporation into a romantic couple, but also emphasises his incorporation into a family as well. Before the war his dreams included "a home of my own and a wife and children" (*Simply Love* 157). His desire to be a father is emphasised throughout the novel; he thinks enviously of a friend "[a]nd there was a baby in Bewcastle's nursery" (64). At the same time, though, he fears that children will recoil from him because of his appearance: "He would try at least to remain out of sight of the children. He did not want to frighten them. The worst feeling in the world was to see fear, revulsion, horror, and panic on the faces of children and to know that it was his own appearance that had caused it" (21). With one child describing Sydnam as "the monster" (86), his fears are not unfounded. Once engaged to Anne, Sydnam worries that David, her son, will not be able to love him: "And who could blame him if he did not? What child would choose a one-eyed, one-armed father whom most children and even some adults feared as a monster?" (231). However, drawn together by a shared love of painting, Sydnam and David develop a close relationship. Anne thinks, "[t]hey were a family" after Sydnam refers to David as "my boy" (304). Sydnam's status as father is cemented on the novel's final page by David calling him "Papa" for the first time, as the three of them arrive at their new family home together. Accepted as a father by David and married to the mother of his unborn child, Sydnam is at the heart of a new family unit.

Rosemarie Garland-Thomson's comment that "sexuality and community" are "two narrative currents which are seldom included in the usual stories we tell about disability" ("Shape" 114) suggests a link between sexuality and community that is borne out in *Simply Love*. Sydnam's incorporation into a romantic relationship and a family are connected, but so too is his integration into a wider social community. Anne and Sydnam are thrown together by the matchmaking efforts of various members of the house party. On their wedding day, the hasty nature of their wedding means that none of Sydnam's family and friends are present. Although overjoyed to be marrying Anne, Sydnam remembers his brother's wedding with some envy, where the couple were "surrounded by their families and friends, the church packed with people"

(*Simply Love* 237). On learning of their marriage, though, their friends and families organise a surprise celebration. This event serves not only as celebration of their marriage but as affirmation that they have been fully accepted into a wider social community. In a recent article, Hosey suggests that the authors she discusses make the significant move of "present[ing] stories about disability that situate characters in communities and traditions," rather than in isolation (48). Balogh's novel goes further than the mainstream narratives Hosey analyses, emphasising multiple levels of union or belonging: romantic couple, family, wider community. While not all romance novels explicitly position their protagonists becoming part of family and community units, the movement towards union inherent to the romance plot always entails the rejection of segregation and isolation.

On the Margins

My discussion so far has focused on romance novels featuring disabled heroes or heroines, arguing that novels which depict disabled characters as romance protagonists offer significant potentials for challenging a range of negative stereotypes. Two questions follow: Firstly, how often do disabled characters feature in romance novels, and what about works where disabled characters appear in secondary roles? Schwab writes that in romance novels the hero "is often physically impaired," while "[i]mpaired heroines tend to be much rarer" (276). Baldys claims a "recent proliferation of disabled characters in popular romance novels" (125). However, in the absence of large scale quantitative studies of the genre it is infeasible to make firm statements about the frequency with which disabled characters appear in the genre.[11] I therefore focus on the potentials the depiction of disabled characters in the genre offers. These potentials are relatively clear-cut when disabled characters appear in the role of hero or heroine, but less so where disabled characters appear in secondary roles.

Whilst *Simply Love* shows disabled characters moving from a state of isolation to one of community, *Slightly Married* begins with a community where disabled people are valued and included. Heroine Eve's fortune supports a host

---

11 | Baldys cites the list of 200+ novels featuring characters with disabilities on the *All About Romance* website as evidence ("Disabilities in Romance"). However, I claim that (a) this is not a particularly large number in the larger context of the genre, and (b) the function of the "Special Title Listings" on this site (of which the "Disabilities in Romance" list is one) is to guide readers to niche categories within the romance genre - those which the reader is unlikely to encounter through casual browsing. Other listings in the same section include twin romances, sports romances, and romances involving courtroom dramas.

of people unwanted by or excluded from society. Her two foster children are orphans, and she provides for "Aunt Mari," a distant relative lamed by years of mine work. Her staff includes Charlie, a cognitively disabled odd-job man unwanted elsewhere after the death of his father, and Ned, an amputee war veteran. Her housekeeper is an ex-convict, and the governess to her foster children is an unmarried mother. Even Eve's dog is the victim of past abuse and has lost an eye and a leg. With the death of her brother, Eve is disinherited and the estate and income that supports the household is lost. It is largely to save the home and livelihood of these others that Eve enters into a marriage of convenience with the hero, Aidan, since marriage will allow her to keep her home and income, and therefore keep the community intact.

Aidan is initially dismissive of the community Eve has created. He accuses her of having a "bleeding heart" and filling "her home and neighbourhood with lame ducks" (*Slightly Married* 59). His primary motive in marrying Eve is the gallant one of preventing her from losing her home, and his intention that the marriage be in name only. However, Aidan is gradually drawn in to Eve's life, and ultimately has a change of heart about the community Eve has created: "I have sometimes spoken with irritation and even contempt of your lame ducks. I am sorry about that. I honor your generosity and your love for all creatures, no matter their looks or their station in life or their history" (303). This declaration is the final piece of evidence that Aidan is worthy of Eve's love. The novel ends with Aidan leaving the army to assist Eve's steward in setting up and running a farming project that will provide work for disabled, destitute ex-soldiers. The community depicted at the start of the novel is not only secured but expanded.

While *Slightly Married* depicts disabled characters as valued parts of a community, the novel bears out Garland-Thomson's assertion that "[d]isabled literary characters usually remain on the margins of fiction" (*Extraordinary* 9), with the individual disabled characters remaining relatively peripheral. Lennard J. Davis notes that where disabled characters appear in literature "the disabled character is never of importance to himself or herself. Rather, the character is placed in the narrative 'for' the nondisabled characters – to help them develop sympathy, empathy, or as a counterbalance to some issue in the life of the 'normal' character" ("Crips" 45). In *Slightly Married* the disabled characters' collective function is to advance the story of the (able-bodied) heroine and hero; they exist primarily as a means of illustrating the heroine's kind and generous nature and providing impetus for her to marry. Later, Aidan's change of heart regarding Eve's 'lame ducks' is evidence that he is worthy of her. In most analyses, the next step would be to move from the statement that these characters are on the margins of the narrative to a claim that they are marginalised – as disabled people have so long been marginalised in a prejudiced society. However, the particular context in which these representations appear problematises this logical leap. In popular romance, where "the love story is the main focus of the novel" (Romance Writers of America, "About" n. pag.), the only two characters that are essential to the narrative are the hero and heroine. *All* other characters are by definition peripheral or marginal. While some romance novels offer a range of fleshed-out secondary characters, even in these works the majority of the textual space is occupied by the central couple, and the secondary characters function in relation to them.[12] While romance novels can (and do) marginalise disabled characters on ideological grounds, it is important to note that there may be structural factors at work as well. Genre context is thus a crucial factor in analysing representations of disability.

YARDSTICK ROLES

One tool for analysing the depiction of disabled secondary characters in romance is David T. Mitchell and Sharon L. Snyder's notion of disability as "narrative prosthesis." Rather than attempt to engage with the full complexity of narrative prosthesis in the limited space available here,[13] I focus on a single aspect of disability representation that falls within that rubric, adapting Patricia M. Puccinelli's work on "retarded characters" in fiction. Puccinelli defines the "yardstick quality" as "the capacity to act as or provide a measure against which other characters in the narrative are assessed. From this measurement the reader makes judgements about the other characters" (15). Therefore: "The other character's responses to the retarded character reveals much about his or her own true nature. For example, if a character responds to a retarded

---

12 | Advice from Mills & Boon on "How to Write the Perfect Romance" makes this explicit: "I *don't like* secondary characters – use with caution! You're writing a romance, readers are interested in your hero and heroine so keep the focus on them" (n. pag.; emphasis in original). Whilst Mills & Boon category romances have more restricted word limits (typically 50,000-75,000 words) than other types of romance novel, the focus on the central couple holds more generally.

13 | Narrative prosthesis "enables a contrast between [...] mainstream discourses that would disguise or obliterate the evidence of physical and cognitive differences, and literary efforts that expose prosthesis as an artificial, and thus, resignifiable, relation" (Mitchell and Snyder 9). Although the term 'mainstream discourses' is never defined, it seems likely that genre fiction would fall into this category. Further, genre fiction is marginalised in *Narrative Prosthesis*: there is a lack of engagement with genre texts, and the ways in which some types of genre fiction might complicate their assertions about the representation of disability in literature are never acknowledged. Finally, although it is often invoked in a simplistic way, the notion of narrative prosthesis as outlined by Mitchell and Snyder is both complex and multifaceted and to engage with it meaningfully requires an amount of space not available here.

character with kindness and patience (even if the responding character appears villainous in other situations), the reader is likely to attribute at least some positive qualities to the non-retarded character" (ibid.).

As the terminology suggests, Puccinelli's engagement with a disability studies perspective is minimal, and consequently her work has been little used within cultural disability studies. Though aspects of her work are problematic, the yardstick concept is particularly useful when considering romance novels. Developing empathy for the heroine and/or hero is vital in romance, and yardstick characters are frequently deployed in romance novels to achieve this, as highlighted by Janice A. Radway. Radway had her participants identify "ideal romances," and found that in these works, the heroine "is always portrayed as unusually compassionate, kind, and understanding. Typically, some minor disaster occurs in the early stages of the story that proves the perfect occasion for her to display her extraordinary capacity for empathetic nurturance and tender care" (127). Frequently it is the deployment of a yardstick character that allows the heroine to demonstrate this capacity for 'tender care.' In Balogh's novels, all of the following function as yardsticks at various points: children, orphans, servants, animals, older people, people with impairments, the dead, prostitutes, and those marginalised by their class position or financial status.

In *Simply Perfect*, one of the key secondary characters is the hero's eleven year old daughter Lizzie, who has been blind since birth. Her father Joseph is searching for a way to educate and care for her after the death of her mother, and suspects that the boarding school run by Claudia, the heroine, may offer the solution. Unsure if Lizzie is ready to attend school, Claudia proposes a trial where Lizzie will join a group of charity girls – girls from impoverished backgrounds who attend the school for free – whom she is taking to the house of an acquaintance for the summer. The scheme allows Joseph, visiting family nearby, to have some contact with his daughter, although it requires the pretense that they are unrelated. Although he loves Lizzie deeply, her illegitimacy means that Joseph is unable to publicly acknowledge her, and his family is unaware she exists.

Lizzie joins the group of girls, and her identity remains hidden, despite frequent contact with her father. Whilst most characters accept Lizzie, one person's attitude stands out in sharp contrast: Portia Hunt, the appropriate bride selected for Joseph by his parents, and to whom he becomes engaged during the novel. When Joseph, Portia and others see Lizzie playing with the other girls, Portia is the only one to comment negatively: "Is that the *blind* girl I have heard about? ... She is spoiling the dance for the others. And she is making a spectacle of herself, poor girl" (*Simply Perfect* 211). Portia also comments within Lizzie's hearing that Lizzie is a clumsy dancer (224). Yet another character offers a very different view of the same scene: "They were a delight, were they not, Joseph, all dancing about the maypole? And that little blind girl was quite undaunted by her affliction" (222). Portia's hostility to Lizzie is partly based upon her class background, but also specifically relates to her impairment. After Claudia and her pupils attend a local event to which they have been invited, Portia comments that it is disrespectful "to have brought *charity* pupils to mingle with such a gathering. [...] And a *blind* charity girl is the outside of enough" (251). Portia's attitude is in marked contrast to the other members of the aristocratic group, who are universally accepting of Lizzie. One comments that Lizzie "is a delightful child" who "has become everyone's pet" (232); she is "something of a favourite with the duchess and her other guests" (223). After Lizzie's true identity is revealed, the same group is surprisingly, and perhaps a little implausibly, sanguine: "I do believe most people are secretly charmed by the fact that she is his daughter. Everyone had fallen for her anyway" (257). The secret out, Joseph seizes the chance to have Lizzie live with him, but Portia rejects this idea absolutely, referring to Lizzie as "that dreadful creature" and "that dreadful blind child" (263, 280), and saying she will marry him only if she never sees Lizzie or hears her name again. Their broken engagement clears the way for Claudia and Joseph to be united.

Lizzie therefore acts as a yardstick character in the novel. The only characters who respond to Lizzie less than positively are those who function as barriers to the union of Claudia and Joseph, including Claudia's former lover, who wants to rekindle their romance, and Joseph's father and sister, who want him to marry Portia. The reader is invited to judge the characters in the text based on their reaction to Lizzie. Were this the full extent of her role in the text, we might read this as a representation which reinforces the marginalisation of disabled people – the character placed in the narrative 'for' the non-disabled characters as described by Davis. However, this is not the case. Much attention is given to her character development, including a section where she is the viewpoint character (see *Simply Perfect* 235-240). Lizzie's presence undoubtedly serves the romance narrative, both in her role as yardstick and as justification for bringing the hero and heroine together across class boundaries. However, the romance narrative also serves Lizzie, whose life is transformed in the course of the novel. At the end of the novel she is starting a new life where she can live with her father all the time, and has a new stepmother whom she has already grown to love. Lizzie's role suggests, then, that a disabled character can function as a yardstick without necessarily being marginalised.[14]

---

14 | Lizzie's position not only as a disabled person but as a disabled child is also significant. Child characters are frequently deployed in romance novels in a yardstick role, or as a device to advance the plot in some other way (e.g. the heroine is employed as a governess for the hero's child). Characterisation of these characters is often minimal, to the extent that one romance website coined a specific term for this phenomenon:

In *Slightly Scandalous* (2003), another disabled female character problematises a straightforwardly negative interpretation of the yardstick role. Prudence Moore, who is cognitively disabled, is the hero's cousin. Initially Prudence appears to be in the novel to function as a yardstick for a number of the other characters, including the hero, the heroine, and the major villain of the piece, Prudence's own mother. The hero's evident love and regard for her, and the actions that he takes to protect Prudence and secure her happiness – he refuses to let her mother put her in an asylum, and liberates her from the nursery to which she is largely confined despite being eighteen – serves as evidence of the essential goodness of his nature. However, Prudence does not just disappear from the text after fulfilling the yardstick function; she remains one of the major secondary characters. By the end of the novel, with the hero's blessing and acknowledgement of her status as an adult able to make her own choices, Prudence chooses to leave her mother and marry the man she is in love with.

This in itself would be significant, but it is not the end of the story. Because of the way the novels are interlinked we learn more about Prudence's life. In *Simply Love* we learn that Prudence now has two sons, and the heroine of that novel envies her happiness. Two books later, in *Simply Perfect*, we get a further update: Claudia describes her as "the sweetest young woman imaginable. She married a fisherman and bore him sturdy sons and runs his home and is as happy as it is possible to be" (329-30). Prudence's story, then challenges particular negative stereotypes about disability. Like the disabled hero Sydnam Butler in *Simply Love*, she moves from a position of isolation (segregation within the family home, and the threat of institutionalisation) to being part of a couple, a family, and a wider community. As the wording of Claudia's comment highlights, Prudence has achieved her happily ever after. In finding an enduring love, and building a family and home upon it, her fate is indistinguishable from that of the non-disabled romance heroine.

Characters in Balogh's novels are part of the romance world in the obvious sense of featuring in a romance novel. However, these characters are also part of the romance world in the specific sense of being potential romantic actants – regardless of their disability status. Lizzie's father is concerned with finding "a husband who will be kind to her" in the future (*Simply Perfect* 117), rather than about whether she will or will not eventually marry. One of the key pleasures for readers of Balogh's novels is catching glimpses of characters whose love stories will be told in future novels, and being updated on the status of couples from earlier books (in *Simply Perfect*, for example, Sydnam and Anne from *Simply Love* appear as minor characters). In some cases, as with Prudence and with Sergeant Strickland in *Slightly Sinful*, these love stories are told in

---

"Plot Moppet: a small child who has no purpose or development except to drive the plot forward" (Wendell n. pag.).

secondary romance plots which run parallel to the central narratives. In other cases, the disabled characters are heroes or heroines of later novels: the "lame and pretty Lady Muir" (*Simply Perfect* 252), who appears occasionally in both series, is the heroine of *The Proposal* (2012). Balogh's work therefore not only features disabled heroes and heroines achieving the HEA, but also positions the secondary disabled characters as doing the same or likely to do the same.

REPRESENTATIONS AND THEIR EFFECTS

Balogh's novels, then, challenge particular negative stereotypes through their depictions of disabled characters achieving the HEA. More broadly, I suggest that romance novels featuring disabled heroes and heroines have significant potentials to do the same. Yet, as Mitchell and Snyder write, "The issue of representation and what it produces in readers is extremely complex" (41). Radway's early feminist work on popular romance reminds us that there may be a significant gap between what one person perceives as the ideological positioning of a particular text and what another actually takes away from reading it. In claiming Balogh's novels as challenging various negative stereotypes, I am not aiming to fix these novels as "positive" representations which should be placed on some hypothetical list of "acceptable" representations of disability (Mitchell and Snyder 42). Rather, I am arguing for a positive *interpretation* of these novels: one which sees them as being potentially useful in the struggle to break down social barriers.

In particular, I suggest that Balogh's novels encourage the reader to reflect upon how they conceptualise disability: by challenging particular negative stereotypes as noted above, but also through explicit discussion and exploration of what it means to be 'disabled.' Sergeant Strickland rejects the label of unfit implicit in his discharge from the army, identifying other venues where his changed physical abilities are irrelevant: "I can dress you and shave you and look after your clothes with one eye the same as two" (*Slightly Sinful* 113). Other characters note that definitions of normality are socially constructed: one character refers to Prudence as "a child who was not normal according to the definition of normality that society had concocted" (*Simply Love* 32). Characters' own ideas of disability change and develop – her contact with Lizzie leads Claudia to comment "I have just realized that *all* girls are different from the norm. In other words, the norm does not exist except in the minds of those who like tidy statistics" (*Simply Perfect* 114). Not only is what is "normal" constructed, contingent, and subject to change, but non-disabled people acknowledge the limitations of their understanding. The hero of *Slightly Scandalous* acknowledges that in viewing those with "physical and mental abilities different from the norm" he and other able-bodied people are only able to "view them from our own limited perspective" (256).

Balogh's work also encourages a reflexive approach to disability through the depiction of disabled characters experiencing prejudice. Portia's reaction to Lizzie in *Simply Perfect* is one example, but a deeper engagement with this theme is seen in *Simply Love*. In this novel, Balogh offers an extended description of the first meeting between Anne and Sydnam. Each of them is walking alone, entertaining romantic fantasies about the other, but the mood is shattered when they get closer, and Anne sees him clearly for the first time:

"[S]he stood transfixed again – but with horror this time. [...] He was a man with half a face, the extraordinarily beautiful left side all the more grotesque because there was no right side to balance it. He was beauty and beast all rolled into one. And all of a sudden his height and those powerful thighs and broad shoulders seemed menacing rather than enticing." (*Simply Love* 30)

Shocked, Anne runs away, and though she returns shortly after to apologise, she is too late and Sydnam is gone. Several pages are devoted to Anne's reflection upon her actions, and the guilt she feels leaves the reader in no doubt that her behaviour is unacceptable. She is "mortified" (31), and reflects "she had recoiled from him, run away in fright and revulsion. How had he felt?" (33). This question is answered a few pages later when the encounter is presented again from Sydnam's point of view, with his romantic daydreams abruptly shattered: "He gazed after her and was again Sydnam Butler, grotesquely ugly, with his right eye gone and the purple scars of old burns down the side of his face, paralyzing most of the nerves there, and all along his armless side to his knee" (35). Despite having "left self-pity behind long ago," "it would take him days to recover his equilibrium" (36).

Writing about film and television representations of disability, Paul Longmore identifies a recurring motif whereby disabled characters "spurn opportunities for romance because of a lack of self-acceptance," while the nondisabled characters "have no trouble finding the disabled persons attractive or falling in love with them, and have no difficulty in accepting them with their disabilities" (142). This type of representation, Longmore suggests, differs greatly from "the real-life experiences" of disabled people, who often find "even the most minor impairments result in romantic rejection" (142). Overall, such depictions "invert social reality and allow the nondisabled audience to disown its anxieties and prejudices about disabled people" (142). Rather than allowing the reader to disown their prejudices, *Simply Love*'s uncompromising depiction of disability-related prejudice brings these issues to the foreground, confronting the reader with what it might feel like to be on the receiving end.

Even after Anne apologies to Sydnam, and the two start afresh, their interactions remain strained. Anne's mind "chattered incessantly with questions she knew she could not ask" about how he acquired his injuries (*Simply Love* 58), and she is highly conscious of how she looks at him, "how difficult it was to look at him as if he were any normal man" (57). As with the earlier scene, the reader is presented with both viewpoints, but in this case the dual perspective is used to illustrate the difference Anne's efforts make: "She was looking directly into his face. Most people, he had observed, either did not look quite at him or else focused their eyes on his left ear or his left shoulder. With most people he felt the urge to turn his head slightly to the side so that they would not have to be repulsed quite so badly. He did not feel that urge with her" (68).

Rather than a facile depiction where "good" characters simply are not prejudiced, Balogh explores the causes and effects of disability-related prejudice, and shows the characters working to overcome them.

CONCLUSION

Simply Love, then, foregrounds the difficulties those with extraordinary bodies face in interactions with able-bodied others, and stresses the importance of attitudes and behaviours in creating an environment that is welcoming or hostile. In this novel as in others, Balogh's depiction of disabled characters encourages readers to reflect upon their own attitudes and beliefs with regards to disability. The rapid expansion of popular romance scholarship in recent years indicates how much romance novels have to offer to scholars in a whole range of fields. This analysis of selected works by Balogh illustrates some of the productive potentials of bringing together cultural disability studies and popular romance studies: a union that is surely to the benefit of both fields.

REFERENCES

Baldys, Emily M. "Disabled Sexuality, Incorporated: The Compulsions of Popular Romance." *Journal of Literary & Cultural Disability Studies* 6.2 (2012): 125-141. Print.

Balogh, Mary. *The Proposal*. London: Piatkus, 2012. Print.

—. *Simply Love*. 2006. London: Piatkus, 2007. Print.

—. *Simply Perfect*. 2008. London: Piatkus, 2009. Print.

—. *Slightly Married*. 2003. London: Piatkus, 2006. Print.

—. *Slightly Scandalous*. 2003. London: Piatkus, 2007. Print.

—. *Slightly Sinful*. New York: Dell, 2004. Print.

—. *Slightly Tempted*. 2004. London: Piatkus, 2007. Print.

—. *Slightly Wicked*. 2003. London: Piatkus, 2007. Print.

Barnes, Colin and Geof Mercer. *Disability*. Cambridge: Polity, 2003. Print.

Bly, Mary. "On Popular Romance, J. R. Ward, and the Limits of Genre Study." *New Approaches to Popular Romance Fiction: Critical Essays*. Ed. Sarah S. G. Frantz and Eric Murphy Selinger. Jefferson: McFarland, 2012. N. pag. *Kindle* digital file.

Bolt, David. "Social Encounters, Cultural Representation, and Critical Avoidance." *Routledge Handbook of Disability Studies*. Ed. Nick Watson, Alan Roulstone and Carol Thomas. London: Routledge, 2012. 287-297. Print.

Davis, Lennard J. "Crips Strike Back: The Rise of Disability Studies." *Bending Over Backwards: Disability, Dismodernism and Other Difficult Positions*. New York: New York University Press, 2002. 33-46. Print.

"Disabilities in Romance." *All About Romance*. June 2013. Web. 19 Aug. 2014. <http://www.likesbooks.com/disability.html>.

Garland-Thomson, Rosemarie. *Extraordinary Bodies: Physical Disability in American Culture and Literature*. New York: Columbia University Press, 1997. Print.

—. "Shape Structures Story: Fresh and Feisty Stories about Disability." *Narrative* 15.1 (2007): 113-23. Web. 27 Aug. 2008. Academic OneFile.

Hosey, Sara. "'One of Us:' Identity and Community in Contemporary Fiction." *Journal of Literary & Cultural Disability Studies* 3.1 (2009): 35-50. Print.

Kaplan, Deborah. "'Why Would Any Woman Want to Read Such Stories?': The Distinctions Between Genre Romances and Slash Fiction." *New Approaches to Popular Romance Fiction: Critical Essays*. Ed. Sarah S. G. Frantz and Eric Murphy Selinger. Jefferson: McFarland, 2012. N. pag. *Kindle* digital file.

Longmore, Paul K. "Screening Stereotypes: Images of Disabled People in Television and Motion Pictures." *Why I Burned My Book: And Other Essays on Disability*. Philadelphia: Temple University Press, 2003. 131-146. Print.

Miller, Kathleen. "'A Little Extra Bite: Dis/Ability and Romance in Tanya Huff and Charlaine Harris's Vampire Fiction." *Journal of Popular Romance Studies* 1.1 (2010). Web. 19 Aug. 2012. <http://jprstudies.org/2010/08/a-little-extra-bite-disability-and-romance-in-tanya-huff-and-charlaine-harris-vampire-fiction-by-kathleen-miller/>.

Mills & Boon. "How to Write the Perfect Romance!" *Mills & Boon.co.uk*. Harlequin Mills & Boon Ltd. Web. 19 Aug. 2014. <http://www.millsandboon.co.uk/Content/ContentPage/14>.

Mitchell, David T. and Sharon L. Snyder. *Narrative Prosthesis: Disability and the Dependencies of Discourse*. Ann Arbor: University of Michigan Press, 2000. Print.

Mollow, Anna and Robert McRuer. "Introduction." *Sex and Disability*. Ed. McRuer and Mollow. Durham: Duke University Press, 2012. 1-34. Print.

Puccinelli, Patricia M. *Yardsticks: Retarded Characters and Their Role in Fiction.* New York: Peter Lang, 1995. Print.

Radway, Janice A. *Reading the Romance: Women, Patriarchy, and Popular Literature.* Chapel Hill: U of North Carolina Press, 1991. Print.

Regis, Pamela. *A Natural History of the Romance Novel.* Philadelphia: University of Pennsylvania Press, 2003. Print.

Romance Writers of America. "About the Romance Genre." *Romance Writers of America.* Web. 19 Aug. 2014. <http://www.rwa.org/p/cm/ld/fid=578>.

—. "Romance Industry Statistics." *Romance Writers of America.* Web. 19 Aug. 2014. <http://www.rwa.org/p/cm/ld/fid=579>.

—. "Romance Subgenres." *Romance Writers of America.* Web. 19 Aug. 2014. <http://www.rwa.org/p/cm/ld/fid=580>.

Schwab, Sandra. "'It is Only with One's Heart that One Can See Clearly:' The Loss of Sight in Teresa Medeiros's *The Bride and the Beast* and *Yours Until Dawn.*" *Journal of Literary & Cultural Disability Studies* 6.3 (2012): 275-89. Print.

Selinger, Eric Murphy and Sarah S. G. Frantz. "Introduction: New Approaches to Popular Romance Fiction." *New Approaches to Popular Romance Fiction: Critical Essays.* Eds. Frantz and Selinger. Jefferson: McFarland, 2012. N. pag. *Kindle* digital file.

Thomas, Carol. *Female Forms: Experiencing and Understanding Disability.* Buckingham: Open University Press, 1999. Print.

Wendell, Sarah. "The Bitchery Glossary." *Smart Bitches Trashy Books.* 21 Nov. 2011. Web. 19 Aug. 2014. <http://smartbitchestrashybooks.com/blog/the-bitchery-glossary>.

Responses to Ria Cheyne

Martin Roussel
LITERALLY AND LITERARY DISABLED BODIES

In my comment on Ria Cheyne's paper I would like to discuss the idea of *fiction* and its possibilities for dealing with disability. For this purpose, I will explore, as Cheyne summarizes her analysis of selected works by Mary Balogh, "productive potentials of bringing together cultural disability studies and popular romance studies: a union that is surely to the benefit of both fields" (214). However, my argument does not stress the applicability – or extension – of disability studies within the field of literary and cultural studies, but goes the other way around: How can we define the idea of 'disability' not only as a topic or motif in narrative discourses but in a more specific literary sense? How does literature contribute to the idea of something or someone being 'disabled?' What kinds of narratives structure our understanding of disability? And is there something that a literary perspective might add to our understanding of disability? I understand my remarks as generally in accordance with Cheyne's basic arguments about an evaluative criticism specifying the necessity for interpretation rather than simply depiction in the sense of retelling. Interpretation means taking a position. Yet, this kind of social responsibility should take into account the differences between a representation or fictional text and its depiction or interpretation. The question is: How can we morally judge fiction?

I will start addressing these issues by quoting a phrase Franz Kafka wrote between 1922 and 1924: "Once I broke my leg, it was the greatest experience of my life" (Kafka 548; translation by author).[15] Whether intentionally or not, Kafka did not finish these words with a full stop. It is not by chance that I quote this detached if not scattered sentence instead of commenting on a longer narrative structure or the whole of an œuvre. The statement lacks any context within Kafka's fragments. If we take this very brief but also highly emphasized

---

15 | Original quote: "Einmal brach ich mir das Bein, es war das schönste Erlebnis meines Lebens."

phrase by a first-person narrator as a miniature story about disability, this story tells us about the luck of dysfunction. The general function of the fragmentary sentence – to articulate a special relationship to dysfunction – is highlighted by the indifference Kafka demonstrates towards the question of whether he, or the narrator, broke his right or left leg, or both legs; it simply states that somebody broke "mein Bein [my leg]," which indicates not the function of one of his legs, but the function of 'leg' in general. How are we to understand Kafka's emphasis? Maybe he (or a she, or an it) was lucky to break a leg because having broken his/her leg he/she/it was unable to do whatever might have to be done if he/she/it had sound legs? One might also ask why we should necessarily think of a human being with two legs, one of them injured, and not of a horse or an elephant with four legs? Why should we recognize Kafka's, we might assume, temporary experience as a highly positive one if it means having to deal with an impairment, with dysfunction, and a lack of capacity to act the way one 'normally' acts?

Eventually, two different perspectives in reading this Kafka story might come to mind. From one angle, we might acknowledge numerous perspectives in reading the sentence. We would therefore reflect upon the representational meaning of the broken leg and the ways of understanding it as a comment on impairment and why this ailment might involve happiness. A second option is not at first hand concerned with the different readings of this partly delightful, partly peculiar story. Kafka's note ties us back to the question of the meaning of being disabled: Do we, in fact, know what it means to consider an impairment as 'good' or 'bad,' as 'positive' or 'negative?' Are we to consider impairment as lack of something – of health, of wholeness, of functionality? And how does this correspond to the use of the term 'disability' in the field of disability studies that refers to socially constructed barriers? At the very least, we might say that Kafka's fragment first selects the act of becoming impaired as its central theme and, secondly, emphasizes this incident as a most beautiful/joyful/satisfying one.[16] Are we to find in Kafka's phrase a certain kind of 'counter-narrative' to the way we think of 'disability' as being confronted with socially constructed barriers?

And, what I think is the most important question in this context, are we to consider a lack of something as 'wrong' in the sense that there should be something 'more? In this sense, what could it mean that Kafka's phrase goes the other way round? The sudden emergence of an impairment, which is literally, and also metaphorically, connected with his ability to stand on his own feet, becomes an experience of deep impact. Of course we know of Kafka as a major example of a 'loser son' struggling with his authoritative father. As Avital Ronell has recently shown in her book *Loser Sons*, Kafka, in his literary works,

---

16 | The German *schönstes Erlebnis* (most beautiful/joyful/satisfying experience) links to the traditional aesthetic discourse of the late 18th century.

puts fundamental mechanisms of authority on the table. The German term "schönstes Erlebnis" is difficult to accurately translate into English: It means "greatest experience," but also includes an aesthetic dimension like "most beautiful experience." Then, why could we speak of a disabling event as in itself being beautiful? What kind of beauty is thus revealed? In a sense, this could be the beauty of life, of emotional and physical presence.

According to my understanding of the history of disability studies, one of the concerns within this field has been to deconstruct the hierarchy between the non-impaired and the disabled body or to deconstruct our prior knowledge of the body (and the mind) as normally normalized phenomena, i.e. as phenomena that have become 'normal' in an unnoticed manner. If one must acknowledge normalizing procedures, one also must accept that there is not *yet* the 'normal.' Consequently, there may not exist anything like a normal body without the procedure of normalization. As early as 1989 in *The Telephone Book: Technology, Schizophrenia, Electric Speech*, Avital Ronell wrote about the non-existence – in a natural sense – of the perfect body. According to Ronell, humans have always tried to complete something – something that we, the humans, are – or to implement the idea of completing ourselves in the processes of learning, growing up, or aging. An effect of this has been that technology has always played the role of a supplementary factor. Ronell argues that the prosthesis as "godlike annexation to a certain extent enjoys the status of the fetish, covering a missing or inadequate body part, amplifying the potentiality of a constitutively fragile organ" (Ronell 88). Following Ronell and her reading of Sigmund Freud's *Das Unbehagen in der Kultur [Civilization and Its Discontents]*, we understand that what Kafka suspends is the phantasm of becoming godlike. By facing his own physical and non-prosthetic existence, Kafka (or his first-person narrator) figures a non-Christian incarnation of a human being becoming human. "How to become what you are," wrote Friedrich Nietzsche in the subtitle of *Ecce homo*. By this means, Kafka refuses the fulfillments and salvations that eventually, in modern times, turn out to be remedies for denying mortality, for eternalizing oneself. Again, I quote Ronell:

"As has been the case with all such infinitizing inventions (one thinks of the works of Edison, Bell, or Dr. Frankenstein), the fulfillment of a fairy-tale wish, coming very close in omnipotent sway to a god, emerges from a traumatized zone to establish some form of restitutional services: the typewriter originally intended for the blind, the gramophone for the deaf, the telephone clandestinely for those afflicted with speech and hearing impediments." (Ronell 88)

Let me take my remarks on Kafka and the insufficient, but also prosthetic human nature, as a starting point to comment on Cheyne's paper. Her main argument focuses on what she calls a "reflexive approach to disability" which is encouraged by literature, for example "through the depiction of disabled characters experiencing prejudice" (213). The invitation to reflect upon a narrative or representational element implies a certain relief of accountability that is fundamental for fictional texts. Fictitious representations thus present themselves without at the same time being evaluative. Fiction suspends the field of social acting; the producer of fiction does not have to take on responsibility for everything that happens to his/her text. An evaluative criticism is foregrounded by the distinction between representation and interpretation. I quote Cheyne who follows David T. Mitchell and Sharon L. Snyder's argument on "disability as narrative prosthesis:"

"[...] I am not aiming to fix these novels as 'positive' representations which should be placed on some hypothetical list of 'acceptable' representations of disability [...]. Rather, I am arguing for a positive *interpretation* of these novels: one which sees them as being potentially useful in the struggle to break down social barriers." (212)

I generally agree with Cheyne in the sense that interpreting representations means to accept responsibility for what one's interpretation suggests. But does that imply that fictitious texts cannot provide the reader with evaluative arguments? One might think of how John L. Austin in *How to Do Things with Words* suspended literature from the realm of successful speech acts:[17] Can we, as a result, make an advantage out of this disadvantage attributed to literature's speech acts, if not their dismissal?[18]

How then do we conceive the role of 'reflection' when talking of *reflexive representations*? Are we, on the one hand, to follow a reader response theory that is based on blank spaces in the text? Where does reflection take place in representational processes? If there is a mediated space, a communicative (or

---

17 | The discussions that followed Austin commented on his distinction between 'serious' speech acts and 'parasitic' speech acts, in which the latter indicate fictional speech acts as 'not serious' in the sense of not including perlocutionary effects.

18 | Of course, one might turn Austin's argument against itself: If language is designated by something Jacques Derrida calls 'iterability,' literature cannot be suspended from speech acts or, to take it a step further, any speech act may be 'read' as literature. The question is, what makes us believe in a certain responsibility (or power, or insistence, etc.) when someone is saying something. The case of literature in speech act theory, thus, is the case of a larger metaphysical argument: Is there something 'present' when someone is saying something to someone, and is this 'presence' (force, power, etc.) going 'through' language (the act of saying something) from someone to someone else (by saying something)? And how can we describe analytically the importance of speech acts of literature for a - more philosophical - field of discussion in this sense? (see Miller 2001).

evaluative) break, between representation and interpretation, where do we find the opposing idea of closeness in the sense of 'a status without the interrupting of reflection?'

In the case of literature, one might point out that literary texts are associated with both the distance from and open spaces for the reader's imagination, as well as proximity, closeness to life. I therefore point out the topos that literature has its "setting in life" ["Sitz im Leben"], as described by Romance scholar Erich Köhler (Köhler 11). To me, it is most likely that the differentiation between 'reflexive' and 'immediate' representation links back to phantasms of literature itself. Probably, the idea that a representational structure might have hallucinating, presentational effects and might therefore potentially be identified with life itself, sounds like one of the phantasms of the Romantic period. In the words of Friedrich Kittler, one might think of the *Discourse Networks 1800/1900*, i.e. German hallucinating Romanticism and operative modernism with a technical definition of writing as contrasted with media like film or the gramophone. Taking this into account, I would argue for a historical understanding of the function of literature and its representations. This is not to argue against an evaluative criticism, but against grounding it in a supra-historical concept of representation and its effect structure.

'Fiction' means that one does not need to judge it because the arguments implied are not directly related to the 'factual world,' but rather to its own 'aesthetic world.' Nonetheless, frictions occur, and of course literature might be conceptualized as *littérature engagée*. But even literature that is strongly intertwined with concepts of 'reality' deals with the power of fiction and not primarily with facts. In a way, reading in the modern sense of 'silent' reading is very private, and so should be a reader's judgment. It is the voice that occupies public domains. To use literary texts in a polemic manner always throws a reflection back at the usage itself: Why and to what end should we blame fictitious texts as if the positions of figures in the text were those of people in flesh and blood? But sometimes fictitious figures may act like 'real' people and the other way round, as we have learned from the novels as well as academic essays of Umberto Eco (see for example *Name*; *Walks*). The question (which may be the wrong question) is: Does 'good' literature have to be likeable? And, what do we value when reading literature? Probably, in literature we cannot separate questions of content (which might be the object of an evaluative criticism) and form (which might be regarded as 'innovative,' 'old fashioned,' etc.). So I would argue for literature's content as always contingent on its form. We can never know about the reliability of meaning in literature without asking about the enactment of a figure, a narrator, a plot, or an argument.

To return to Kafka, my reading of his brief fragment would stress the distinctive and specific position Kafka expresses. Agreeing to the prosthetic character of existence, Kafka discovers the beauty of a position of being not capable. His kindred spirits in the history of literature are, among others, Fyodor M. Dostoevsky and his contemporary Robert Walser. With a sidestep to Walser, Kafka's congenial soul mate, I conclude my comment. This Swiss author once wrote about the perfection of our earthly imperfection:

"O, how the errors gleam with perfection, and how failures are fragrant with alluring skillfulness, and how everything that seems to be right is wrong, and what truth lies in all that is false and how unimportant is *the* important and how are unimportances taken importantly, and this has to be this way, as it just *suits* us so." (Walser 106 et. seq.; translation by author)[19]

In opposition to all traditions which provide us with ideas of perfection, of wholeness and the holy with the promise of an idealized afterlife, in the works of Kafka and Walser the idea of redemption returns to human existence in its bare sense.

In Walser, by the way, we find a person who embodies all these metaphorizations and incredible reversals in 'real' life. Against his will, he was hospitalized in 1929 with the tentative diagnosis of schizophrenia, although he was never examined again. He stayed in a mental hospital for almost 28 years until his death in 1956, accepting his fatally changed life path. Of course, we can also learn something here about the 'negative' treatment of people displaying behavioral problems, but I think the distinctiveness of his attitude and, in a certain way, superior behavior also poses questions about the relation between the normal and the unique, and how both are found intertwined in this peculiar biography. As far as we know, Walser stopped being an author from the moment he officially became a patient. Asked about whether he received preferential treatment in hospital, Walser briefly answered Carl Seelig, who was one of the few people who remembered the once famous poet, and his answer may be taken as a parable of life in hospital: "Why should I change to a better ward? Wasn't it you who remained a private (lance-corporal), without the conspicuous behavior of an officer? Look, I am a private like you and want to remain one. I have little appetite for becoming an officer as you have. I want to live among the people and vanish into them" (Seelig 93; translation by author).[20]

---

19 | Original quote (italics marks a hypothetical reading): "O, wie schimmern die Fehler vor Vollkommenheit, und wie duften Mißlungenheiten nach verführerischem Gekonnthaben, und wie ist alles, was richtig zu sein scheint, unrichtig, und was liegt in allem Falschen für eine Wahrheit, und wie unwichtig ist *das* Wichtige und wie wichtig werden Unwichtigkeiten genommen, und das muß so sein, es *liegt* uns so."

20 | Original quote: "Warum soll ich in eine höhere Abteilung wollen? Sind Sie nicht auch Gefreiter geblieben, ohne Offiziersallüren? Sehen Sie, so eine Art Gefreiter bin

References

Cheyne, Ria. "Disability Studies Reads the Romance." This volume. 201-216. Print.

Eco, Umberto. *The Name of the Rose.* San Diego: Harcourt, 1983. Print.

—. *Six Walks in the Fictional Woods.* Cambridge: Harvard University Press, 1994. Print.

Kafka, Franz. *Schriften – Tagebücher. Kritische Ausgabe.* Eds. Jürgen Born, Gerhard Neumann, Malcolm Pasley and Jost Schillemeit. *Vol. 2: Nachgelassene Schriften und Fragmente II.* Ed. Jost Schillemeit. Frankfurt a.M.: Suhrkamp, 2002. Print.

Kittler, Friedrich. *Discourse Networks 1800/1900.* Trans. Michael Metter with Chris Cullens. Foreword David E. Wellbery. Palo Alto: Stanford University Press, 1990. Print.

Köhler, Erich. "Gattungssystem und Gesellschaftssystem." *Literatursoziologische Perspektiven. Gesammelte Aufsätze.* Ed. Henning Krauss. Heidelberg: Winter, 1982. 11-26. Print.

Miller, J. Hillis. *Speech Acts in Literature.* Palo Alto: Stanford University Press, 2001. Print.

Mitchell, David T. and Sharon L. Snyder. *Narrative Prosthesis: Disability and the Dependencies of Discourse.* Ann Arbor: University of Michigan Press, 2000. Print.

Nietzsche, Friedrich. *Ecce homo. Wie man wird, was man ist.* Kritische Studienausgabe. Eds. Giorgio Colli and Mazzino Montinari. Vol. 6. München: Deutscher Taschenbuch Verlag, 1999. 255-374. Print.

Ronell, Avital. *Loser Sons: Politics and Authority.* Urbana, Chicago, and Springfield: University of Illinois Press, 2012. Print.

—. *The Telephone Book: Technology, Schizophrenia, Electric Speech.* Lincoln: University of Nebraska Press, 1989. Print.

Seelig, Carl. *Wanderungen mit Robert Walser.* Ed. Elio Fröhlich. Frankfurt a.M.: Suhrkamp, 1977. Print.

Walser, Robert. *Aus dem Bleistiftgebiet. Mikrogramme 1924-1932.* Eds. Bernhard Echte and Werner Morlang. Vol. 4. Frankfurt a.M.: Suhrkamp, 2003. Print.

---

auch ich und will es bleiben. Ich habe sowenig Appetit zum Offizier wie Sie. Ich will mit dem Volk leben und in ihm verschwinden."

Benjamin Haas

DIS-/ABILITY AND NORMALISM:
PATTERNS OF INCLUSION IN ROMANCE LITERATURE

Introduction

The historical and cultural construction of dis-/ability and ab-/normality requires transdisciplinary analyses informed by cultural studies. At the same time, there is a need for adequate theoretical frameworks. Ria Cheyne's approach offers a stimulating way of incorporating aspects of cultural dis-/ability studies into the field of romance studies and vice versa.

In this response, I would like to focus first on the key points of Cheyne's essay. In an attempt to acknowledge the possibility of different interpretations, I aim at scrutinising the potential effects of dis-/ability representations in romance novels as discussed by Cheyne. With this objective in mind, I will not only discuss the relationship between the text and its readership, but also explore how the reader's ways of interpreting depictions might be influenced by their identity, attitudes and conceptions of normality. By showing that interpretations are not determined by depictions but are also actively constructed by readers, I want to underline the need to examine the historically and culturally contingent processes of meaning-making (see Hall "Encoding"), that is, following Stuart Hall I contend that messages have to be meaningfully decoded before they are able to generate effects. In short, how the reception itself might work requires examination before we are able to talk about 'positive' interpretations of dis-/ability potentially developed by the reading public. I therefore propose to historicize the dynamics between the narrative and the reader. From this perspective, it might be possible to develop a better understanding of how stereotypes towards dis-/ability are structured and could be overcome with regards to patterns of inclusion.

Representation of Dis-/ability in Popular Romance Novels

Cheyne states that the representation of dis-/ability in romance novels works differently when compared to other genres of literature. This is primarily a result of the structural factors inherent to the genre, such as demanding a happily-ever-after ending or the necessity of secondary and yardstick roles. Cheyne shows that the de-eroticization and marginalisation of dis-/abled characters which, as other analyses in the field of cultural dis-/ability studies have revealed (see Mollow and McRuer 4), is rather common in romance fiction, does not occur in the novels of Mary Balogh. Instead, in her works characters with disabilities are part of the community and have fulfilling romantic relationships. Furthermore, they do not simply function as a "narrative prosthesis" (see Mitchell and Snyder

6-10), but rather perform their own roles and tasks within the plot. In the novels analysed by Cheyne, dis-/ability seems not to be absent from what is commonly understood as the 'good and normal life.' These interesting research findings demonstrate the potential of applying a cultural dis-/ability studies perspective in popular romance studies, thus extending the scope of both fields.

Representational Effects

Nonetheless, the impact of discriminatory prejudices and stereotypes towards dis-/abled persons is also comprehensively covered in Balogh's novels. Based on this observation, Cheyne argues in favour of the possibility that these representations could encourage readers to critically reflect upon their own conceptualisations of dis-/ability. At this point it is appropriate to take a closer look into how the individual reception of romance novels in particular, and cultural messages in general, might work. In the following, I will discuss whether widening the focus of the individual reader's modes of reception from representation to interpretation advances two consequences: first, a more profound analysis of the relationship between text and readership and, second, the conceptualisation of dis-/ability following the approach of normalism.

As a first step, I will focus on Stuart Hall's model of encoding and decoding to acquire a better understanding of the relationship between the source and the receiver (see "Encoding" 509).[21] Specifically, I will discuss how readers might interpret fluid depictions of dis-/ability and examples of social exclusion within narratives. From here, I want to infer how readers might themselves engage with novels and thus consider the possible impacts this engagement might have upon them. Taking up Cheyne's observation that a character's conceptualization of dis-/ability is connected to their own concepts of normality, I will underline the complexity of the possible representational effects connected to the reading public's concepts of normality.

Meaning-Making

According to Hall's model of encoding and decoding (see "Encoding"), there is always a *lack of fit* between the production (encoding) and the reception

---

21 | While Hall is focusing on the communication processes at play in television, his theory of encoding and decoding is also applicable to literary interpretation (see for example Pavšič 2007; Radway 1991). Novels can be seen as producing and circulating cultural messages, which is why differences in production and consumption should be considered. In light of this reception theory, readers are not seen as passive consumers. Instead, how the text functions in relation to its historical context and how it relates to the individual reader is analysed.

(decoding) of messages. This gap is caused by structural differences and an asymmetry between encoder and receiver. Therefore, discursive aspects must be considered in accordance with the production of a message and individual backgrounds related to its reception. The correspondence between message and meaning is to be seen as constructed, shaping the dynamics of meaning-making and creating a fluidity of meanings. As Hall points out, three different types of decoding or reading positions are possible: Readers can either confirm, negotiate or oppose the presented message (see "Encoding" 508-517).

Hall indicates that the meaning of a reading deduced by a reader is not necessarily the same as that intended by the writer or supposed by other readers. Consequently, there is a need to consider meaning as constructed through both the language and the concepts that readers have in mind. Therefore, meaning is never fixed but historically contingent; it relies upon different cultural and historical backgrounds. Hence, representation and meaning-making should be seen as a process in which the reader, in creating meaning, appears to be more important than the writer (see "Representation" 32 -33).

Thus following Hall and in contrast to Cheyne's argument, I contend that meaning does not reside in the author's narrative depictions, but instead is produced by readers in an active process of interpretation. These dynamics of meaning-making and varied audience interpretations are validated by Alison Wilde's media analyses of popular TV shows, in which she examines responses of dis-/ability depictions by active audiences. Referring to Hall's model of "encoding – decoding" as well as Abercrombie and Longhurst's "Spectacle/Performance paradigm,"[22] audience interpretations are seen as viewing performances. Wilde argues that these viewing performances depend on crucial aspects such as engagement, viewer identity, and, most importantly, how modes of depiction relate to existing attitudes and feelings (see 36-40). She writes: "But *how* people are depicted on television is of greater significance. Viewers are more likely to seek images that reassure them of their own normality or against private feelings of ab-/normality, whatever they may be" (42).

Wilde suggests that it is necessary to approach viewing as a performative act influenced by representation and identity. Hence, "characterisations are used to strengthen or weaken cultural identifications and to articulate, negotiate or maintain patterns of exclusion and inclusion between people" (ibid.). Wilde's analysis shows that the reception of a certain message depends on the

---

22 | Abercrombie and Longhurst argue that media, spectator identities, cultural representations, and outlooks must be investigated in a dialogical manner, where media and everyday life appear to be interwoven. This results in a relational form of performativity, where the cultural distance between performers and audience is eliminated. Consequently, the viewing performances are related to emotional attachment and individual identities.

manner of depiction as well as on social context. Thus, the effects of representations are ambivalent and contradictory, and ultimately identity and representation seem to be mutually dependent. It therefore follows that a qualitatively
and quantitatively more balanced representation of dis-/ability, as observed in
Balogh's novels, is likely to have positive effects on its readers, encouraging
them to have more empathy towards dis-/abled characters, but this relation is
far from inevitable. Furthermore, when considering reading as a performance
influenced by the interplay of representation and identity, one must concede
that personal conceptions of normality and ab-/normality might also play an
important role (see ibid.).

Interpretations of Normalism

Following the assumption that interpretation is linked with identity and, as
demonstrated by Wilde, with personal beliefs of normality in particular, it is
worthwhile to take a closer look at the latter. Such an approach is also supported
by Cheyne's essay, which analyses examples in Balogh's novels that are
explicitly concerned with the discussion of norms. This becomes particularly
obvious when non-dis-/abled characters – like Claudia in *Simply Perfect* – make
their 'narrow' conceptions of normality, or the social construction of norms, a
subject of discussion in their personal responses to dis-/abled characters. In
addition, a focus on normality emerges, since narratives of (de-)normalization
have certain effects on the construction of dis-/ability (see Link "Erzählen").

In light of the reader's concepts of normality and in order to specify the
historical and culturally contingent processes of reception, I will refer to
Jürgen Link's concept of normalism (see "Versuch"), which distinguishes
between normativity and normality. Link claims that it is essential to
differentiate between "normative norms" and "normalistic norms." Normative
norms can be described as social and legal norms that are imposed on only
a few people, whereas normalistic norms function through all individuals
comparing themselves to each other in accordance with a standard. Hence,
normality appears less static, functioning as a range norm based on change
and dynamics while requiring self-normalization by individuals. Conversely,
normativity works as a point norm aiming at stability and conformity. With
regard to normalistic norms, the two strategies of protonormalism and
flexible normalism must also be differentiated (see Link, "Versuch" 77-82).
Protonormalism is orientated towards normativity. It has a narrow normal
range and works through a strict separation of the normal and the pathological.
Flexible normalization, in contrast, has a wide normal range and expanded
boundaries where temporary separations and categorisations are possible. It
is thus possible to analyse intersections and ambivalences between the two
strategies in order to recognize new boundaries of inclusion and exclusion.

Even in flexible normalism exclusion remains an option since the normal range cannot be widened endlessly, whereas a return to narrow zones of normality and protonormalistic strategies is always possible (see Link, "Grenze" 136). Dis-/ability provides a good example for considering this dilemma. Even when strategies of a flexible normalism can be witnessed, for example in services for dis-/abled persons and in rehabilitation policies, the polarity of normality and dis-/ability still continues without being dissolved (see Waldschmidt "Normalisierung"). With regards to readers' "own normality" (see Wilde 42) and how they respond to depictions of certain characters, the focus of analysis needs to be widened. If it is true that 'everybody wants to be normal' (see Waldschmidt, "Who is Normal" 195), we need to explore in greater detail what this means nowadays both socially and culturally.

A Need for "Critical Frameworks"[23]

As mentioned above, while the relationship between the text and the reader evaluated with reference to normality makes possible a positive interpretation by the reader, it does not make it inevitable. On the contrary, when speaking of individual interpretations by readers, protonormalistic strategies as well as temporary separations of dis-/abled characters are still possible. Therefore, to distinguish between patterns of in- and exclusion, the ambivalent processes of meaning-making need to be analysed in conjunction with different conceptions of normality. This makes it essential to consider the identity and attitudes of the reader and his or her conception of normality, which can serve to strengthen or weaken cultural identifications of dis-/ability.

With regard to the obvious complexity of representational effects, I would like to stress two additional aspects concerning modes of reception and their analyses. First, a historical perspective on the dynamics between spectacle and spectator might be beneficial (see Garland-Thomson 136). Focussing on the culturally and historically specific construction of dis-/ability in contrast to the idealised bodies and identities or "normate subject positions" (see ibid. 8), this type of approach could call into question the ideological structures that constitute 'otherness' and therefore make and interpret dis-/ability (see ibid. 135). Second, a 'discursive approach' according to Michel Foucault could deepen the understanding of subject-positions depending on relations of power and knowledge. These two perspectives seem not only to be compatible with Hall's call for a constructivist approach (see "Representation" 25), but they are also

---

23 | In her book *Extraordinary Bodies*, Rosemarie Garland-Thomson underlines the need for a "critical framework" focusing on social relations (Erving Goffman), cultural responses (Mary Douglas), and historical delineations (Foucault) in order to analyse dis-/ability as a historically and culturally specific social construction (see 141).

favourable in acknowledging the contingent cultural and historical backgrounds that could affect individual reception. Thus, the attempt to stimulate potentially positive interpretations of dis-/ability would require a critical reconstruction of meaning-making. Taking into account discursive formations (see Foucault) influencing concepts of dis-/ability and normality could contextualize the dynamics between narrative and reader.

Conclusion

In this essay I have tried to illustrate that the complexity of meaning-making demands critical frameworks which focus on the social, cultural, and historical aspects of a reader's reception. Starting with Cheyne's observation of the different depictions of dis-/ability in romance literature and her suggestion that they stress the importance of attitudes creating welcoming environments, I wanted to emphasise the need to analyse the underlying structures of stereotypes in terms of *techniques of normalization*. Referring to Link's concept of normality and considering the flexible-normalistic character of inclusion (see "Denkanstöße"), it must be taken into account that even a widened normal range with regard to depiction and reception can be accompanied by exclusive practices. In other words, strategies of flexible normalism do not necessarily have to be identical with patterns of inclusion. This claim highlights the need for further research on normality as a discourse-framing category (see Lingenauber; Waldschmidt "Behindertsein"). Finally, I have argued for a perspective that not only supports interdisciplinary dialogues between cultural studies and dis-/ability studies, but one that also serves as an example for developing a framework of critical dis-/ability analysis by drawing on different fields of research.

References

Foucault, Michel. *The Archaeology of Knowledge*. London: Tavistock, 1972. Print.
Garland-Thomson, Rosemarie. *Extraordinary Bodies: Figuring Physical Disability in American Culture and Literature*. New York: Columbia University Press, 1997. Print.
Hall, Stuart. "Encoding, Decoding." *The Cultural Studies Reader*. Ed. Simon During. London: Routledge, 1995. 507-517. Print.
—. "The Work of Representation." *Representation: Cultural Representations and Signifying Practices*. Ed. Stuart Hall. London: Sage, 1997. 13-64. Print.
Lingenauber, Sabine. *Integration, Normalität und Behinderung*. Leverkusen: Leske + Budrich, 2003. Print.
Link, Jürgen. *Versuch über den Normalismus. Wie Normalität produziert wird*. Opladen: Westdeutscher Verlag, 1997. Print.

—. "'Radikal Umdenken': Wie? Denkanstöße angesichts der Denormalisierung nach dem 11. September 2001." *DISS-Journal* 9 (2001). Web. 20. August 2014. <http://www.diss-duisburg.de/2001/12/radikal-umdenken-wie/>.

—. "Irgendwo stößt die flexibelste Integration schließlich an eine Grenze. Behinderung zwischen Normativität und Normalität." *Ethik und Behinderung. Ein Perspektivenwechsel.* Ed. Sigrid Graumann. Frankfurt: Campus, 2004. 130-139. Print.

—. "Erzählen, wie man in andere Zustände kommt. Mentale Denormalisierung in der Literatur (mit einem Blick auf Zola und Musil)." *Andere Bilder. Zur Produktion von Behinderung in der Visuellen Kultur.* Eds. Beate Ochsner and Anna Grebe. Bielefeld: transcript, 2013. 179-194. Print.

Mitchell, David T. and Sharon L. Snyder. *Narrative Prosthesis: Disability and the Dependencies of Discourse.* Ann Arbor: University of Michigan Press, 2000. Print.

Mollow, Anna and Robert McRuer. "Introduction." *Sex and Disability.* Ed. McRuer and Mollow. Durham: Duke University Press, 2012. 1-34. Print.

Pavšič, Brigita. "Understanding Racism and Sexism in Harry Potter and Stuart Hall's Modell of Three Reading Positions." *ELOPE* 4.1/2 (2007). 69-80. Print.

Radway, Janice A. *Reading the Romance: Women, Patriarchy, and Popular Literature.* Chapel Hill: University of North Carolina Press, 1991. Print.

Waldschmidt, Anne. "Flexible Normalisierung oder stabile Ausgrenzung: Veränderungen im Verhältnis Behinderung und Normalität." *Soziale Probleme. Zeitschrift für soziale Probleme und soziale Kontrolle* 9.1/2 (1998). 3-25. Print.

—. "Ist Behindertsein normal? Behinderung als flexibelnormalistisches Dispositiv." *Wie man behindert wird. Texte zur Konstruktion einer sozialen Rolle und zur Lebenssituation betroffener Menschen.* Ed. Günther Cloerkes. Heidelberg: Universitätsverlag Winter, Edition. 2003. 83-101. Print.

—. "Who is Normal? Who is Deviant? 'Normality' and 'Risk' in Genetic Diagnostics and Counseling." *Foucault and the Government of Disability.* Ed. Shelley L. Tremain. Ann Arbor: University of Michigan Press. 2005. 191-207. Print.

Wilde, Alison. "Spectacle, Performance, and the Re-Presentation of Disability and Impairment." *Review of Disability Studies: An International Journal* 6.3 (2010). 34-43. Print.

The Inarticulate Post-Socialist Crip

On the Cruel Optimism of Neoliberal Transformations in the Czech Republic[1]

Kateřina Kolářová

INTRODUCTION

In 2009, twenty years past the collapse of state socialism in Czechoslovakia, Jan Potměšil,[2] disabled in a car-accident during protest work in 1989, is reported to have said: "If I was to choose between the rule of communists and being able to walk again, I would take the chair" (cited in Remešová, translation by author). The quote is illuminating even if its tabloid source may make us doubt its authenticity. It reveals that discourses of post-socialism were rich with prosthetic narratives of disability, rehabilitation, and cure. It also reveals the importance of discourses of post-socialist 'transformation' for shaping political consciousness in the Czech Republic of today. This short anecdote foreshadows some of the central questions of my article: What does the symbolic juxtaposition of dis/ability and "the rule of communists" mean for the introduction of (neoliberal) capitalism into the Czechoslovakia? And – most importantly – how did it influence epistemologies of disability and the im/possibility of what we might term, adapting José Muñoz, 'crip horizons?'

The possibility of critical imaginaries and visions of the political are central to my exploration here. In my reading of the early years of post-socialist

1 | This essay originally appeared in *Journal of Literary & Cultural Disability Studies* 8.3 (2014): 257–274. It is reprinted here with the kind permission of the editor of JLCDS for which I am grateful.

2 | In the revolutionary autumn of 1989, Potměšil was one of the students, artists and activists travelling around the Czech Republic to spread support for the regime change. Interestingly, becoming disabled turned Potměšil into an impromptu embodiment of the revolution as his 'incapacitated' body was transfigured into a symbolic sacrifice for the collective freedom (and capacity).

transformation I am looking for a "structure of feeling," the name Raymond Williams uses for the residue of shared historical experiences (128), or what Lauren Berlant terms "affective attachments," "a structure of relationality" (Berlant 13); a structure of feeling that reflects how much "[i]t matters how we arrive at the places we do" (Ahmed, *Queer* 2), individually as well as collectively. The affective politics of the post-socialist transformation leads me to explore the conditions for intelligibility of political and social concepts and imaginaries; this is one of the meanings I invoke with the concept of horizon. The affects, I argue, help to pose the questions of 'political horizon:'

"What are the factors that make political action conceivable at all, or that make some forms of activism thinkable while others are, or become, wholly unimaginable? How do attitudes within a social group or collectivity about what is politically possible, desirable, and necessary – what I call a political horizon – get established, consolidated, stabilized, and reproduced over time, and with what sorts of effects on political action?" (Gould 3)

The following discussion traces two lines of argument. First, I reveal how disability metaphors and broader ideological structures of health and compulsory able-bodiedness were appropriated to fuel the optimism of the post-revolutionary years. I argue that a curative logic smoothed the way and provided legitimation for the neoliberal transformations. Second, I cruise through the disability journalism of the early 1990s to explore the disability positionalities articulated there.[3]

The larger question that underlies my ruminations on the 1990s addresses the cultural and contextual contingencies of toxic attachments to optimism, progress, and an affective politics of positivity in the present moment of austerity. The theses that I propose complicate the affective attachments to optimistic visions of free, democratic futurity by arguing that these visions cruelly reduced the meaning of freedom to the freedom of the market and foreclosed more complex negotiations of the meaning of 'the social.' As my analysis indicates, the post-revolution euphoria transmuted quite rashly into the form of affectivity that Berlant defines as "cruel optimism" and which she summarises as a relation in which "something you desire is actually an obstacle to your flourishing" (2). The cruel optimism of the post-socialist moment in Czechoslovakia, I propose, has been forclosing the possibility of crip epistemologies. In the post-socialist moment when social belonging

---

3 | Specifically, for the purposes of this article, I lean on an analysis of two journals: *Elán* (*Vigour*) and *Vozíčkář* (*The Wheelchair User*); the former is a journal platform of the official and state-sanctioned *The Union of Invalids* (*Svaz Invalidů*) and as such represents a continuity with the era of the state socialism. The latter, on the other side, is a new journal founded after the regime change and as an explicit critique of *Elán*.

appears defined (and conditioned) by the compulsory affects of curative positivity, cripness is an impossible location; it is unintelligible and lies beyond the conceivable, thinkable, and imaginable political horizon.

Yet, there is a different meaning of horizon that speaks to this impossibility of crip(ness) in the times of post-socialist rehabilitation into/through neo-liberalism. Making Muñoz's imagination more generously accommodating and accessible, we could envision "[cripness] [as] not yet here [and as] ideality [...] that can be distilled from the past and used to imagine a future" (*Cruising* 1). The metaphor of the inarticulate crip that I offer here gestures towards such a horizon transgressing the "presentness" (25) and of the normatively progressive futurity of straight *and* abled time (of rehabilitation, shock therapies and cure) and thus, as I argue toward the end of the article, allows us to revisit and complicate the past to forge different versions of desires for crip futures.

The following image elucidates the metaphor and the ways in which it allows for imagining a cripness defiant to compulsory positivity and optimism.

Jan Šibík, "Untitled." [4]

The image captures two women, half-clad/half-naked, sitting face-to-face, one on a hospital bed, one in front of it. The drab environment, the pills, used cups, and fashion magazines surrounding the women tell a story of sickness and an improvised/impoverished home. However, the women are so engrossed in each

---

4 | Photograph used with permission of the photographer.

other that the markers of illness, death, and destitution seem to disappear in a momentous bliss of erotic and mutual care.

The image is a part of larger series titled *I Do Not Want To Die Yet* (Šibík, *Chci ještě žít*; translation by author), which received a lot of attention as well as critical acclaim in the Czech Republic in 2004. The work of Jan Šibík, a Czech photographer well-applauded for his 'humanitarian projects,' the series documents life in an asylum in Odessa, Ukraine, where people with AIDS were left to themselves; those who still could cared for those closer to death.

The whole series is waiting for an overdue critical intervention: it fetishizes AIDS and death, it exploits narratives of tragedy and despair, it objectifies both the people photographed and their ill bodies, and, most importantly, it traffics in images of a post-Soviet 'AIDS-infested Ukraine' to bolster Czech pride in capitalist success and post-socialist overcoming. And yet, the images invite *crip signing*, a crip version of "homosexual hearing," a stratagem for reading culture (and cultural texts) against the grain for the purpose of survival and crafting alternative futures (Marga Gomez cited in Muñoz, *Disidentifications* 3). "Crip signing," like "homosexual hearing," is a form of "disidentification," a tactic "that neither opts to assimilate [...] nor strictly oppose [dominant ideologies]" but rather "works on and against dominant ideology" (Muñoz, *Disidentifications* 2) at its seams. Crip signing is a critical gesture towards something that is not fully articulated, something that cannot be expressed in the language of identity and political pragmatism. Taking its cue from Marga Gomez, who heard the calling of homosexuality in moments of ambivalence that combined desire with shame, or recognition with abjection, crip signing in this particular image can be imagined as a moment that 'disses' the ideologies of (heterosexual) sexuality but also ideological notions of health, reproductive femininity, able-bodied longevity, and, most acutely, the compulsorily optimistic visions of cure. Crip signing, like homosexual hearing, paradoxically crafts survival out of abjection and stigma.

This (lesbian) crip picture captures a powerful clash between failure and sustenance.[5] In their 'AIDS-as-death-sentence' existence, the two women are meant to embody 'failure' in relation to ideologies of vitality and able-bodied health, as well as ideologies of (hetero)normative femininity. Yet despite its rawness and the ways in which it actually emphasises the visual markers of illness, the image signifies (however ephemeral, however crip) thriving. It attaches the women's bodies to each other by acts of interdependent care, while their ambivalent positioning allows – even calls for – sexual fantasies, turning the two women into subjects of (each other's) desire. In this, they paradoxically embody a moment of careless sorority and of mutual care/pleasure. The ways in which the 'failure' of AIDS/illness can be turned into sustaining cripness;

---

5 | I use the term 'lesbian' here to denote forms of gendered intimacy, closeness, care, and erotics *neither* dependent on nor wholly defined by the notion of lesbian identity.

the intimate relationality that challenges the individualising medical narrative; the pleasure/desire that is an "angry fist in the eye" (Wade 24) to narratives of fatality and despair; and the embodiment and practices of care reveal not only the negligence of the Ukrainian state but, more importantly, a challenge to the narrative of capitalism's global success and the vision of capitalism as the only chance at futurity.

Yet, the crip signing so clear now remained long inarticulate to me despite the fact that the series of photographs was on my syllabus for an AIDS politics class for several years. How had I not responded to the complicated network of pleasures/hurt the image embodies and speaks to? What cripistemological lessons can be drawn from this personal experience with the un/intelligibility of *crip signing*? These are some of the questions that inspire the remainder of my analysis. Genealogies of disability in a post-socialist Czechoslovakia may shed more light on why crip epistemologies have been unintelligible (and not viable) in this specific geo-political location. But despite the focus on a specific location, the theses and questions that I put forth in this article have a broader radius. Cruising the geopolitical time and place that no longer exists poses challenges to discussions and critical reflections on neoliberalism and austerity in the present moment. More specifically, it opens a critical dialogue with epistemologies of disability and cripness developed mostly from Western/global North experiences. In particular, the various figurations of the inarticulate/inarticulable crip problematize epistemologies of disability that expunge ambiguity and require fully-developed and articulated identity positions. In brief, the post-socialist crip appears to be precisely the "disorientation device" (Ahmed, *Queer* 171) to attune us to what has been slipping to "the point at which things fleet" (172) away from safe and 'positive' epistemologies. Such a disorientation is necessary if we are to imagine crip horizons.

DISABILITY SEMANTICS OF TRANSITION AND CAPITALIST REHABILITATIONS

Exploring the 'post' of socialism, Katherine Verdery prefaces her book *What Was Socialism, and What Comes Next?* by a short retort, which in its beautiful irony seems to capture the prevailing logic of the historical moment: "Q: What is the definition of socialism? A: The longest and most painful route from capitalism to capitalism." Similarly, one of the sociological studies led by an ambition to provide a concise version of the Czech history in the 20th century reflects the same sentiment in its title *On the Road from Capitalism to Capitalism* (Kabele). It presents a vision of the modern Czech/oslovak history as a cyclical move 'from capitalism to socialism and back,' where the 40-year period of state socialism is posed as a temporary deviation, an unfortunate false turn "on the road from capitalism to capitalism." Indicated already in the rhetorical exercise of Verdery's Q and A, the belief that there is no other future than global capitalism punctuated cultural imaginations of the 'transformation' of post-socialist Czechoslovakia: it ran through pop culture, academic representations of the process, and the many foreign reflections on the events of the period. In this preliminary archaeology of the discourse of transformation, I am interested in unearthing its dependence upon ideologies of cure and recuperation that have played a crucial role not only in situating discourses of disability but, even more crucially, *all* visions of the social.

Elaine Weiner organised the dominant significations of socialism and capitalism that circulated (not only) in the 1990s into a neatly illustrative table that helps to draw out the highly normative evaluations of both political regimes (58):

Planned economy	Market economy
Evil	Good
Failure	Success
East	West/Europe
Past	Future
Constraint/Captivity	Opportunity/Freedom
Premodernity/Uncivilised	Modernity/Civilisation
Stagnation/Regression	Development/Progress
Abnormality/Artificiality	Normality/Naturality
Human design	Human nature
Irrationality	Rationality
Immorality	Morality
Collectivism	Individualism

The binary structure makes it sardonically clear that ascribing failure to socialism/communism functions as a projection enabling the imagined successes of capitalism. Weiner's table reveals also the extent to which economic markers and structures became the criteria and defining characteristics for evaluating societies; indeed, the conflation of freedom with a market economy persists as the hegemonic vision until the present. This is the cruel aftermath of the transformation period.[6]

Even if unreflected in Weiner's analysis, these binaries reveal the extent to which an epistemology of the socialist other is hoisted upon a negative semantics of disability and the extent to which the passage from a failed communism/socialism – state of regression, immorality and irrationality – corresponds to semantic and ideological structures which, drawing on work of Henri-Jacques Stiker, Robert McRuer terms a "cultural grammar of rehabilitation" (*Crip* 108-116; for the term 112; see also Stiker).[7] Semantics of illness and disability crop up everywhere in early evaluations of a post-socialist and post-revolution Czechoslovakia. Already the first New Year's Presidential address introduced a metaphoric of malady as Václav Havel opened his message to the citizenry with a bitter pill and spoke of the state's decline: "our country does not flourish" (Havel "Novoroční projev;" translation by author).[8] He later made references to sickness explicit and added a clear moral impetus: "[In socialism] we became morally ill" (ibid.). The same rhetoric also pervades the State of the Czech Republic Address from March 1990 delivered by the then Prime Minister, Petr Pithart. He characterised communism as a health risk, blamed it for "the loss of general *immunity*" of the whole population, and identified it as "the most dangerous *bomb ticking away in our organisms*" (Pithart, "Zpráva" 9; emphases added). These brief examples hopefully suffice to indicate not only the extent to which the political imaginary of the post-revolution moment relied upon visions of sickness and malignancy, but also that these visions – as is very clearly indicated by the metaphor of ticking bomb – could be deployed as part of a moral appeal for (rehabilitative) transformation.

Thus the process of 'transition' from socialism into the new social order could be dubbed literally the 'path to recovery' and 'cure' ("The prevention is not enough, cure is necessary here;" Pithart "Programové"), while the immediacy

---

6 | A few days prior to finalizing this article, the Czech Republic held pre-term elections, following the fall of the right-wing government responsible for austerity measures. In a bizarre outcome representing the general frustration and growing precarity, Andrej Babiš, a billionaire and entrepreneur, was close to winning the election. He promised to "run the state as a firm" in order to be a good manager in this state/entrepreneurship hybrid.

7 | Notions of rehabilitation resound in the dominant significations attached to the process of the transition. Phrases such as "the return to Europe" or the "rediscovery of civil society" (see Hann 10) attributed to the development in post-socialist countries is illustrative of the process of othering of (post-)socialism and of the power dynamic between the 'East' and 'West.'

8 | All subsequent quotations from Czech sources have been translated into English by the author.

and desperate acuteness of the metaphoric ticking bomb legitimised the shock nature of this recovery: "The path to recovery will be very difficult. [...] Every step of the reforms will cause a shock from which we will have to learn again and again how to recover" (Pithart, "Zpráva" 10). Arguably, the trauma caused by the process of recovery (from the malignancy of the communist past) functions as both a means to overcome the sickness and as a means of (moral) cleansing.

The extent to which ideologies of *ability and health* are utilised to celebrate/ legitimise the new social order of neoliberal capitalism raises new questions for the critical exploration of discourses of transformation and their formative impact upon the present. What does it mean for future visions of society and sociality that socialism and communism are signified as harmful and unhealthy anomalies to the presumed universal (and universally capitalist) social order, to the "assumed prior, normal state" (Stiker cited in McRuer, *Crip* 111)? Why and how do ideologies of health and ability give legitimacy to the new social order? What repercussions for crip and disability politics follow from figuring the post-socialist and current political regime as the result of successful rehabilitative therapy?

The import of these questions goes well beyond the scale of disability critique. The rehabilitative grammar of post-socialist transition had ramifications for all critical projects and transformative visions of social parity and social justice in post-socialist Czechoslovakia. Understanding this genealogy is important for understanding the politics of austerity governing the present moment in the Czech Republic.

CRUEL VELVET PROMISES

The semantics of rehabilitation bequeaths us a language propelled by promises: promises of health, normalcy, functionality, and prosperity – all that seemed to be encapsulated in the early 1990s by the promise of the new social order and of capitalist democracy in post-socialist Czechoslovakia. Yet, as Lauren Berlant assures, some promises are cruel. She cautions, "[w]here cruel optimism operates, the very vitalising or animating potency of an object/scene of desire contributes to the attrition of the very thriving that is supposed to be made possible in the work of attachment in the first place" (Berlant 24-5). In the following section, I trace more thoroughly how post-revolution euphoria transmuted into the form of affectivity Berlant terms "cruel optimism." As I read these cruel velvet promises, my main interest is in drawing out the ways in which people with disabilities identified with the 'affective public' of post-socialist Czechoslovakia, thereby investing in visions of the promising future that proved cruel to crip horizons.

The most powerful promise is articulated through visions of reparation and overcoming of the failings of the past regime. The change in regime brought hope for an end to "the long-standing rule of clichés, promises and unfulfilled demands and needs;" it generated the expectation that *"even in* our Czechoslovakia, everyone with a health disability (*zdravotním postižením*) [will be able to] enjoy full rights" (Váchalová n. pag.; emphasis added). In a letter to the then prime minister, *The Union of Invalids* (Svaz Invalidů) claimed to be ready to cooperate with the government on their "shared mission" to remedy "the painful aspects of life in our state" and to secure that *"every citizen* of this country fe[els] *content and happy"* ("Vážený" 2; emphasis added). Interestingly, these visions seem to share the rehabilitative investment in the 'assumed prior, assumed normal' (see Striker and McRuer above). The moment of reparation is imagined as the moment when "the ideals of humanism *will again become* the inherent part of the [social] consciousness" ("El Rozhovor" 1-2; emphasis added).

These statements exemplify that post-revolutionary euphoria and positivity are in truth a specific instance of "cruel optimism." Perhaps, indeed, to go beyond Berlant, cruel optimism materializes even more rapidly in locations where capitalism had been least naturalized and thus could be (in the neoliberal era) more readily packaged as a supposed miracle cure for the failures of the past. Such a miracle cure would have you feeling yourself again in no time. Of course, regime change *could have been* a moment for renegotiation of visions of the social, yet these references to an idealised, phantasmatic, 'assumed prior' no-place inhibited (crip) fantasies of different presents and futures. Furthermore, the grammar of rehabilitation is an ethical and moral discourse; curative logic always pairs optimism and euphoria with negative affects and bad feelings.

I want to examine this juxtaposition of promises alongside what I call an "affectivity of debt" to map out how promises were set against demands of overcoming and reparation of the failed, sick, disabled state (of being) of socialism. As darkly ironic as it is, the assuring and optimistic visions of good futures became the ways to curtail utopian visions, critical projects, and critical epistemologies. Petr Pithart said in the early 1990s: "We lived our lives on credit. [...] We have to realise that [...] *so frequently proclaimed 'social securities' and the living standard were secured at great costs.* [...] We lived above our means, on credit and this debt [...] needs to be paid off" (Pithart, "Zpráva" 10; emphasis added). The early 1990s were teeming with similar pronouncements (strangely, or perhaps predictably, similar comments have reappeared with eerie echoes in the present moment of austerity); they carried a notion of 'debt' as the source of negative affects (shame, guilt, abjection) and, most importantly, contained a moral imperative. David Graeber summarises the normative force of the modern idea of debt when he describes its "basic problem" as "the very assumption that debts *have* to be repaid" (Graeber 3).

The need to 'pay off' the debt of failed communism has become instrumental in articulating the moral imperatives that bound every citizen into the collectivity Berlant calls an "affective public," a collectivity knit together both by a shared aspiration to an optimistic future, but also by the shared shame, guilt, and enforced responsibility for the past failure in the project of recuperation *into capitalism*. The statement of the first post-socialist government puts it laconically yet with shrilling clarity: "The *moral recovery* of the nation will not be possible without wise *social policy*" (Pithart "Programové"; emphasis added).

These visions of sociality provide us with one tangible example of a promise transforming itself into a factor that actually inhibits thriving (of the disabled). The project of rehabilitative transition was made synonymous with 'paying off' the debts accumulated by 'living on credit' or 'living above *our* means;' 'social securities' were satirised and put forth as the main source of the crisis. The notion of overextended credit contravened crip visions. The price for social belonging and the symbolic (self-)inclusion into the affective public was, in a cruel paradox, the impossibility of expressing any political demands that would reveal the violence of ableism. The moral weight of the 'affectivity of debt' required that one's critiques and demands be deferred and postponed:

"It is impossible to change everything by a blink of an eye and *even we, the disabled, should be patient!*" (Juřenová 82; emphasis added).

"Do you not believe that this is *not* the most appropriate moment to [...] burden the state budget *further*?" ("Náš mikrorozhovor" n. pag.; emphasis added).

It appears only too convenient – and illustrative of the cruelness of the post-socialist cure – that Klaus's text vindicating a market-based vision of justice,[9] and tellingly entitled "The Chimera of Equality," relies upon a complicated disability metaphor. Employing this metaphor, he likens equality to something "which is hoped for but is *illusory* or *impossible to achieve*" ("Chimera" *OED*; emphasis added). It is not a useless diversion to look up the figurative meanings of the "chimera:"

"(2) a fire-breathing female monster with a lion's head, a goat's body, and a serpent's tail [...]; (3) an organism containing a mixture of genetically different tissues, formed by processes such as fusion of early embryos, grafting, or mutation [...]; (4) a DNA molecule with sequences derived from two or more different organisms, formed by laboratory manipulation; (5) (chimaera) a cartilaginous marine fish with a long tail, an erect spine before the first dorsal fin, and typically a forward projection from the snout." (ibid.)

---

9 | See Klaus: "only the market relations will show us who really *deserves* what" ("Chiméra Rovnosti" 1; translation and emphasis by author).

All of these meanings call up visions of abnormality, monstrosity, and bodily difference, all of which are conceptually akin to disability. In fact, the chimera is itself a disability metaphor, a figuration of monstrosity, where references to abnormality and deviation from 'natural order' connote its impossibility. As Michel Foucault elaborates in his lectures on the 'abnormal,' the monster is a *mixture*, either a combination of the human and the animal, a mixture of forms, two species, or two sexes (see Foucault 55-6 and 63). Defying unity and coherence of various sorts, the monster – the chimera – produces confusion that threatens to overthrow the natural order.

By weight of such significations, equality becomes a monstrosity that endangers both social and natural laws and poses a threat to survival and (future) life. Conversely, inequality is legitimised as a natural part and an inevitable consequence of the healthy state/economy and the healthy result of rehabilitative recuperation. The full force of this diatribe against equality and the idea of social solidarity can be seen in the following comparison: "[social welfare is] only at the first sight less dangerous [than] inhuman *communist* and *social nationalist* (sic!) experiments" (Klaus, "Chiméra Rovnosti" 1; emphasis added).

CRIPPING CRUEL OPTIMISM

Echoing Sara Ahmed's understanding of future as "a question [that] unfolds [...] in the present" (*Promise* 164), I want to come back to the questions that have opened this article and to ruminate on what it means to cruise a geopolitical time and place that apparently does not exist anymore. I want to ask what the vantage point crafted from the specific historical experience of socialism and the post-socialist transition offers to critiques of neoliberalism – more specifically, to critiques formulated from cripistemological perspectives and what we might perceive as reorientations towards crip futures.

In engaging with these questions I come back to Berlant's concept of cruel optimism, which has been extremely helpful in my article as I identify structural attachments to promises of better futures that created the ideological base of the project of transition. The engagement with post-socialist material shows, as well, however, that Berlant's brilliant discussion of the toxicity of the neoliberal version of the promise of good life needs, as I implied earlier, to be reformulated not only to correspond to the specificity of the particular experience of post-socialism, but also to reveal how such a confrontation also brings forth more general challenges and lines of critique.

There is a strange incongruity about Lauren Berlant's book; disability is literally on its cover, as the crip artist Riva Lehrer provided the cover image *If Body: Riva and Zora in Middle Age*. It is embedded in the title of the book, as "cruel optimism" could in fact be a very appropriate naming of the violent, recuperative and compulsory optimism of the cultural logic of rehabilitation to which the disabled are permanently subjected. The book's discussions are haunted by disability; at times disability is even evoked directly, yet it is through the clinical and medicalised language of 'disease,' 'depression,' 'obesity,' 'spina bifida' rather than through the transformative and politicised vocabulary of cripness.

In this sense, Berlant's book replicates the failing of the majority of critical work that exposes the neoliberal debasement of values of solidarity, social justice, and equity. This lack of discussion is startling. Indeed, how is it possible that the bulk of critique of neoliberalism and neoliberal governmentality provides such engaging and incisive insights into the politics of maximising vitality, capitalising on the very act of living, or exposing the morbid utilisation of the mechanisms for which Berlant coined the widely circulating term "slow death," and the necropolitical distribution of death, yet does so without including disability/cripness into its analytical instrumentarium? How can a discussion of 'the politics of life' itself do without a category that is integral to modern definition of life and vitality? Taking up the one crip lead from the book, I speak to the image of *If Body* (differently than Berlant herself does in her closing "Note on the Cover Image" 265-267) and ask what would a critique of cruel optimism look like *if* it thought of *crip bodies, if* it thought of crip bodies *elsewhere* from the Western context and *if* it thought of *crip existence in the context of post-socialist, neoliberal promises.*[10]

In formulating the crip reading of cruel optimism, in *cripping* cruel optimism, we need to address the different affective structures of post-socialist promises. We also need to read those affective structures along with and perhaps against the relationality of cruel optimism Berlant first identified. Most importantly, the concept needs to be expanded so that its more capacious definition would account for the pressures of compulsory able-bodiedness and for the specific experiences of disabled people and crips. In other words, Berlant's concept of toxic and hurtful promises and her repertoire of critical analysis of fantasies of the good life calls for encounters with crip versions of 'life' as well as for a cripping of the notion of the 'good life.' It needs to be read more carefully and specifically along with the realities of lives that were never promised (let alone lived through) this liberal fantasy, lives that are appropriated

---

10 | It is beyond the scope of this article to outline the import of the critical interrogations of "post-socialism." However, disability, again, rarely figures in these analyses. The work of scholars such as Anastasia Kayiatos, Sarah Phillips, Darja Zaviršek and the newest anthology edited by Michael Rasell and Elena Iarskaia-Smirnova, to name just a few, represents a valued and important exception to this prevailing trend.

and colonised by images of 'life not worth living,' or lives that are at times not even granted the recognition of life itself.

The transition into neoliberalism produced forms of affective citizenship based on what Berlant calls "aspirational normativity" (164 and 169-71). In the post-socialist context, the aspiration promising the utopia of the 'good life' was not expressed in the imperative to keep going; the moral aspiration of the post-socialist transition was by definition that of rehabilitation, overcoming the failure and shame of the bad past. It was not the "nearly utopian desire of a prolonged present" (163-4), but the "nearly utopian" desire of a recuperative future.

The cruelness of the post-socialist moment lies – as I hope my analysis above unmasks – in conditioning forms of social belonging by an "affectivity of debt," discourses of overcoming, and fantasies of cure. The cultural grammar of rehabilitation saturated 'the political' and 'the social' so fully that claims to social equity could be disavowed and turned into a *chimera*, the crip monstrous ghost haunting the post-socialist redefinition of sociality and community, where any other form of social belonging for crips than under the rubrics of paternalisingly charitable humanism was (and remains) virtually impossible (see Kolářová).

Registering the temporal coincidence of different structures of compulsory optimism also emphasises their cruel irony. The project of rehabilitating the post-socialist crip virtually overlaps with the moment when, in the West, states started to retract their social-welfare commitments. Even more specifically, the countries in 'transition' served to uphold the fantasies of success, health, and the general 'good life' made possible by capitalism. For instance, with the claims that it was living the "post-communist dream" (cited in Weiner 53), the Czech Republic was in the early 1990s (before the myth of smooth, straightforward, and successful transition was ruptured by the first crisis in 1994) put forth as the model for the countries of the former Eastern Block. The "teleology of 'transition'" (Hann 9) of the post-socialist countries along the identical path that the West passed decades earlier (see Verdery) also served, however, as an important projection space for the 'West,' where the apparent rehabilitative capacity of capitalism in the East was utilized to bolster the "secular faith" in (neoliberal) capitalism as the only possibility for human history (Duggan xiii). This did not go completely unnoticed, as the key figure of the Czech transformation, Václav Klaus, himself notes: "It is nearly paradoxical that the speeches of some of us [sic] delivered in the West are perceived not only as signs of the vital renaissance of thought in the East, but are also sought after as a support in their own ideological skirmishes [...]" (Klaus, "Síla" 1). Yet, in his ego-centrism, Klaus did not draw the conclusions at hand: that the project of rehabilitation/transformation in the 'East' and its shock method helped to sustain the 'West' – and at the same time inhibited the development of a critical crip consciousness in both locations.

IMAGING CRIP FAILURES, CRIP HORIZONS

The aspiration of post-socialism was progress, moral emancipation, and eventual happiness. Recall the earlier quote from a letter to the former prime minister of Czechoslovakia that attempted to articulate the vision of the optimistic future as a moment when 'every citizen of this country fe[els] content and happy.' Yet, Sara Ahmed cautions, happiness is a troubled notion. Ahmed asks us: "What are we consenting to, when we consent to happiness?" and offers a troubling answer: "perhaps the consensus that happiness is the consensus" (*Promise* 1). Ahmed's questioning of happiness as the normative horizon of our orientation, resounds with the key issues that I wanted to address; the promise of happiness is a twin of "cruel optimism." Most acutely, Ahmed's critical discussion focuses on revealing how (the vision of and desire for) happiness participates in establishing structures of consensus, which are in fact structures of dominance. With (falsely) positive energy, recuperative logic said, 'you should be happy communism is over;' the promise of happiness was used to justify the oppression of the disabled through ideologies of ableism constitutive to liberal individualism and liberal humanism.

The impossibility of seeing and envisioning crip(topias) in the situation of (post-)shameful identity illustrates not only the harmful and utterly disabling work of certain affective attachments, it also and as vividly illustrates the equally harmful impacts/effects of attachments to affects, in particular attachments to affects of positivity, affects that seemingly are necessary to foster self-embracing identity and subjectivity. In other words, the post-socialist crip challenges Western-developed theories of (disabled) identity that argue that positive affects are necessary to foster self-embracing and affirmative understandings of disability and disabled subjectivity. The symbolic violence embedded in recuperative positivity offers us the opportunity to think about crip failure and crip negativity. The violence also points toward conditions that (could) make (some forms of) failure useful for cripistemologies and that (could) map crip horizons.

Cripness *is* already rich with failure; cripness *is* infused with negativity that sustains. The crip negativity I plead for is a critical strategy rupturing ideologies of cure, rehabilitation and overcoming, ideologies that inflict hurt and violence (not only) on crips. I wish to initiate a discussion about crip negativity as a political practice working towards (if never reaching) crip utopian horizons. Still, the post-socialist crip opens other and new questions about what crip failure would mean if it were to foster and sustain life, what forms of crip negative energies would allow for crip utopias and make possible the desire for crip survival.

J. Jack Halberstam's theory of failure elucidates how the compulsory positive nature of optimism, hope, pride, and success precludes the realisation that failure can be a form of sustenance and strategy of critique/survival. In failing the normative prescriptions of compulsory heterosexuality (and ablebodiedness), failure "imagines other goals for life, for love, for art, and for being" (Halberstam 88). And coming back to the image of the women failing/ surviving with AIDS at the post-socialist Odessa hospice, failure also imagines signs of crip solidarity and sustenance where the visions of an optimistic future create spaces of abandonment for subjects who will never be offered a fantasy of the 'good life.'

Despite its lack of substantial attention to cripness that would surpass the level of metaphorics, Halberstam's *The Queer Art of Failure* does offer some lines along which to also think *crip* failures. The most helpful to my current analysis of post-socialist affects would seem to be Halberstam's discussion of the failure to remember. Forgetting, losing, looping between past and future are the techniques of resistance to normative temporalities.

Such failures at temporalities of progressive and curative futurity, I argue, could offer forms of sustenance (for the post-socialist crip). The failure to remember would produce a rupture into the dominant narratives of shame (of a failed socialism) and the futurity of 'getting better.' It would forget visions of pride based on overcoming the failed socialist crip, and it would loosen/lose the compulsory vision of optimism of (neoliberal) humanism. It would forget the ideologies that we have seen to hurt and violate crips and our futures. Cripping, disjointing the normative forms of (linear) knowing about the past-present-future, could offer resistance to the cruel hope that directs our desires into (an evacuated) future, while foreclosing the negotiation of difficult yet important relationships past and the present.

The rejection of the curative and always already deferred future opens up a space for developing a more complicated relationship with failed pasts. Queer theorist Heather Love devises the politics of 'feeling backwards/backwards feelings' as an affective strategy of resistance to liberal understandings of the repressive hypothesis and emancipation (see Love). Her concept is both a corrective to the deeply problematic progressivism of 'gay pragmatism' with its compulsorily positive futurity of 'getting better', as well as an affective reaching backwards to legacies of difficult pasts. As she puts it, "[b]ackward feelings serve as an index to the ruined state of the social world; they indicate continuities between the bad gay past and the present; and they show up the inadequacy of queer narratives of progress" (Love 27); I wish to add, they show up continuities between crip pasts and presents obscured by the undisputedly "good intentions" of rehabilitation (McRuer, *Crip* 110). Halberstam for his part appreciates the strategies of backward feeling as a way of recovering the past of queer and racially marked subjects erased in the tidy versions of the past, "[w]hile liberal histories build triumphant political narratives with progressive stories of improvement and success, radical histories must content with a less tidy past, one that passes on legacies of failure and loneliness as the consequence of [ableist] homophobia and racism and xenophobia" (Halberstam 98). To retrieve lives undone by ideologies of ableism, homophobia, racism and xenophobia, and practices of institutionalisation, forced sterilisation, ethnic segregation, and on and on, we need backward-feelings.

The project of "reformulated histories" (see Kafer's discussion of Halberstam 42-44) feels backwards to past forms of *crip survivals* and past experiences that have been erased. Alongside this move, I also want to 'feel backwards' to the hurt caused by the shame of the bad past itself. This is not a naïve reclamation of the idealised communist past ignorant of the violence committed by the communist regime (violence and hurt inflicted on disabled people still remains mostly undocumented, unspoken, and unanalysed). What I argue is that the notion of the bad and failed past is too comfortable and too tidy and serves only the ideology of capitalist recovery that prescribes only one version of futurity, a futurity – I argue – that is constructed upon abjection of cripness. To open critical discussion I propose that we need to continue to produce untidy, crooked, queer, twisted, bent, crip versions of pasts. Only they will provide for more generous horizons of the present and future.

Acknowledgements

I dedicate this text to all crip boys and girls that taught me to long for and read crip signing; most importantly it is a love letter to A., the Crip Boy who also taught me to desire cripness. I also wish to express my gratitude to Merri Lisa Johnson, Robert McRuer, Anastasia Kayiatos, Aly Patsavas, Moritz Ingwersen and the other editors of this volume; their critiques have pushed me to extend, clarify, and make bolder my arguments. Earlier versions of the article were presented as "Cruising for a crip(topia) in the context of neoliberal transformations of the Czech republic" and I owe thanks to audiences for their insightful comments. This text has been facilitated by a grant support awarded by Czech Science Foundation (GAČR 13-18411S).

REFERENCES

Ahmed, Sara. *Queer Phenomenology: Orientations, Objects, Others.* Durham: Duke UP, 2006. Print.

—. *The Promise of Happiness.* Durham: Duke University Press, 2010. Print.

Berlant, Lauren Gail. *Cruel Optimism.* Durham: Duke University Press, 2011. Print.

"Chimera." *Oxford English Dictionary.* Oxford: Oxford University Press, 1989. Print.

Duggan, Lisa. *The Twilight Of Equality?: Neoliberalism, Cultural Politics, And The Attack On Democracy.* Boston: Beacon Press, 2003. Print.

"'El Rozhovor' s prezidentem československého červeného kříže, MUDr. RNDr., PhMr. Václavem Burianem, CSc., s první víceprezidentkou ČSČK MUDr. Olgou Královou, s ředitelkou Českého výboru červeného kříže pověřenou řízením úřadu FV ČSČK PhDr. Václavou Marešovou" ["Interview with the president of the Czechoslovak Red Cross et. al."]. *Elán: časopis svazu invalidů* 41.7-8 (1990): 1-2. Print.

Foucault, Michel. *Abnormal: Lectures At The Collège De France, 1974-1975.* New York: Picador, 2003. Print.

Gould, Deborah B. *Moving Politics: Emotion And ACT UP's Fight Against AIDS.* Chicago: University of Chicago Press, 2009. Print.

Graeber, David. *Debt: The First 5,000 Years.* Brooklyn: Melville House, 2011. Print.

Halberstam, Judith. *The Queer Art Of Failure.* Durham: Duke University Press, 2011. Print.

Hann, Chris, ed. *Postsocialism: Ideals, Ideologies and Practices in Euroasia.* London: Routledge, 2002. Print.

Havel, Václav. "Novoroční projev prezidenta ČSSR Václava Havla" ["Václav Havel's New Year's Presidential Address"]. 1 January 1990. Web. 15 Nov. 2013. <http://vaclavhavel.cz/showtrans.php?cat=projevy&val=327_projevy.html&typ=HTML>.

Juřenová, Ivanka. "Problémy mají i jinde." *Vozíčkář* ["The Wheelchair User"]. 4.2 (1991): 82. Print.

Kabele, Jiří. *Z kapitalismu do socialismu a zpět: teoretické vyšetřování přerodů Československa a České republiky* ["From Capitalism to Socialism and Back"]. Praha: Karolinum, 2005. Print.

Kafer, Alison. *Feminist, Queer, Crip.* Bloomington: Indiana University Press, 2013. Print.

Kayiatos, Anastasia. "Shock and Alla: Capitalist Cures for Socialist Perversities at the End of the Twentieth Century." *Lambda Nordica* 4 (2012): 33-64. Print.

Klaus, Václav. "Chiméra Rovnosti" [The Chimera of Equality]. *Literární noviny* 2 August 1990: 1. Print.

—. "Síla Idejí" ["The Power of Ideas"]. *Literární noviny* 25 April 1991: 1. Print.

Kolářová, Kateřina. "Affective Politics of Disability Shame in the Times of Neoliberal Exceptionalism." *Export-Import-Transport: Queer Theory, Queer Critique and Activism in Motion.* Eds. Sushila Mesquita, Maria Katharina Wiedlack and Katrin Lasthofer. Wien: Zaglossus, 2012. 263-80. Print.

Love, Heather. *Feeling Backward: Loss and the Politics of Queer History.* Cambridge: Harvard University Press, 2007. Print.

McRuer, Robert. *Crip Theory: Cultural Signs Of Queerness And Disability.* New York: New York University Press, 2006. Print.

McRuer, Robert and Abby Wilkerson. "Desiring Disability: Queer Theory Meets Disability Studies." *GLQ: A Journal of Lesbian and Gay Studies* 9.1-2 (2003): 1-23. Print.

Muñoz, José Esteban. *Disidentifications: Queers of Color and the Performance of Politics.* Minneapolis: University of Minnesota Press, 1999. Print.

—. *Cruising Utopia: The Then and There of Queer Futurity.* New York: New York University Press, 2009. Print.

"Náš mikrorozhovor s Petrem Anderlem, jedním z těch, kteří byli a jsou u toho" ["Interview with Petr Anderle, One Of Those Who Were At It"]. *Elán Express.* 41.4 (1990): n. pag. Print.

Phillips, Sarah D. *Disability and Mobile Citizenship in Postsocialist Ukraine.* Bloomington: Indiana UP, 2011. Print.

Pithart, Petr. "Zpráva o stavu České republiky přednesena v ČNR Petrem Pithartem" ["The State of the Czech Republic Address"]. *Lidové Noviny* 10 March 1990: 9-10. Print.

—. "Programové prohlášení vlády" ["Policy Statement of the Government of the Czech Republic"]. 2 July.1990.Web. 15 Nov. 2013. <http://www.vlada.cz/assets/clenove-vlady/historie-minulych-vlad/prehled-vlad-cr/1990-1992-cr/petr-pithart/ppv-1990-1992-pithart.pdf>.

Rasell, Michael and Elena Iarskaia-Smirnova. *Disability in Eastern Europe and the Former Soviet Union. History, Policy and Everyday Life.* Routledge: London. 2014. Print.

Remešová, Michaela. "Potměšil: Raději vozík než komunisty!" ["Potměšil: Wheelchair Better than the Communists"]. *Blesk.* 2009. Web. 15 Nov. 2013. <http://www.blesk.cz/clanek/zpravy-17-listopad/126864/potmesil-radeji-vozik-nez-komunisty.html>.

Stiker, Henri-Jacques. *A History of Disability.* Ann Arbor: University of Michigan Press, 1999. Print.

Šibík, Jan. *Chci ještě žít [I Do Not Want To Die Yet].* 2004. Photo Exhibition.

Váchalová, Anna. "Jak dál svaze invalidů?" ["*The Union of Invalids,* Where To Now?"]. *Elán Express.* 41.3 (1990): n. pag. Print.

"Vážený pane ministerský předsedo" ["Dear Mr. Prime Minister"]. *Elán: časopis svazu invalidů* 41.9 (1990): 2. Print.

Verdery, Katherine. *What Was Socialism, and What Comes Next?* Princeton: Princeton University Press, 1996. Print.

Wade, Cheryl Marie. "I'm Not One of The." *Sinister Wisdom* 35 (1988): 24. Print.

Weiner, Elaine. *Market Dreams: Gender, Class and Capitalism in the Czech Republic.* Ann Arbor: University of Michigan Press, 2007. Print.

Williams, Raymond. *Marxism and Literature.* Oxford: Oxford University Press, 1977. Print.

Zaviršek, Darja. "Pictures and Silences: Memories of Sexual Abuse of Disabled People." *International Journal of Social Welfare.* 11.4 (2002): 270-85. Web. 15 Nov. 2013.

Responses to Kateřina Kolářová

Heidi Helmhold

CRUEL OPTIMISM, CRIP EPISTEMOLOGY, AND THE LIMITS OF VISUAL ANALYSIS

Kateřina Kolářová's essay, "The Inarticulate Post-Socialist Crip," provides an interesting and terminologically dense reading. Overlaps with topics of my own research[11] covering visual arts, material culture, affect politics and space arise particularly in relation to terms such as 'structure of feeling,' 'affective attachments,' as well as the image-text relation in the context of visual arts. In the following, I will present three responses to this text. First, with reference to Laurent Berlant's terminology of 'cruel optimism,' as cited by Kolářová, I will present an argumentation differing from the one she follows. According to my understanding, no 'toxic attachment' to the cultural and contextual contingencies of the 'inarticulate crip' as described by Kolářová can be derived from Berlant's 'cruel optimism.' The second response refers to the neoliberal transformation processes in post-socialist Czechoslovakia, which Kolářová regards as responsible for the prevention of a crip epistemology. I believe, instead, that the university is accountable for such transformation processes, since academia should be understood as a place where epistemologies are included and excluded, hence it is also responsible for the formation of precarities. Third, my response deals with Kolářová's interpretation of Jan Šibík's photo "Chci ještě žít" from the series "Každý desátý! – Ukrajina, Oděsa, 2003-2004." Here I wish to defend the right of an artistic achievement in professional art (and the work in question is professional photo art) to be protected against misreading for the sake of supporting one's own argumentation.

---

11 | See Heidi Helmhold, *Affektpolitik und Raum* (especially 9-33).

First Response:
Cruel Optimism Describes Positive Processes

In Kolářová's line of argumentation, Berlant's term 'cruel optimism' is considered as a concept that is supposed to identify the strategic dynamics of post-socialist transformation processes and fundamentally to depict these in their cruelty. However, in terms of her own definition, Berlant's 'affective attachments' are only construed with reference to what she calls 'the good life,' which is unattainable for so many, but – and this perspective is decisive – still holds potential that principally offers everyone the opportunity to participate in it:

"As an analytic lever, it is an incitement to inhabit and to track the affective attachment to what we call 'the good life', which is for so many a bad life that wears out the subjects who nonetheless, and at the same time, find their conditions of possibility within it. [...] Cruel optimism is in this sense a concept pointing toward a mode of lived immanence, one that grows from a perception about the reasons people [...] choose to ride the wave of the system of attachment that they are used to, to syncopate with it, or to be held in a relation of reciprocity, reconciliation, or resignation that does not mean defeat by it." (Berlant 27-28)

Attachment as a 'structure of relationality' is linked to a wide range of experiences taking into consideration affects and emotions, so that Berlant concludes: "I therefore make no claims about what specific experiential modes of emotional reflexivity, if any, are especially queer, cool, resistant, revolutionary, or not" (13).

In order to dissociate from Berlant's notion of affective attachment, Kolářová establishes the category of "toxic attachment (232)," whereby cripness should become an "impossible location." (233) From my point of view, it does not really make sense to introduce this term. On the one hand, Kolářová convincingly illustrates that there exists a dis/ability semantics in the process of post-socialist transformation. But this does not explain that a crip epistemology was in actual fact *prevented* by this dis/ability semantic. Kolářová neither provides specific, empirical details nor does she present a direct addressee or an historical sphere of activity for this prevention. On the other hand, the term 'cruel optimism' seems to me fundamentally unsuitable in this context. According to my understanding, Berlant is interested in positive processes of change within neoliberal conditions. As cited above, "[c]ruel optimism is in this sense a concept pointing toward a mode of lived immanence" (Berlant 28), which means that cruel optimism ultimately aims to overcome the impasses. If this assumption of a positive dynamic intrinsic in the system is followed, then this constitutes a condition precedent that leads to the articulation of a language proper to 'crip expression' and definitely not to an 'inarticulate crip.' Rather, this inarticulate crip exists, precisely in the sense of Berlant, in "a relation of reciprocity, reconciliation, or resignation that does not mean defeat by it" (28).

In other words, a counter-culture can result in 'guerilla techniques.' The impact and power of these techniques should not be underestimated; intrinsically they hold a great potential for articulation. Berlant describes such guerilla activity with the example of "The Surveillance Camera Players," "a comic project with a DIY aesthetic, inspired by underground or guerilla activity" (Berlant 240). She relates how the group's book, *We Are Watching You* [2001], "provides rich documentation of their tactical, ephemeral, spectatorial events," events which involve actors confronting public surveillance cameras with cardboard signs displaying humorous messages that exemplify the "enactment of the body politic's refusal to be docile" (ibid.). "This aesthetic project," Berlant maintains, "reconstructs the body politic as an institutional actor who addresses the state as an interlocutor, not a structure, and whose pleasure is not in an unconscious or random freedom but in the production of interference, noise in the system" (242).

Second Response:
Neoliberalism, University and the 'Inarticulate Crip'

My next response discusses neoliberal transformation processes with reference to academia. Such processes, which Kolářová reflects on with respect to post-socialist Czechoslovakia, have now become global instruments. They have also reached institutions of knowledge, in particular universities, and have resulted in the official restructuring of knowledge itself within these institutions. Again, I am drawing on Berlant:

"Speaking of cruel optimism, it may be that, for many now, living in an impasse would be an aspiration, as the traditional infrastructures for reproducing life – at work, in intimacy, politically – are crumbling at a threatening pace. [...] What Jacques Rancière calls 'the distribution of the sensible' appears here not only in the class-based positioning of sensibility, but also in gestural economies that register norms of self-management that differ according to what kinds of confidence people have enjoyed about the entitlement of their social location. The way the body slows down what's going down helps to clarify the relation of living on to ongoing crisis and loss." (Berlant 4-5)

In this sense, I cannot follow Kolářová and her highlighting of cruel optimism as the agent of the prevention of a crip epistemology in post-socialist Czechoslovakia, because I understand cruel optimism as containing a rather positive, modifying dynamic. For me, the more relevant term – and Berlant also emphasizes this – would be precarity. Neoliberal transformation processes are immanently precarity-forming processes, which describe a global process and consequently a process relevant to society and social inequality as a whole. In Berlant's words: "At root, precarity is a condition of dependency – as a legal term, *precarious* describes the situation wherein your tenancy on your land is in someone else's hand" (192). Precarity designates managing systems which govern resources and capital, and which continually decrease temporal and spatial units of work and social participation. This process undermines and prohibits the formation of certain epistemic systems if they do not fit into the neoliberal administrative system of knowledge.

In the following, I aim to trace this dynamic by discussing the example of German academia in order to indicate how knowledge machines based upon neoliberal patterns function. Further, I will relate this discussion to Kolářová's assertions related to the 'inarticulate crip' and its connection to the neoliberalization of the university. Since the 1980s, the reorganization of 'university' as a place of knowledge and education has been conducted in Germany with a clear tendency towards a focus on achievement, following the motto 'strong academia results in strong achievement.' But how can strong achievements be established? In Germany, academic achievement is increasingly assessed according to quantifiable criteria that can be visualized in external and internal rankings and subsequently converted into financial and other forms of capital.

To implement neoliberal policies in academia, in its 1993 "10 Hypotheses On Higher Education Policies," the German Council of Science and Humanities suggested a stronger orientation towards employment and vocation as well as an alignment with the requirements of the economy, such as permanent evaluation, adherence to standard periods of study, and other measures (see "10 Hypotheses"). The tenth hypothesis demanded autonomous (i.e., non-state) institutions of higher education which are capable of acting on their own account; their destiny was to be placed in the hands of a "higher education institution management capable of making decisions" (ibid.; translation by author). The effectiveness of this neoliberal 'university' is reflected in particular in the raising of external funds: If individual faculties and departments are successful, they can gain external funding bonuses, which will enable them to engage in internal monetary allocations according to the principle of 'achievement-oriented allocation of funds.'[12] Thus, neoliberal university management relies on the measurement of achievement, which is published in university rankings – similar to the premier league rankings – in economic journals. The criteria for these rankings are devised in accordance with standards of quantifiable measurability. In these rankings, students are referred to as 'customers,' a terminology that has symptomatically been coined in the neoliberal higher education transformation process itself.

---

12 | In German: Leistungsorientierte Mittelzuweisung (LOMZ).

In the context of the Bologna Process starting in 1999, a further instrument of neoliberalising academia in Europe and therefore also in Germany has been developed: the two-tier BA/MA program structure, which aims at inter-European comparability of university degrees. Since then, the formats of university courses have been centrally predefined. To be established, a course needs to pass an accreditation process, which is controlled by private agencies. These accreditation agencies are appointed by a national accreditation council which, by way of a statutory mandate, monitors whether university courses consist of a corset of a specific length, examination performance and workload for students; output orientation plays an important role in this respect.

Last but not least, in 2005/06 Germany developed the "Excellence Initiative" instrument: An elite of top universities was created and endowed with an increased volume of equipment and financing. Professors who carry out research in these elite clusters are exempted from teaching, while teaching is conducted by highly qualified, massively underpaid academics who are employed through precarious employment contracts. This formation of an 'elite' through the 'Excellence Initiative' has had exclusionary effects on the academic community as a whole: It outshines the rest of the faculty which now appears as underachieving and unattractive. Academics, who are not affiliated with the neoliberal formation of achievement, visibility (affective public), university ministration (curative positivity), excellence, and scientific potency (i.e. funds and personnel equipment) stay behind and do not face an optimistic future. Their forms of knowledge fall by the wayside in the prevailing mentality of quantifiable scientific achievement, orientation towards employability, and standardization of studies, or, to assimilate Kolářová's terminology: They remain 'inarticulate.'

Thus, remaining inarticulate does not only apply to traditionally 'minor subjects' such as crip theory, but it concerns any epistemology which fails to find a place in neoliberal academia or cannot even be taught. This invisibility can *also* refer to 'crip epistemology,' but in my view, processes of suppressing 'other' forms of knowledge should be considered from the perspective of the neoliberal university system, rather than attributing it to 'crip epistemology' itself. Contrasting planned economy and market economy, as Kolářová (236) does in line with Elaine Weiner, does not, in my opinion, provide specific indicators for 'the inarticulate post-socialist crip'. Instead, it would have been interesting to be offered an analysis of *university* disability semantics during the period of transition in post-socialist Czechoslovakia.

Third Response:
Social Creativity, Beauty, Visual Culture

My last response deals with the work of Jan Šibík, who I know as an internationally active photographer who intervenes in political and social contexts while applying professional methods, creating good and profound artistic work. In her essay, Kolářová discusses a photograph by Šibík called "Chci ještě žít" or "I Want to Live" from a series of photographs supporting people suffering from AIDS in Odessa, Ukraine, which Šibík photographed in the early 2000s. The series comprises 19 photographs, which are currently on view on Šibík's website under the title "Každý desátý! – Ukrajina, Oděsa, 2003-2004." The images document various spatial situations in an asylum for AIDS-infected people in Odessa, "where people with AIDS were left to themselves; those who still could cared for those closer to death" (Kolářová 234). Disparately placed beds, tables and chairs on which sick people sit, lie, and sleep are depicted. The images show visitors sitting on beds together with residents and in one photograph also with a priest, who, unnoticed by the people in the room, seems to be reading a mass. They also show several people sleeping, being self-absorbed, or looking unemotionally into the camera. The pictures show roommates looking at people in the bed next to them or seemingly thinking about them. They show a nurse turning to a woman who is lying on a bed naked waiting to be taken care of. They show women talking or exchanging caring gestures. They show a deceased man being mourned by his wife. And they show another deceased man who, adorned with flowers, is publicly carried on the street, and people in the background, who are probably his relatives – although no specific mourning clothes can be seen here. In these photographs people's gestures are introverted, partly focusing on conversation, partly with long lingering gazes. Many of these photographs show physical contact – visitors touching patients who are lying on beds, a nurse touching another bed-ridden woman, patients touching each other, or people being engrossed in thought while touching themselves. Almost all of the photos depict instances of social interaction – humans, rooms and objects appear as *spacing* (see Löw 108-115, 158-161). There is one specific photograph that does not show a social interaction but a body segment: On a bed sheet we discern human legs 'bandaged' with plastic bags. The legs are marked by wounds, some of which are bleeding. Bloodstains can be seen on the bed.[13]

Kolářová chose image number 7 as an example of the inarticulate crip. Two women in their underwear sit facing each other, one of them on the bed, the other one on the floor in front it. The woman sitting on the bed carries out a

---

13 | See Photograph 12 on Jan Šibík's website: <http://www.sibik.cz/reportaze/aids_odesa_ukrajina/index.html>.

nursing or cosmetic gesture on the woman sitting beneath her – a focused gesture of care that is received by the woman sitting below with equal attention. Kolářová describes this scene as follows: "The drab environment, the pills, used cups, and fashion magazines surrounding the women tell a story of sickness and an improvised/impoverished home. However, the women are so engrossed in each other that the markers of illness, death, and destitution seem to disappear in a momentous bliss of erotic and mutual care" (Kolářová 233-234). Put into context with the other photographs of the series, this description itself is a projection. Indeed, many of these photos show a "drab environment" that fits the description of "pills, used cups, and fashion magazines [that] tell a story of sickness and an improvised/impoverished home" (233). But this photo in particular *does not* show a story of sickness with regard to its tangible, spatial setting. In my reading, it is an attentive and intimate scene between two women who are engrossed in physical affection. The surrounding space is densely equipped and could therefore also be a small room in a residence hall – insignia of sickness and hopelessness are spatially eliminated if one compares it with the other photographs. And crucially: In contrast to Kolářová, I contend that the affection shared by these women is *not* of an erotic nature, at least not in an intentional sense. The gestures between the two women are full of trust and tenderness, which corresponds with the seemingly mutual affection between them. To speak of a 'momentous bliss of erotic and mutual care,' as Kolářová does, projects, from my point of view, a (male or eroticized) gaze onto an intimate situation of devotion.

Moreover, with this interpretation Kolářová underestimates the narrative dimension of the entire series. I understand this photo as the most 'touching' photograph of the series – touching in a double sense: touching the beholder by means of the devotion between the two women and touching as an act of mutual physical contact. There is no visual reference to sickness, death or destruction in this image. It is – in all of the fragility of the place, the asylum, in all of the hopelessness of the situation – the most socially creative photograph in the series. Furthermore, it is significant that this social creativity is iconically carried out by two women, in contrast with the iconic hopelessness of individual men in other photographs of the series (see for example image number 4 on Šibík's website). Against this background I cannot comprehend why this photograph should show "a powerful clash between failure and sustenance," as Kolářová puts it (234). She sees the two women depicted here as embodying the failure of the ideologies of vitality and able-bodied health. And she goes on to say that the image

"attaches the woman's bodies to each other by acts of interdependent care, while their ambivalent positioning allows – even calls for and invites – sexual fantasies, turning the two women into subjects of (each other's) desire. In this they paradoxically embody a moment of careless sorority and of mutual care/pleasure." (Ibid.)

But there is no pictorial evidence to suggest a sexual phantasy constructed between the two women and/or which would evoke sexual phantasy in the viewer. Additionally, I cannot *see* that this photograph shows "[t]he ways in which the 'failure' of AIDS/illness can be turned into sustaining cripness," as Kolářová argues (ibid.). Since Susan Sontag we have known of the subtle but effective instruments which the photography of Postmodernism has introduced into photographic narratives:

"But notwithstanding the declared aims of indiscreet, unposed, often harsh photography to reveal truth, not beauty, photography still beautifies. Indeed, the most enduring triumph of photography has been its aptitude for discovering beauty in the humble, the inane, the decrepit. At the very least, the real has a pathos. And that pathos is – beauty" (Sontag 102).

With this ability of visual culture to 'beautify' the ugly, an implicit vehemence and horror is often amplified rather than taken away. But pathos occurs in the sense of affectivity and emotionality. However, there is one particular thing that is not accomplished in works such Jan Šibík's (and works of visual art in general): They do not allow themselves to be instrumentalized. This photo, like the others in the series, is undoubtedly a statement about a time of political and moral re-orientation in East Europe, in particular in the Ukraine. But its iconic program has its own hermeticism which can illustrate a theoretical or cultural context only to a limited extent: "But photographs do not explain; they acknowledge. Robert Frank was only being honest when he declared that 'to produce an authentic contemporary document, the visual impact should be such as will nullify explanation'" (Sontag 111).

If this photo and some others in the series show something *in the image*, then they show gestures of affection in a hopeless environment (asylum, society, political re-organization). What they do not display is 'failure' or 'ambivalence' – there are definitely no signs and no iconographic program which would indicate these aspects in this particular photograph. In Šibík's photographs, the subject matter is the same as in all narrative images in critical documentary photography, namely humanity and the lack thereof. This is a lot and should not be underestimated; it has the potential to shape our views about political and social injustices. In this regard, the photo itself appears as a "dissociative point of intersection," as Susan Sontag (97) describes it, between the camera and the human eye, and it is therefore never congruent with what is generally

258 Heidi Helmhold, Arne Müller

called 'reality' or 'truth.'[14] Consequently, we cannot derive a valid structure of a pictorial *crip signing* from the majority of the photos in this series by Jan Šibík. Kolářová's attempt to see this in his visual artwork appears inexplicable to me.

References

"10 Thesen zur Hochschulpolitik" ["10 Hypotheses on Higher Education Policies"]. Eds. Der Wissenschaftsrat 1993. Web. 22 Juni 2015. <http://www. die-soziale-bewegung.de/hochschule/10thesen.PDF>.

Berlant, Lauren. *Cruel Optimism.* Durham & London: Duke University Press, 2011. Print.

Helmhold, Heidi. *Affektpolitik und Raum: Zu einer Architektur des Textilen* [Affect Politics of Space: Architecture of Textiles]. Köln: Walther König, 2012. Print.

Kolářová, Kateřina. "The Inarticulate Post-Socialist Crip: On the Cruel Optimism of Neoliberal Transformations in the Czech Republic." This volume. 231-249. Print.

McRuer, Robert. *Cultural Signs of Queerness and Disability.* New York: New York University Press, 2006. Print.

Šibík, Jan. *Každý desátý! – Ukrajina, Oděsa, 2003 – 2004.* Photography Series. Web. 17 July 2014. <http://www.sibik.cz/reportaze/aids_odesa_ukrajina/ index.html>.

Löw, Martina. *Raumsoziologie* [Sociology of Space]. Frankfurt a.M.: Suhrkamp, 2001. Print.

Sontag, Susan. *On Photography.* First Ebook Edition (2011). New York: Farrar, Straus and Giroux, 1973. Kindle file.

---

14 | Also see: "Photographic seeing, when one examines its claims, turns out to be mainly the practice of a kind of dissociative seeing, a subject habit which is reinforced by the objective discrepancies between the way that the camera and the human eye focus and judge perspective" (Sontag 97).

Arne Müller

CRIP HORIZONS, THE CULTURAL MODEL OF DISABILITY, AND BOURDIEU'S POLITICAL SOCIOLOGY

While reading Kateřina Kolářová's essay for the first time and coming across what she names 'crip horizons,' I was reminded of the cultural model of disability developed by researchers like Anne Waldschmidt (2005) and Patrick Devlieger (2005) in Europe, or Sharon L. Snyder and David T. Mitchell (2006) in North America. The implementation of this model is intended to initiate a paradigm shift: By offering a different research perspective it shifts the analytical frame away from individualistic or socio-political aspects of impairment and disability towards the cultural norms of the temporally able-bodied majority. The cultural model presents an alternative model of disability, as it focuses on the cultural practices and normative grounds that are responsible for the marginalization of disabled persons[15] within a given society. In the social model of disability, exclusion results from social behaviors (like discrimination) and insurmountable barriers (like inaccessible buildings), whereas the cultural model focuses on cultural patterns that are causing exclusion by defining what is considered normal for a culture or, as Devlieger states, "disability is a symbolic reflection of dominant categories in society, a mirror" (Devlieger 9). According to this model, disability is a foil that is used to divide normalcy from deviation. So from my point of view, the main function of the cultural model is to analyze in which ways considering people as disabled contributes to the discourse of normalcy within a society.

In this response I want to concentrate on three different aspects. First, I would like to discuss how Kolářová's remarks about the rehabilitative rhetoric of the Czech transition period provide vivid examples of what is addressed by the cultural model of disability. Then, I will concentrate on the sociological ramifications of considering disabled persons as a specific social group, and I will try to show that the theoretical approach of French sociologist Pierre Bourdieu is helpful in understanding disabled or 'crip' resistance to neoliberalism. Finally, I discuss implications for the research of social inequality and inclusion with particular regard to disability.

Although Kolářová does not explicitly refer to the cultural model of disability, her essay can be read as a contribution to this approach. Unfortunately, she does not provide a definition of the term 'crip horizons,' but refers instead to political horizons which, following Deborah B. Gould, she considers as a state that is

---

15 | In this essay the term 'disabled persons' is used instead of persons (or people) with disabilities. According to Barnes (20), the term 'people with disabilities' focuses on disability in the sense of impairment and thus denies or neglects that these persons are actually more disabled by the societies they live in than by their impairments.

imagined as "possible, desirable and necessary" (Kolářová 232). Assuming that this definition applies to 'crip horizons' as well, such a desired horizon appears to be opposed to current concepts of normalcy that are normative in so far as "disabled people serve the nondisabled to define themselves as normal" (Devlieger 9). This is the point where the cultural model of disability comes into play.

By starting with normative structures of a society that considers some of its members as deviant and provides rehabilitative solutions for them, one can analyze both the concept and the treatment of disability within this society. In a time of the worldwide ratification of the UN Convention on the Rights of Persons with Disabilities, it would appear that the inclusion of disabled people has become a judicially codified cultural norm. However, despite the Convention the exclusion of disabled persons is still a common everyday practice. In most countries academic discourses and public speeches continue to use a rehabilitative rhetoric which disabled people find offensive, as the will to rehabilitate implies that one also needs to eliminate the pathological parts.

This last point is addressed by Kolářová, and in this respect one of her main aims is to examine this rehabilitative rhetoric as part of the dominant narratives in the Czech Republic during its post-socialist transition period. By doing so, she addresses the normative complex of disability at that time. By showing that the 'affective attachments' (Kolářová 232) which underlay the country's transitional period were influenced by promises of hope and cure even for disabled people, Kolářová provides vivid examples of strategies of exclusion during this shift to capitalism and neoliberalism. Demands of disabled persons were not fulfilled but rather postponed, accompanied by what Kolářová calls in reference to Laurent Berlant "cruel optimism" for better futures. To promise these better futures, the narratives of the Czech post-socialistic transition period used a vocabulary of rehabilitation, cure, and recuperation.

Taking the cultural model of disability and using it to analyze the post-socialist transition period in Eastern Europe can, as Kolářová's essay shows, be helpful in highlighting the idea that the normative grounds in the 1990s were largely based on medical implications and the promise for better futures without 'crippled deviance'. Such futures could be considered as proud, bright, and tempting for those who wanted to escape the communist past that was no longer considered as a model opposed to a glorified capitalism. To emphasize this deviation between 'evil' communism and 'good' capitalism in the time of the transition period, Elaine Weiner's table (see Kolářová 236) is a useful tool that illustrates how the deliberate use of a certain diction contributed indirectly to the exclusion of disabled people. The good capitalist future is regarded as the 'normal' result of hard, able-bodied work, and will allow no room for those considered 'abnormal' and who do not contribute on an equal footing because they live with impairments.

In the second part of my response, I will concentrate on some aspects of social structure analysis that seem pertinent to Kolářová's intervention. As she uses the term 'cripness' throughout her article and refers to the 'disabled,' she seems to address disabled persons as a social group that could be regarded according to Bourdieu as an "objective class" (Bourdieu, *Distinction* 570 et. seq.).

In such an "objective class" all members of a group are imagined as socially close because they share the same experiences, live similar lives or, as Bourdieu would say, they share a "class habitus" (101). But, in my point of view, disabled people do not share the same habitus just because they have impairments. I would rather argue that they share a habitus only when they have the same social class which is based on similar economic, cultural and social resources or forms of capital, but not a result of the same impairment experiences. This differentiation is of importance where agent-based questions are concerned, especially when disabled people turn out to be a "mobilized class" (570). Following Bourdieu, such a mobilized class is "a set of individuals brought together [...] for the purpose of the struggle to preserve or modify the structure of the distribution of objectified properties" (ibid.). For reasons of fighting for a shared goal this mobilized class might function for a short span of time, but having Bourdieu's theory in mind implies that the habitus of different members of the imagined mobilized class of disabled people might differ due to the different class backgrounds of its members which thus will challenge the coherence of common aims in the long term.

According to Kolářová, disabled people in the Czech Republic's post-socialist transition period considered themselves to be part of the new capitalist society, but were confronted with a request for patience and, finally, the postponement of their demands (see Kolářová 239). To me it appears like a trade-off to sacrifice one's own demands as a mobilized class for the sake of being an inclusive and equal part of a better future. It seems even more astonishing that disabled people in the Czech Republic postponed their demands when the analysed rhetoric of that time used a disability-adverse and excluding language.

Within the framework of Bourdieu and his critique of neoliberalism, one could argue that people who postpone their demands opt, at least in the midterm, for a strong "right hand of the state" (Bourdieu, *Acts of Resistance* 2), although they are in need of what he calls "the left hand of the state" (ibid.). This left hand symbolises the traces "of the social struggles of the past" (ibid.), such as social security systems, social work, etc., which might be considered cost-intensive areas of a state's budget from a neoliberalist point of view. The right hand of the state includes, among others, "the technocrats of the Ministry of Finance" (ibid.) who focus on reducing state expenses. In other words, according to Bourdieu neoliberal strategies aim to eliminate 'cost factors' like the results of past social struggles and encourage individual achievement and competition instead. Thus, the social structure of neoliberal societies is presented as the result of individual merit and what Bourdieu calls "neo-Darwinism [...] the product of the natural selection of the most capable" (Bourdieu, *Firing Back* 34). As disabled persons are often regarded as less capable of contributing merits they face new inequalities in neoliberal economies and their situation turns out to be precarious. In my opinion, neoliberal politics focusing on individual effort does not offer promises for disabled persons at all; the mobilized class of disabled persons should rather concentrate on engaging more strongly in new social movements by engaging in acts of resistance against neoliberalism and austerity measures.

These short remarks with reference to Bourdieu and his approach to neoliberalism introduce another pressing issue. Discourses about disabled persons often start from the assumption that they own a social status of deprivation or poverty, i.e. the reflection of disabled people's life situations usually implies talking about class issues. But this aspect is seldom explicitly mentioned. In this respect, Kolářová's essay is just one striking example among many others. She never ever uses the term 'class,' but is in fact focusing on precisely this point.

So why is class so important in this context? I would argue that failing to address disabled persons' problems as class issues is another mode of a politics of exclusion which makes it easier to ignore or postpone the demands of the group of disabled persons. To better discuss this point it might be useful to have a closer look into today's concepts of inequality.

Current research on social inequality distinguishes between so-called vertical and horizontal inequalities (see Stewart et al.). It considers individual inequality, such as income and wealth or knowledge, as vertical inequality and differentiates these individual attributes from those that are considered as collective because they refer to attributes not considered to be a result of individual achievement. These collective attributes are designated as horizontal inequalities, for example gender, ethnicity, or disability (ibid.). For analytical purposes, the distinction between vertical and horizontal inequality has some enlightening implications for my context. As already mentioned, from a non-disabled perspective disabled people are considered as less able to contribute merits that serve to secure a reasonable living. In addition, current research for Germany shows that provisions of social security such as legal protections against dismissal on the labor market often hinder the hiring of disabled persons at all (see Niehaus and Bauer). Ascribed restrictions of the productivity of impaired people and the reverse effect of dismissal protections have a strong disabling effect for the entire social group. Addressing the social group of disabled people as a collective with shared disabling experiences (i.e., addressing them only as horizontally unequal) results, in my point of view, only in obscuring the vertical dimension, or what I would call the "vertical effect" of a horizontal inequality like disability.

With this argument I do not want to suggest that all disabled people are always excluded or poor, but I would rather like to call for the necessity of research into social inequality concerning disabled people that broadens its analytical framework and analyzes the functional interactions between vertical and horizontal inequalities. As I have already pointed out, considering a person as horizontally unequal does not necessarily mean that this person is poor or a member of an inferior class, but sociological research should aim at identifying to which extent one's vertical position is (also) caused by horizontal effects. Additionally, there might be other reverse effects. Being a member of the dominant class or having access to a good living can diminish or soften horizontal, i.e. disabling, experiences.

Currently, there is a lot of research analyzing these functional interactions of different inequalities under the rubric of what is called 'intersectionality' (see Hess et al.). The concept of intersectionality may be well-suited to the analysis of disability-related inequalities and systematic oppression, especially when horizontal and vertical inequalities intersect. But general intersectional analyses still tend to ignore disability and prefer to focus on other categories such as race, class, and gender. Future disability research should take the approach of analyzing marginalization and promote the inclusion of disability as an important inequality in intersectional analyses.

Referring to Kolářová's essay, using the cultural model of disability as a background, and drawing on Bourdieu's political sociology, this essay has tried to elaborate the argument that the culturalist concept of 'crip horizons' is helpful, but it should be supplemented by a broader analytical framework considering class theory, social inequality approaches, and intersectionality. What is needed is a figure of thought capable of challenging cultural norms and of irritating established concepts of normalcy. In so doing, the potential to establish 'crip existence' as a new mode of existence is likely to arise.

References

Barnes, Colin. "Disabling Imagery and the Media: An Exploration of the Principles for Media Representations of Disabled People". Krumlin: Ryburn Publishing, 1992. Web. 25 March 2015. <http://disability-studies.leeds.ac.uk/files/library/Barnes-disabling-imagery.pdf>.

Bourdieu, Pierre. *Distinction: A Social Critique of the Judgment of Taste*. London: Routledge, 1984. Print.

—. *Acts of Resistance: Against the New Myth of our Time*. Cambridge: Polity Press, 1998. Print.

—. *Firing Back: Against the Tyranny of the Market 2.* New York: The New Press, 2003. Print.

Devlieger, Patrick. "Generating a Cultural Model of Disability." *Lecture at the FEAPDA Congress, Geneva 14-16 October* 2005. Web. 15 Oct. 2013. <http://www.feapda.org/FEAPDA%20Geneva%202005/culturalmodelofdisability.doc>.

Hees, Sabine, Langreiter, Nicole and Elisabeth Timm (eds.). *Intersektionalität Revisited: Empirische, theoretische und methodische Erkundungen.* Bielefeld: transcript, 2011. Print.

Kolářová, Kateřina. "The Inarticulate Post-Socialist Crip: On the Cruel Optimism of Neoliberal Transformations in the Czech Republic." This volume. 231-249. Print.

Niehaus, Mathilde and Jana Bauer. "Chancen und Barrieren für hochqualifizierte Menschen mit Behinderung. Übergang in ein sozialversicherungspflichtiges Beschäftigungsverhältnis. Pilotstudie zur beruflichen Teilhabe." 2013. Web. 18 March 2014. <http://publikationen.aktion-mensch.de/arbeit/AktionMensch_Studie-Arbeit_2013_09_30.pdf>.

Schneider, Werner and Anne Waldschmidt. "Disability Studies. (Nicht-) Behinderung anders denken." *Kultur. Von den Cultural Studies bis zu den Visual Studies: Eine Einführung.* Ed. Stephan Moebius. Bielefeld: transcript, 2012. 128-150. Print.

Snyder, Sharon L. and David T. Mitchell. *Cultural Locations of Disability.* Chicago: University of Chicago Press, 2006. Print.

Stewart, Frances, Brown, Graham and Luca Mancin. "Why Horizontal Inequalities Matter: Some Implications for Measurement." *CRISE Working Paper* No. 19. Web. 22 October 2013. <http://r4d.dfid.gov.uk/PDF/Outputs/inequality/wp19.pdf>.

Waldschmidt, Anne. "Disability Studies: Individuelles, soziales und/oder kulturelles Modell von Behinderung?" *Psychologie & Gesellschaftskritik* 29.1 (2005). 9-31. Print.

Notes on Contributors

Hanjo Berressem is Professor of American Literature at the University of Cologne, Germany. His publications include *Pynchon's Poetics: Interfacing Theory and Text* and *Lines of Desire: Reading Gombrowicz's Fiction with Lacan* (1998). He has edited, together with Leyla Haferkamp, *Deleuzian Events: Writing|History* (2009) and *site-specific: from aachen to zwölfkinder – pynchon | germany* (2008).

Konstantin Butz is a researcher and lecturer at the Academy of Media Arts Cologne. He completed degrees in American Studies and Cultural Studies with a dissertation on the American subculture of skate punk published as *Grinding California: Culture and Corporeality in American Skate Punk* (2012). His research interests include subcultures, youth cultures, and (un-)popular literature and music.

Ria Cheyne is a lecturer at Liverpool Hope University. Her research focuses on representations of disability in contemporary literature and culture, and bridges the fields of literary studies, disability studies, and medical humanities. She is currently completing a book on disability and affect in contemporary genre fiction.

Lennard J. Davis is Distinguished Professor of Liberal Arts and Sciences at the University of Illinois at Chicago in the departments of English, Disability and Human Development, and Medical Education. He is the author, most recently, of *Enabling Acts: The Hidden Story of How the Americans with Disabilities Act Gave The Largest US Minority Its Rights* (2015) and is the editor of *The Disability Studies Reader* (2013).

Rosemarie Garland-Thomson is Professor of English at Emory University. Her work develops critical disability studies in the health humanities to promote access and inclusion within and outside of the academy. She is author of *Staring: How We Look* (2009) and other books. Her current project is *Habitable Worlds: Toward a Disability Bioethics*.

Dan Goodley is Professor of Disability Studies at the University of Sheffield. His research is engaged with the dual processes of ableism and disablism and recent work includes *Dis/ability Studies* (2014) and *Disability Studies* (2011). He is co-director of iHuman, a research centre in Sheffield and a Nottingham Forest FC fan.

Benjamin Haas is a lecturer for inclusive education at the University of Bremen. His teaching and research activities include special and inclusive education, inclusive school development, disability studies and disability studies in education. He is currently working on his PhD thesis about the construction of ADHD in the discourse of German Special Education.

Karin Harrasser is Professor of Cultural Theory at the Kunstuniversität Linz. Her research is concerned with techniques and media of the body, popular culture and science fiction, gender and agency, genres and methods of cultural studies. Together with Elisabeth Timm, she is the editor in chief of *Zeitschrift für Kulturwissenschaften*. She is the author, most recently, of *Prothesen: Figuren einer lädierten Moderne* (2016).

Heidi Helmhold is Professor of Aesthetic Theory at the Department of Art and Art Theory at the University of Cologne. Her research focuses on user-related/user-oriented space performances. Her publications include *Affektpolitik und Raum. Zu einer Architektur des Textilen* (2012). At the intersection of the sociology of space, spatial theory and artistic space intervention, she works in social heterotopias such as refugee camps and penal institutions.

Moritz Ingwersen is a Ph.D. Candidate at the Cultural Studies Department of Trent University in Ontario studying under a Cotutelle agreement with the Department of English at the University of Cologne. Building on a degree in English and Physics his research and teaching address the intersections between American literature and culture, science fiction, science studies, media philosophy, and disability studies.

Arta Karāne is an M.A. student of North American Studies at the University of Cologne. She is originally from Latvia where she earned her B.A. in Political Science. In her Masters studies she focuses on historical, postcolonial, literary and cultural aspects of North America. Her main research interests are the intersection of disability and sexuality, abject and affect in extreme body performances, material culture, and literary and cultural theory.

Kateřina Kolářová is Assistant Professor of Cultural Studies and Chair in the Department of Gender Studies at Charles University, Prague. She is currently working on a monograph tentatively titled *Capitalist Rehabilitations: Assembla-ges of Gender, Sex, Disability and Race in Affective Economies of Belonging and Abandonment between Post-Socialism and Neoliberalism*, as well as a research project exploring neo-liberal politics of biological citizenship, HIV/AIDS and chronicity.

Robert McRuer is Professor of English at The George Washington Universi-ty. He is the author of *Crip Theory: Cultural Signs of Queerness and Disability* (2006) and co-editor of *Sex and Disability* (2012). He is currently completing a manuscript titled *Crip Times: Disability, Globalization, and Resistance.*

Arne Müller is a sociologist and a Ph.D. Candidate working in the field of Disa-bility Studies. Stations of his career as a researcher are the University of Colog-ne, University of New England, Australia, and the Center for Disability Studies at the University of Sydney.

Martin Roussel is Associate Director of the Morphomata Center for Advanced Studies at the University of Cologne (since 2009). He completed his studies in German, Education and Philosophy with a dissertation on Robert Walser's Micrography (2009). He has been the editor of the Kleist-Jahrbuch since 2007 and a board member of the Directorate of the Heinrich-von-Kleist-Gesellschaft since 2008.

Rouven Schlegel studied special needs education at the University of Cologne. He published on the body and discourse and worked as a research assistant at the specialized library for special needs education and rehabilitation at the University of Cologne. Currently he teaches at Schule der Jugendhilfe, Jülich.

Margrit Shildrick is Professor of Gender and Knowledge Production at Linkö-ping University, and Adjunct Professor of Critical Disability Studies at York University, Toronto. Her research covers postmodern feminist and cultural theory, bioethics, critical disability studies and body theory. Her books include *Leaky Bodies and Boundaries: Feminism, (Bio)ethics and Postmodernism* (1997), *Embodying the Monster: Encounters with the Vulnerable Self* (2002) and *Dange-rous Discourses of Disability, Sexuality and Subjectivity* (2009).

Tobin Siebers was V. L. Parrington Collegiate Professor of Literary and Cultural Criticism at the Department of English Language and Literature at the Uni-versity of Michigan. His numerous books include *Disability Aesthetics* (2010), *Zerbrochene Schönheit: Essays über Kunst, Ästhetik und Behinderung* (2009), *Di-sability Theory* (2008), and *The Mirror of Medusa* (1983, 2000).

Jan Söffner works as a program director at Wilhelm Fink Verlag, Paderborn. He holds a Ph.D. and a habilitation in Comparative Literature and has worked at the Universities of Cologne and Tübingen, as well as Zentrum für Literatur- und Kulturforschung Berlin (ZfL). His research focuses on embodiment and phenomenology. His publications include the monographs *Partizipation: Metapher, Mimesis, Musik* (2014) and *Metaphern und Morphomata* (2015).

Andreas Sturm (M.A.) is a Ph.D. student and worked as a junior researcher at the International Research Unit in Disability Studies (iDiS) at the University of Cologne, Germany. His research focuses on the cultural and political sociologies of 'dis/ability,' the disability rights movement and representations of persons with disabilities.

Olga Tarapata completed a degree in English, Biology and Educational Sciences at the University of Cologne. She joined the Institute of American Literature and Culture in 2009 and continued as a research assistant in 2014. She is a scholarship holder at the a.r.t.e.s Graduate School for the Humanities Cologne and her research interests include the work of William Gibson, U.S. American literature, literary theory, radical constructivism, and disability theory.

Eleana Vaja studied English, Philosophy and Education at the University of Cologne, the University of Birmingham, and as a scholarship holder at the University of Berkeley. In April 2013 she entered the a.r.t.e.s. Graduate School for the Humanities Cologne with her dissertation project "Renegotiations of Epilepsy Metaphors in U.S. American Literature (1990-2015)." She works as research assistant at the Institute of American Literature and Culture in Cologne.

Anne Waldschmidt is Professor of Disability Studies, Sociology and Politics of Rehabilitation, and Director of the International Research Unit in Disability Studies (iDiS) at the Faculty of Human Sciences of the University of Cologne. Her research focuses on the cultural and political sociologies of 'dis/ability,' body sociology, contemporary disability history, the political participation of persons with disabilities and transnational disability policies. Her books include *Selbstbestimmung als Konstruktion. Alltagstheorien behinderter Frauen und Männer* (2012); she is co-editor of *Kontinuitäten, Zäsuren, Brüche? Lebenslagen von Menschen mit Behinderungen in der deutschen Zeitgeschichte* (2016), *Disability History: Konstruktionen von Behinderung in der Geschichte* (2010), and *Disability Studies, Kultursoziologie und Soziologie der Behinderung* (2007).